T0147104

FOUR FIELDS

ALSO BY TIM DEE

The Running Sky: A Birdwatching Life
The Poetry of Birds (co-editor with Simon Armitage)

Tim Dee

Four Fields

COUNTERPOINT
BERKELEY

Library of Congress Cataloging-in-Publication Data Is Available

ISBN 978-1-61902-621-6

Cover design by Julia Connoly
Interior Design by Palimpsest Book Production Ltd, Falkirk, Stirlingshire

Counterpoint Press
2560 Ninth Street, Suite 318
Berkeley, CA 94710
www.counterpointpress.com

Printed in the United States of America

husbandry

for Claire

CONTENTS

A man keeps and feeds a lion. The lion owns a man.

Diogenes

HOME FIELD

I was driving home in the dark. The stop-start charms of the A14. Lorries, boxy with containers heaving into the night, metal bergs not long off the sea struggling over the land, Stonehenge and Easter Island heads to be delivered to the interior. Body shunts and heart attacks on every incline. The Midlands up in front. Dusk had taken the fields next to the hurrying road out of sight. The lit trench was all. I was thinking of nothing, as you must to survive, when stems of grass suddenly glanced in my beams and crowded at my windscreen, their straight thin bars of strobing light tinkling against the glass. Somewhere in front of me a hay lorry was travelling and throwing behind it this green storm. The traffic slowed. As I braked, the hectic sprinkle fell away and I could see in my headlights and then feel beneath my tyres that the whole of the road's surface was covered in the thinnest spread of hay. A cigar butt or two of the stuff must have bounced from the back of the lorry and split on the road. We were all driving on grass. It brought a smile to my face. I might have strayed into some nativity scene of straw carried into a church and spread across a stone floor to make a point. I might have drifted into the story of the Princess and the Pea. The road had been transported or turned over into a kind of field and the grass was announcing itself in our ungreen and ungrowing world. My car and all the cars and lorries around me inched forward over the strange luxury beneath our tyres and, though the hay blades were thin and crushed thinner, I could still feel the new field under me with its tiny ridges and furrows briefly repossessing the road.

Throughout my life much of my happiness has come from being outside. That brief smile on the A14 was declaring it. I became a serious

1

birdwatcher at the age of seven in 1968. I've grown less serious with time but, ever since my childhood, going out *into the field* has been part and parcel of what I do. The *field* might mean the fields of a farm but it can also mean anywhere that birds live and especially places where you deliberately look for them. Mostly this has been away from towns and cities, but not always: a back garden would do on a good day, or a park. My wanting to see birds simplified the world: if you didn't go out, you didn't see anything; if you did go out, regardless of what you saw, you seemed to have been somewhere and to have done something. Thoreau used the same phrase having spent a day kneeling to the earth to collect fallen sweet chestnuts in October 1857. Any day out for me, any day in the field, was better than a day indoors – I think that is what Thoreau meant too. Being outside was never a waste of time: even a day in July in a wood in the middle of England at the year's green midnight, when no birds sing; even an expedition in February with a grumpy girlfriend to an urban sewage farm; even a day with only a pitiful species list or wet feet to show for your efforts. Without any fieldwork of this kind, life inside stalled. Long before I read it, I knew the damp grey constriction – in my chest and between my eyes – of the first page of *Jane Eyre*: 'There was no possibility of taking a walk that day.'

Indoors, looked at from the field, seemed at best to be talk about life instead of life itself. Rather than living under the sun it fizzed – if it fizzed at all – parasitically or secondarily, with batteries, on printed pages, and in flickering images. I realised this around 1968 in my seven-year-old way. At the same time, however, I learned that I needed the indoor world to make the outdoors be something more than simply everything I wasn't. I saw it was true that indoor talk helped the outdoor world come alive and could of itself be living and lovely, too. Words about birds made birds live as more than words. Jane Eyre, held inside by bad weather, takes Thomas Bewick's *History of British Birds* to the window and reads looking out into the wind and rain.

A yellowhammer on a flaming gorse a mile from my childhood home, my first ring ouzels on spring migration on the grassed bank of a slurry pit – these birds, once found and named (real, flighty, not interested), started something off like a shock into living. The world leaned on me, as it were, and the green gears of outside became part of the machinery of my mind, and 'a language of my whole life', as Ted Hughes described animals in his. Ever since, being in the field, following the field's seasons and its birds, and, at the same time, moving words from indoors out, and outdoors in, has more or less dominated my years.

Without fields – no us. Without us – no fields. So it has come to seem to me. 'This green plot shall be our stage,' says Peter Quince in *A Midsummer Night's Dream*. Fields were there at our beginning and they are growing still. *Earth* half-rhymes with *life* and half-rhymes with *death*. Every day, countless incarnations of our oldest history are played out in a field down any road from wherever we are. Yet these acres of shaped growing earth, telling our shared story over and over, are so ordinary, ubiquitous and banal that we have – mostly – stopped noticing them as anything other than substrate or backdrop, the green crayon-line across the bottom of every child's drawing. It is in the nature of all commonplaces that they are overlooked, in both senses of the word: fields are everywhere but we don't see them for they are too familiar and homely; being the stage and not the show, they are trodden under-foot, and no one seeks them out, no one gives a sod. For Walt Whitman, prairie-dreamer of the great lawn of men, grass fitted us and suited; it was a 'uniform hieroglyphic'. It grew and stood for us and, because it goes where we are, we tread where it grows. Yet because it meant everything it could easily mean nothing.

Might it be possible to look again and to see the grass and the fields afresh? Our making of fields, first of all from that grass, has tied us to nature more than any other human activity. The relationship is rooted yet simple, ancient yet living. Fields offer the most articulate description and vivid enactment of our life here *on earth*, of how we live both within the grain of the world and against it. We break ground to lay foundations, sow seeds and begin life; we break ground to harvest life, bury our dead and end things. Every field is at once totally functional and the expression of an enormous idea. Fields live as proverbs as well as fodder and we reap what we sow.

'The fields!' urged John Ruskin, early conjuror of cultural landscapes, 'follow but forth for a little time the thoughts of all that we ought to recognize in those words.' What follows here is an attempt to say some more about the fields in my life; to understand why these four fields mean as much to me as they do and how they have given me the sentimental education, the heart's journey, that they have; to explore what they have meant to others; to discover the common ground they make, the *midfield*; to walk and work them in the only way I know, to name their birds and to read their words; to remember their other workers, their makers, mappers, gleaners, fighters; to count their flowers and to smell them; to link wild fields to factory fields; to argue that the most meaningful green squares might be the most banal, the most beautiful meadows the most ruined; to learn how they all work and how they all fail; to find the future of some in their past and, in others, their present enduring through change; to dive into their grass and sneeze alive, to lie in their grass and feel it a grave; to enlist every acre.

My beginning is the simple discovery of a simple truth. The outside places that I like are the places that I know. And being born in the 1960s and growing up in southern England, the places I know best, apart from the A-roads and the paved and heaped-up world of towns and cities, are the man-made fields close to home in between them. A *terra cognita*.

I hardly know a single wild place. There is none left in England. 'Natural England' is a government department. I am not actually sure that you can know a wild place. Not knowing how to be in a rainforest, I couldn't wait to get out of the only one I have ever been in. I am equally frightened of the open sea. In 1972, I thought I was going to drown when the father of a schoolfriend lost his nerve as we sailed a little dinghy off the Isle of Sheppey and the sea slopped over the side of the boat. The nearest I have come to divorcing my wife was just last year when she scampered on ahead and left me frozen in terror on a (humiliatingly) small cliff on Table Mountain above Cape Town.

For Claire the mountain isn't wild – it is her outside place, a

4

mountain as it happens, and which begins at the end of the street where she grew up. I would say the same for most of the fields in this book. They are places where I find myself. My plots and theirs overlap. I am not a farmer but like almost all of us I am a fieldworker. Jane Eyre peers at Thomas Bewick's Arctic vignette of 'forlorn regions of dreary space' and makes the English weather outside her window speak. Seamus Heaney digs with his pen as outside his window his father lifts potatoes with a spade. The plough was the first constellation in the night sky that I learned. It remains the only one I can point to reliably.

In what follows I want a field to mean most often a man-made outside place, but my definitions will run wild at times and be close-cropped at others, my facts and my metaphors (those carried into and out of the fields) will change with every ground. Come with me, then, as I plough my own furrow, but forgive me, knowing that we all must.

The word *field* is almost as big and elusive as its neighbour *nature*. And fields are talk of nature as well as ways of talking to nature. One of our oldest words, speaking of one of the first things we made and one of our oldest concepts, is alive and growing still. Fields are ordinary, universal, tamed and practical, but they are also none of those things or their opposite; they are strange, particular, wild, and as far beyond money as human-inflected things can be. The hedged allotment and the open prairie coax different poems as well as different meals. Kept places keep us in all sorts of ways. Fields are pay dirt but also the greatest land art on the globe. There is a story that John Ruskin once took a plough into an art lecture at Oxford to ensure his students – who, like me, might have known the plough of the night sky better – would recognise what one of the most effective sculptural tools ever invented by man looked like.

What is predictable in a field is never quite understood and what is extraordinary about them often seems familiar. 'Visionary dreariness', Wordsworth reported in *The Prelude*, and fields mist with the same negative capability or paradoxical potential. A fallow field is life in waiting. But so are all fields. In their ubiquity and in their endless difference, they are places of continuity and of security but also of risk and of transformation. In a dream scene in the Taviani brothers' film

The Night of San Lorenzo, a troop of Italian partisans in World War Two hides below the ripe wheat of a field and then, moments later, stands up armoured as Virgilian heroes to fight the Black Shirts with pitchforks. A bread field becomes a battlefield. In a ballad sung by Nic Jones, a smart lady is tempted and lies outdoors all night with seven yellow gypsies. A green field becomes a seamy bed of grass. Who wouldn't smile?

For a year or so around my tenth birthday I was perhaps the only subscriber in Croydon to *Farmers Weekly*. Before I fell in fully with birds, I had wanted to be a zookeeper or a farmer. But I have never had a field of my own nor worked in one. I have never cut hay nor driven a tractor. Once I rode on a horse. It tried to throw me into a puddle. More recently, I abandoned a walk across a fen field because a herd of cows was gathered at its gate and I was frightened to cross into their bulky company. I don't like milk, fatty meat, gravy, thick butter, or runny eggs.

For a few months in my twenties I had a girlfriend who was a farmer's daughter. We ended in a mess, strung out in different cities in different countries, but the beginning of our end happened I think near our very beginning, in her bed in her old childhood bedroom down the farmhouse corridor from her parents' room. Not that anyone was asleep, except for me; not that anyone was even in their bedrooms, except for me. Me – the visitor who knew about the early whitethroat singing in the hawthorns along the farm hedge but who wasn't expected or even invited to join the rest of the family out in the lambing barn in the middle of the night. Shifts had been allocated: my girlfriend's visit, even with a new boy, didn't excuse her, and when they weren't pulling lambs from ewes, or forking bloody straw from the cobbles, or cutting the fleece off dead lambs to wrap others that had been orphaned at birth so they might be fostered by the mothers of the dead, she and her family were behind the lines at the big range in the farmhouse kitchen on tea-making duty (the slab-tongue of milk into a mug), or cutting crumbling ham slices for midnight sandwiches (a brick of butter oiling its own dish). Eventually the farmer's daughter came back to bed and she smelled of the ewes and the lambs, of birth and afterbirth, of grass and wool, of everything that I wasn't, and I smelled of nothing at all, and we were never to work.

I had though, aged six, loved my little silvery-grey rubber milk churns that were part of my Britains toy farm set. I also loved how I could have a Ford tractor (blue) and a Massey Ferguson one (red) and could fix on the back of either my Lely Snipe Rotary Tedder (four words I have never written in that order until now nor uttered to anyone ever but which I know to be as indelibly true as anything in this world). When you steered the tractor with your finger the tines on the tedder spun round. And at the same time, in the next field, made with plastic drystone walls that clicked together, you could have a one-inch tall shepherd carrying a crook in one hand and a lamb in the other, and put next to him a shire horse with great feathered feet, some tiny saddleback piglets, and a blonde girl wearing wellingtons and a short 1960s sky-blue dress who spooned maize for chickens or ducks forever. And I loved it, and her for getting it for me, when my mother persuaded a greengrocer to part with some of his plastic display grass so that I might lay out on the proper ground my whole farm, barns, fences, tractors, farmers, animals, and so be installed in heaven, irked only by a problem of scale that meant that the blades of greengrocer grass came too high up the sides of my livestock and they tended to fall over in it.

I did the falling over, on a family holiday to Skye in Scotland, when I was ten. My sister and I were encouraged to feed two orphaned lambs with bottles of fresh milk from the farm cow. The lambs were small and stood only to our knees, but they butted us with surprising force, knocking me over in their haste and my nervousness. I got up and patted them, and their fleece was thick and my fingers came away greased with lanolin. The next time I knew that same strange ointment was holding for a quick minute in my surprised arms the oily purple body of my first son, just after he was born and before he was dried and delivered to his mother's breast. On Skye, my sister and I were dragged around the sheepfold by the amazing suck of the lambs on their teated bottles which they pulled at as if everything they needed was in the milk. I next knew that sensation when after his first feed I slipped my finger into the warm wet pucker of my baby's mouth and felt concentrated there all of his world.

The farmer's wife did the milking on Skye. She was a farmer too, though we have no word for her despite her centuries of toil. 'The farmer wants a wife', was the end of the round we sang at school of cattle and chattels. The wife followed 'the farmer wants a sheep' and 'the farmer wants a pig'. One morning she invited me into the byre to watch her milking. The Old English *byre* is related to *bower*, which is related to the German *Bauer* or birdcage. Sure enough, as I followed her muddy boots, swallows flew in and out above us, cutting into the dark, twittering one quick tune as they arrived and another slightly amended one as they left. The cowshed was heavy with the catching smell of sweet-grass-made-shit, a half-dirt-half-dream smell, rising up out of an old world that you find, even aged ten, you know already. I stood against the stone doorway and watched.

The farmer's wife pulled the pail of new milk towards me from between the cow's dirty legs. She had leaned in there on a little low stool, her cheek pressed against the cow's flank, a great black furry wall, while her hands moved on the swaying full moon of udder. The jet of milk rattled like peas at first in the empty bucket and then, as it frothed and filled, like nothing so much as the sound of my own desperate peeing after a run home from school. And, like my pee accidentally touched, it was surprising for being warm, almost hot. In the dark of the byre, the brightest things were all the same washed creamy colour: the farmer's hands, her cow's udder, and the rising disc of milk. 'Try it,' she said, and I knew I should even though I already knew that it wasn't for me. I drew her enamel cup through the bubbles and they burst into tiny flecks of curd that fell back on to the skin of the milk. I wanted to pour it direct to my throat but it covered the inside of my mouth in a warm chalky paint. As it went down it pulled just below my ears, at the place where my jaw was joined to my head. One mouthful was enough. I gave up on *Farmers Weekly* not long after.

Two grass truths I have learned anyway. Like anyone in the temperate world I lived these without knowing them. If you cut grass it doesn't die. If you eat its tops it doesn't mind, because it grows from near its base at what is called an intercalary meristem. This is the joint-like node on the stalk, the bump you feel beneath your fingers when you pluck a stem from the side of a path. Grasses and intercalary meristems are inseparable. In the growth tissue at the meristem, rapid cell division occurs and pushes the grass upwards. A simple and beautiful adaptation has brought us to where we are: hay can be cut, lawns mown, plains grazed. Herbivores – grass-croppers – drove this evolution. Grazing by buffalo maintained the prairie. A savannah is a wildebeest.

The second unknown known: our bodies are grass. We are grass 'carnified' as Thomas Browne said: 'all those creatures we behold, are but the hearbs of the field, digested into flesh in them, or more remotely carnified in our selves'. A cow eats grass and makes milk; a steer eats grass and becomes beef. We toast our cheese and barbecue our burgers and wrap the ensemble in a bread roll made of grass. The three great food crops of the north (now of the whole world) are grasses: rice, corn and wheat. They made us but we made them, as well. We have more than grown up together. Our domestication of the wild has drawn the wild after us. The transubstantiation of the earth works on.

Grass, like us, is young, fresh and green across many time zones. Our bodies are grass, and our days, as the Psalmist said, are 'as' grass. Grass has been a metaphor for our short life as long as we have known it. Land plants have been around for more than 400 million years but grasses evolved only 50 or 60 million years ago. The world's grasslands are young landscapes. Grass has dominated the temperate northern hemisphere only in the last 10,000 to 12,000 years. We appeared in these places about the time they became grasslands. And grass itself seems endlessly young while endlessly dying. Nowhere do its blades grow older than any autumn makes them. A meadow is a year.

Fields are not often famous for what they are. But begin to make a list of those you recall and it is hard to stop. South of the High Atlas Mountains of Morocco there is pitifully little grass. In this rock-desert the soil is thin. The last fields before the Sahara are here. Some giant has unpacked, tearing impatiently at a parcel, and the surface of the

Earth is littered like a new planet with the debris of its making, with black shattered stones that might have fallen from above or sliced their way up from beneath. They are hot from the sun or with the smoulder of the core. In the hills east of N'kob, a Berber family was making a field near a dry riverbed, clearing stones and raising low walls from them, twisting thorns into shrunken hedges. Seeing my friend Mark and me looking for scrub warblers, they said hello and invited us for tea. The young mother, forever pulling her headscarf across her shy smiling face, bent to a pile of thorn twigs and made a fire from them under a soot-blackened kettle. Her two teenage boys brought more kindling. Their father stooped lightly to their field, with a familiarity that made the stones at his feet seem like his crop. He collected an armful as he walked through the cleared place he was making and dropped the stones at the field edge, then crouched to the kettle and leaned in to his wife. I smiled and bent too. We had no language in common. The boys were picking at a thorn; in the next bush along I could see a scrub warbler, my first ever, carrying smaller twigs for its own purposes. The new field beyond the little fire of sticks and its three hearthstones ran for no more than fifty feet in one direction and thirty in the other. There were still many stones to clear. The soil without the stones was as dry and as hard as the stones. The mother shook green tea leaves from a box into their blue enamelled teapot and took a rough block of sugar from the folds of her clothes and passed it to her husband. He hit it with a stone and dropped shattered angular chunks into four blue tea glasses. The boys had to wait while Mark and I drank. The warbler came closer and scolded us with a call as dry as the grey thorn it hid among. The family would try to grow a few lines of wheat here, for couscous. When the kettle had finished a small cooking pot replaced it on the tiny flames; in the pot were a few slices of potato in dilute harissa, their lunch.

Two days later we came down from the mountains into Marrakesh, descending through white storks and cattle egrets planing to their roosts, and arriving as the high violet dusk gave way to a night of blue velvet above the Djemaa el-Fna, the teeming square at the heart of the old medina. There was drumming and singing and a thousand mopeds.

Wood smoke from the grills thickened the air and the lanterns of the cafes floated in it like so many full moons. We ate and then walked into the souk, losing ourselves within moments between the beetling cliffs of goods bursting from the fronts of crowded stalls that deepened giddily beyond like tunnels without end. There were reclining torsos of pungent leather bags, star clusters of verdigris-stained copper lamps, forests of rusty carpets. The vendors were packing up, getting everything that had been laid out in front of their stalls back into the narrow spaces beyond. We were chased down alleys by the judder of metal roller-blinds and we stumbled out of the maze to stop in front of the smallest unit of any that we had passed: a lit green cave, fluorescent bright and deeply scented, a mint stall. The mint-man in a khaki greatcoat was tiny-faced and old and he stood (there was only standing room) framed or wrapped by bunch after bunch of countless serrated green leaves in a sweet and clean-smelling cloud. For the female customer ahead of us, he selected eight or so handfuls from beneath a freshening wet sack at the front of his stall. We spoke briefly (me in halting French) and she said that the carrier bag of mint she had bought was all for tea, would keep in the fridge, and would last about a week. We smiled at the green man in his green cave, the smallest, freshest and greenest field in the world, and walked on out into the riot of the dusty old city.

At the other end of Europe, a few months later, I slept in the final field before the Atlantic.

After the last of the mainland fell away behind us, there was an hour and a half of open water. The sea rolled and slapped the boat. The engines churned, roaring when the propellers rose out through the swell. The seabirds thinned. I tried not to be sick. More slapping, the sea's leer and its bully lean. Then the auks came again, flying ahead of us now, towards where we were going. Slowly out of the marine-blue rose a low grey whaleback. It calmed my guts, grew up, and turned island-green. The engines were cut and we sunk down in the boat, finding our level in the sea at the base of a cliff. We landed in a tender, clambering down to the sea's surface, touching it as we gripped the dinghy, then scrambled up again, wet rocks, then dry, then grass. We dragged barrels of fresh water up the rough slope, its green rising in front of me to fill my sweating eyes, as the salt sea had done minutes before. At the top, I threw my bags from my back and found myself sitting in a field – fifty miles out into the ocean west of Cape Wrath, and the only field on North Rona.

I pitched my tent in a grassed ditch at what looked like the field edge. Away from its cliffs most of the top of the island is grass; on its gentlest slope looking back towards the mainland is the remains of its one field. My friend Kathleen had a bunk in the hut where seal scientists stay. No one has lived on North Rona since 1844; no one could live there now. It and its neighbour, Sula Sgeir, twelve miles off to the south-west, are like accidental islands, crumbs brushed from the table of the mainland and lodged in the sea. Even huddling into the bank there is no real shelter to be had from the wind. But once, under the same oceanic barrage, the island was farmed. The ditch was dug to raise an adjacent bed of soil in order to grow things to eat. Dug and re-dug between the eighth century and the nineteenth, the lazy bed (a mean name far removed from the effort needed to make it) marks the land still, just as it did on the day it was cut from the turf and soil. It is part of a beautiful sinuous geometry, a delta of green corduroy, which drains furrows and ridges, runs and rigs, down the island's sloping southern flank to the sea. It is as human a mark as we have made anywhere before or since.

There is an unmanned lighthouse on Rona now, and the hut is used by the seal people for a few weeks of the year. Both buildings are too recent to look anything other than garish and temporary, ludicrously – and vulnerably – square-angled and blocky in this place of rounded and winded things. The grass blows into a permanent wave along the lazy beds; the ruined houses and chapel in the old village with their turf roofs and drystone walls curve out of and back into the land as if they have grown from it. Storm petrels and Leach's petrels now breed in burrows they dig between the stones of the village.

The ditches, like the ruins, are an imposition on Rona; they mark a clearance, an enclosure, something made in our scale, and yet the space they create has found some natural equivalence in the scale of the island and so of the Earth. The human space has become a land-scape that endures even in its ruin. A centre, somehow, even on the edge. The ripples of green man-made lines spilling down the grass-topped island seem good. If marks have to be made, they seem to be the best marks to make. Thus fields anywhere and everywhere: old but apt; imposed but giving; made in proportions that fit the Earth and us, which bring us together, that allow us to belong, that take the oldest and most searching human measurement – how much land does a man need? – and say, this can be yours, these acres, this plot, your field, man's not nature's, but the best thing of man, and the thing of his that is nearest to becoming nature.

After a midsummer night of the snag and fret of half-light and sea wind, I lay in my sleeping bag with my head out of the tent looking up at the sky. A migrant swallow flew above me along the shelter of the ditch, seeking – as I had – the calmed air made by people shifting earth hundreds of years ago. It fed, as it flew, on the insects that gath-ered in the windless lee. The sea had stilled to the south and tracks and furrows had stretched to meander across its surface, oiled smooth in places, more choppy in others, marking deeper currents beneath, and the way the sea, even in its continuousness, drifts and ripples variously under the wind and around the land. It looked like a field of grass.

If you were not a commoner or a parishioner in early-modern England and you wanted to rent part of a common field or hire rights to pasture, you might seek someone called a *fieldsearcher*, who would act as an agent on your behalf. Without fields of my own, these chapters are my *field-searches*. The field to which I return most often is currently rough grazing land at Burwell in the Cambridgeshire fens, one mile from where I live. This field was once a fen and the intention of its current owners is that it will be fen again, one day. The other three are foreign plots that I have known (in part) across some years: far afield, but not. The first of these is in Zambia on an old colonial farm. This particular field once grew tobacco but is at present overgrown with grasses and scrub. I have already written a little about these Zambian fields. Since those first words the farmer has died (he is buried near his old crops) and I have married Claire, the woman who showed me the field, the farm and the farmer. The second foreign field is a battlefield, and the remnant shortgrass prairie and adjacent croplands, in Montana in the USA where Sioux and Cheyenne warriors killed George Custer and his party in June 1876, in a battle which as much as anything was a fight over grass. The last field is in the abandoned village of Vesniane in the Exclusion Zone near the exploded nuclear reactor at Chernobyl in Ukraine. Until April 1986 it was a meadow grazed by cows. When I went there, the last thing I saw was an empty aluminium milk churn lying on its side, in the open doorway of a ruined byre at the field edge.

Each of these four fields has been turned over in one way or another for as long as they have been fields – it's in their nature. But now each is at a more angled point in its life. Fields cut from cleared scrub are abandoned back to thorns and thickets. Wild grasslands have become battlefields and then the holding place for the dead of those battles. Pasture is poisoned. A plot will be unplumbed. Territory, ownership, the exploitation of land, its meaning and value, the grass itself – all has been and is being argued over. There are tangled human voices in each field but there is also the sound of the grass. Just as fields aren't famous, grass isn't heroic of itself. It works anonymously. But I am trying to hear that as well. In John Clare's great poem 'The Lament of Swordy Well' a put-upon, enclosed field talks back. It's worth listening.

I'll begin by taking us once again to the worst so we might get it behind us. The road, encore. The anti-field. A place that is not even a place, which is the opposite of where you want to be, but where you find yourself again and again. I grow old even thinking about it, even as I tell you. This time we will walk up to it, in order to best catch the sting of its slap, but so that we might also have a means of escape. Stand at the last field edge before the asphalt. In front of you is a main road, the A14 once more, sunk into the ditch of a cutting. You don't see it until you arrive at the lip of its wound but you have heard it already, forever, the crenellated din of combustion and hardware passing without end. If you are lucky it sounds like a sea heard from the top of a cliff; more likely it puts a boxed fever into the brain, a swarfed headache driving between your ears. You have been here many times before; indeed, part of you lives here, though you are never at home. Your car will dip below the earth's surface, angle down the slipway, and latch on. But today, on foot, turn your back on the road and walk west down the green path through the wheat fields. Right now you must start away from here.

The dual carriageway of the A14 marks the eastern edge of the English fields of this book. The road forms the county border between Suffolk and Cambridgeshire and also the upland end of the parish of Swaffham Prior where Claire and I live. From the house it takes half an hour to walk to the main road, up a farm lane or along a footpath on the top of a chalk dyke (the Anglo-Saxon Devil's Dyke or Ditch). Depending on the wind's quarter I hear the road between five and fifteen minutes after leaving the front door. Once, when I was near, a crash had stopped the traffic on both sides and I could hear skylarks singing in Suffolk, otherwise I have never heard it quiet. Every day it fights its fight, dug into its trench.

Halfway into the last field before the traffic, a lesser whitethroat rattling from the final hedge stole into my ears. After that the road silenced all apart from itself. I flushed a skylark and it rose nervously and banked to avoid having to fly over the cars. I saw its beak open but couldn't hear its call. In the last wide fields of Cambridgeshire that run to the road there were forty hares spread through the young wheat in twos and threes. The sun streamed through their long black ears flushing them blood-pink. Such ears for such noise. At the road, parallel with it, is a hedged bridleway, just twenty feet from the metal run of traffic. I have never seen any person or horse there. A dead mole was on the path, lying with its head pointing towards the road, *unsoiled* – encumbered by being above the earth and to be buried in the air. It looked, as D. H. Lawrence said of a mole in his story 'Second Best', 'like a very ghost of joie de vivre'. It was earless and its eyes were lost into its soft fur, giving its front a blank and incomplete look. Its mouth grinned half open and showed two tiny canines, ivory needles against its sooted snout. Its fleshy hands and feet hung at its four corners like pink flags.

I turned from the mole and the road and headed west. If you look from the Suffolk hills to the Cambridgeshire fens, the sky leaps up above you and doubles in height. In the spring on days of silvery cloudless sheen it seems higher still and able to further flatten the fields beneath it. The country before me opened but it also disappeared, thinning at the horizon about ten miles away to a level green line. This is a fen effect. Shining green ground hurries like dark water spilled across a tabletop to fill the flat space. The width of the view tugs at the corners of your eyes, its shallowness makes you frown. There is a lot of light to take in and not much else.

I heard a bee flying past my ear. The chalk hills behind me (though they would barely count as hills anywhere but here) made a bony barn of stone and they shouldered the dyke back towards the main road. Ahead, where the bee had gone, the fens were a soft and glistening skin, streaming from beneath me, cambered at either edge, an offering of earth, thin and damp but vividly alive. The green squares of the farms of Burwell, Reach and Swaffham Prior were chopped and trimmed by their hedges and ditches and, rolled hard under the silver-blue noon, they receded like Euclid's geometry or Alice's chessboard. Descending towards them and the fen beyond from the last few feet of altitude on the dyke was like watching from the windows of a landing aeroplane, when distance and spread shrink and narrow until you arrive on the ground as if buried by the near edge of things. But there were consolations: new weather came and conversation. A skylark got up from the path ahead, climbing over a field, its wings and throat rippling in one continuous action of flight and song. A lapwing shadowed a buzzard. Cowslips on the bank shook in the wind like smeared butter. There were swallows laying their slates, one over the other, up above my head. They sang as they worked.

The village of Reach marks the fen end of the dyke. It finishes on the village green but the dyke line continues beyond the cluster of houses and joins another man-made pathway running across the flat fen: Reach Lode, a cut waterway draining west. Though my feet remained dry I had crossed into a world of wet. I felt it beneath me. The calcified spine of the dyke was replaced by stoneless earth banks held together by the lush green grass and the soft dampness of the soil itself. Back on the dyke the molehills had been pale and powdery and bumped with nubs of chalk and blades of flint. A hundred steps away on the banks of the lode they were soft and peaty, smooth and sticky, and as black as mole fur.

My fen field begins here, the first of the four in this book. From here, there is not much to look at. It is the same closer up. But the field, once a stretch of fenland, has worked its way into my life, as have the three others. All four are grassed at the moment. They are real fields: a few hundred acres standing for the world. They could be walked, mapped, mown and known. Each has lived, at least for some time, as an apparently flat and plain place but also as a living sheet on which people sketched or screened various dreams for a while. Yet regardless of their fieldworkers' attentions, each also holds on to its own life, and remains itself even as it is harvested or grazed, preserved or abandoned. All fields are places of outlasting transience. They reset time. Each has a past but each lives in the present; each has a biography but is still a work in progress.

It happens that the same species of bird, the swallow (known internationally these days as the barn swallow), flies and feeds over all my four fields, and I love the bird and our world for that, though that doesn't make the grass beneath the swallows the same. The fields have some things in common but much that is particular. They are site-specific, idiomatic and accented; they are shaped by what they are near and speak of where they are. We made them and we were made by them. 'The land has been humanised, through and through', D. H. Lawrence wrote of rural Italy as he might have of all fields, 'and we in our own tissued consciousness bear the results of this humanisation.' I wonder if there are any two fields in Britain that are identical? I doubt it. I've been keeping watch. I know there are no ways into a field, no field-gateways in the world, that are the same. But I also know in no field anywhere do you feel properly lost.

And yes, as well as being a book of four fields, I want this to be a book *for* fields, a work of advocacy as much as of observation. My field love is different from my swallow love. Swallows I love for not being us, for not knowing they are swallows, for quickening the air while flying so closely and so swallowishly about our lives. I love fields for what they are, parcels of the earth we have gathered to us (almost always beautifully, could there be an *ugly* field?), but also for the picture they give us of ourselves (not always beautiful), the way all fields tell of how we have orphaned ourselves from the world – how hard we must work for even a whisper of Eden – but also how best we can be at home in it.

Winter Fen

Life moves. A year neither starts nor finishes. I went out.

In a field next to Burwell Fen a lit fuse of winter wheat ran bright along the hard earth, its green mocking the cold. Overhead eight white winter swans lowered out of the north sky, cut from its freezing grey canvas, a family of whoopers from Russia flying like a washing line of flapping linen and yelping to one another as they pitched and juddered to a stop in the field. Their booted black feet kicked up the cold peat as they settled, and their long necks straight away dowsed the green where they ate.

A storm beyond the horizon had chased the swans south and was moving on the fen. Ten herring gulls with cold fish eyes and heads of shaved ice sat on another run of the wheat field, as white on the green as mushrooms. In the next-door field, 800 fieldfares spread over the threadbare flint-olive winter turf. Never before had I seen so many together. Each had its allotted grass and bounced over it at the same speed and in the same direction as its neighbour. The flock moved with the tact of a herd. Every few minutes the leading edge of the birds sensed they had come to the rim of something and rose into a flex of grey-brown flight which drew their followers up after them until, fifty yards or so further on, they all landed again, spaced as before, and resumed taking in the grass beneath them.

Even in the winter, because of the lifting and carrying of water, the once great swamp of the fens is now mostly dry. Slub – the evocative fen word for mud – is not what it once was. Drains beneath the grass vein the ground, while pumps and ditches and a thousand cuts (reaches, eaus and lodes, conduits and leams, fosses and sewers, washes and sluices) fetch rain and river water from the fields and beyond and bear it away. For the fens to function as a place for us, their water must be sent somewhere else and turned into the sea's problem. The pumping is non-stop; this country must bail itself out forever if it is to remain country; if the sea broke in and came down from where it rides now, fifty miles to the north, all would drown.

To walk on the flat worn grass of Burwell Fen in the winter is to cross a seabed. Both the North Sea at the Wash and the nearby water are over my head. The zero contour circles the fen and the land dips further at its centre to lie six and a half feet below sea level, the lowest place for miles. To step below the waterline in these fields is to sense a keeping back of a wetter truth across the wider fens: it was once sea here and then was kept from being always-sea by being sometimes-sea, and part of the great porous edge-of-sea that the fens were until we bested them, or tried to.

The wringing of water from the spongy fens and its portage away has put them further under. After hundreds of years of drainage the land has shrunk and lies *against* nature, below the sea but also below the rivers and drains that take its water away. The soil is drying and wasting, six feet every sixty years: 'by the height of a man' it was said sixty years ago, 'in the life of a man'.

Yet even in the time I have known them, the fens ran wet for part of every year and spread their own inland floodlit waters. That we still think of them as *fens* declares the dripping fact. And this is still a wet place in waiting. As fast as we build our dams the fens run back, rippling without contours, flat but edgy, a place where planned outcomes never quite happen and where human intentions forever come up against falling water. No one has nailed them. In an otherwise locked-down southern England, they seem like a work still in progress. Unfinished, you might say, or unfished.

Half a mile from my home, there is a road through the fields to the fens called Commercial End. It's a cul-de-sac. The tarmac ends. Farmers use the track that remains, and dog walkers, and birdwatchers like me. Today the village turns its back on the fens, and the road to town is king. But once the people faced them as if the entire world came to the village from there. And it did. Commercial End is a road, but the oldest villagers remember it as a hythe or a quay. Coal came here from the north-east of England by boat; wine, bricks and timber were also landed. Less than sixty years ago a way to the sea began here.

From the quay at Commercial End you once could have stepped on to a boat and not walked on land again until you were in Cape Town, Odessa, or Nantucket. The sense of the fens as the beginning of the sea is hidden now but still lies locked at their heart. The flat land asks us to feel the marine in it again and again. There doesn't seem to be much to the earth here. The world is spread thinly. The sky does most of the work. You can watch rain from far off steering over the land, and so look around you in time. At the horizon, which is only the horizon because I am five foot ten, the fen peters out, edged but not ended – a bank or a line of willows is merely in the way. Being there would be the same as being here. If I was five foot eleven I could see more, but not much. To see further I would need a mast or a crow's nest.

There is a story from hundreds of years ago that is told and repeated in various histories of the fens about a sea fish, a cod, taken to market in 1626 from the Wash to Cambridge, splashing in a wooden barrel of seawater as the boat that carried it and others sailed inland from the salt to the sweet. Keeping fish fresh by carrying them alive to market was not unusual. A hundred years later, in 1724, Daniel Defoe noted horse-drawn wagons hauling fish through the fens: 'tench and pike, pearch and eels ... [in] ... great butts fill'd with water'. But Cambridge was also a port and much arrived there by boat. The coat of arms of the town – fifty miles from the North Sea at the Wash – included three ships and two seahorses. The city market was busy and barges and boats from the sea often blocked the Cam. When the cod was opened at a fish-woman's stall, a book wrapped in a piece of canvas fell from the fish's guts. It was 'much soyled and defaced, and couered ouer with a kind of slime & congealed matter'. The mess on the gutting slab was given the name of *Book-Fish*.

Someone's book, an inland indoors thing, had fallen overboard and been swallowed into the belly of a fish, and so carried across the lost sea of the fens to a city of stone and readers. The book was made up of three separate religious texts that had been written in prison by an early-sixteenth-century protestant reformer called John Frith: 'The Preparation to the Cross and to Death', 'A Mirrour, or, Glasse to know thy selfe' and 'A Briefe Instruction, to teach a person willingly to die, and not to feare death'. It was a sort of fish-supper, or *Compleat Angler*, for the soul.

The last great thaw in the northern hemisphere began 11,000 years ago. Calculations made of the former extent and thickness of the ice suggest that, after it melted, the sea level rose eustatically (uniformly around the world) by 300 feet. Many fields were lost beneath the waves. Previously, when the sea was locked away in ice to the north, the bed of what we now know as the North Sea made a 'great lowland plain' of dry accessible land, riddled with the rivers Rhine, Thames and Trent (each far longer then than now). In those days a horse might walk east and unhindered from the grass-topped western cliff edge of Ireland all the way through Europe and Asia, across the grassed Bering Bridge and on to the valley of the Greasy Grass River in the middle of the Great Plains of North America.

In the summer of 1929 the fishermen of the *Colinda* out from Yarmouth, trawling between the Leman and Ower Banks, north-east of the Norfolk coast, dredged up from 120 feet of salt water a piece of what they called *moorlog*, the brown fibrous remains of freshwater peat. Breaking it open they found what they thought was a 'harpoon', a pointed piece of worked bone some inches long, serrated on one side with well-fabricated teeth. In fact it was a farm tool, not a fish tool: a Danish Mesolithic implement dating from around 6500 BC, a time when the seabed was worked as a field.

The book lost overboard and carried inland in the belly of a cod here finds its echo or half-rhyme: a man's hand-tool from the land, lost and left, first within the earth and then buried at sea, netted to the surface and carried ashore.

* * *

Other books have come from the earth of the fens over which the cod and its book sailed. Two appeared in the middle of the Second World War made from the few flat acres of Adventurers' and Burwell Fens. At a time of national crisis, when the very earth of Britain was under threat, the fen soil was tilled variously into service. The copies I have of the two are printed on thin but precious wartime economy paper, onion skin to the touch. They are oppositional documents, enemies of one another, and record a battle over a single fen – what it meant, what it was for, and how people might live from it. The battle, in some ways, pitched onions against fish.

The two books, Eric Ennion's *Adventurers Fen* and Alan Bloom's *The Farm in the Fen*, are about precisely the same place: the fen and the fields one mile north-west of where I live. Thirty years ago, as a visiting student birdwatcher, I saw a barn owl overtaken by a hunting male hen harrier there, and this secured the place as always worth watching. Today as I travel towards it, as I have done hundreds of times in the last few years, even when it is still hidden by its surrounding earthen aqueducts carrying away its water, I find I am raising it in my mind's eye and wondering what it will hold.

Snowlight on the fen after an overnight fall. Its white gold spread evenly, a universe of snow: nothing excluded, everything covered. Fields transformed into rooms, walled and ceilinged in muting pink. The whole fen padded. Not a whisper of wind. I talked to myself as if at home as I walked across the sheeted floor. Below me, a dentist packing a tooth, or the squeak of kapok. The sun, an old orange light bulb, eventually leaked through the ceiling, a stain from upstairs. My eyes burned with the spirit glare of reflected snow: the white razorlight pressing from the ground was brighter than the sky. All about me the stopped air ticked like a tube-train rail. Some sort of crystal set had been lowered over the fen. Tiny live-wire *seeps* of meadow pipits came across the frost. Hares moved off stiff-backed with their odd, humping limp. Their long hind legs afflict them with a kind of virile disability, as if to walk were always more taxing than to run.

The snow had come with wind. In the village, the north-east side of both church towers was white; it was the same with the willows on the road, the lower legs of the pylons on the fen, and the reed flags along the ditch: a carpet, flicked from one angry quarter only, had crept up the walls of the room. There were some pigs in a field, in the snow they looked like naked people. Under a hawthorn thrushes had gathered, arriving on hurried flights – the snow made everything fly as if startled into the air. The birds came whiffling down into a space too small for them, crowding into a clear patch of ground the size of a spread handkerchief: two blackbirds and two fieldfares with a redwing more nervous at the edge of the ring. With the desperation of displaced people they had half abandoned and half redoubled their territoriality. The blackbirds – a male and a female – launched themselves upwards from standing jumps to snatch berries from the thin low-slung branches above them. I saw them come back down on the earth with the frozen haws, the colour of old blood, jammed in their beaks. They threw their heads back and swallowed. The fieldfares and the redwing waited.

Thirty years ago, in what seems now like an ancient Elizabethan winter of iron cold and hard freeze, the fens flooded and then fixed: a new Greenland cast in ice. I came out of Cambridge with friends, nudging a car down a slippery road, and we stopped and I put on borrowed Dutch skates and slid across the utter quiet of a frozen field. An iced mist tinkled from one side of the flood to the other. Our voices and the scratch of our skates came back to us. I grew bolder and undid the brass buttons on my old khaki greatcoat, trying to make a sail or wings to catch any wind but there was none. We were somehow inside an outside place.

The flood was only a foot deep and it had frozen solid, and apart from a few milky clouds it had set clear. Clear like old glass is clear: yellowish, a little bumpy and not quite true. Moving out over the fen was like being able to slide over the roof of a Victorian greenhouse. Even as it was freezing the water had passed across the field and the icing flood had stirred the grass until it was fixed in rippling waves and looked like a long-exposure photograph taken as a tide rises into a weedy rock pool. There were imprisoned bubbles strung through the grass stems like wall-eyed pearls. The ice had trapped the earth's breathing.

Burwell is the nearest village to Burwell Fen and Adventurers' Fen. It had an unfinished *burh* or castle that was built on the orders of King Stephen in 1144 to oversee the rebellious Geoffrey de Mandeville who was pillaging across the fens from his captured base at Ely. The castle duly drew Geoffrey in and he attacked it from its watery side but was mortally wounded in the process. The Adventurers came long after the village and its castle were founded, and maybe never *came* at all: they were the investors who put money into fen drainage in the 1600s, the backers of delvers, dykers and ditchers, the fen equivalent of hedge-funders or enclosers. A document from 1717 marks a drained fen as *Adventure land*. But long before (and long since) the fens were (and have remained) risky places for pillage or adventure, indeed for almost every project undertaken on their shifting ground.

Nonetheless the *fens* are almost entirely *Fens* now. Naming them and draining them began at the same time. The capital men made capital Fens. Fen scale became human; they were branded, like wild horses, with a big letter that cut straight ditches and right angles in their swamp and made their wet someone's. Yet once it was all one fen, not just these acres west of Burwell, but for dozens of miles in all directions, and all of it without edge but for the hills to its sides and the sea at its mouth. Lower-case fens were wider, wilder and unbound. They slipped more fishily from the grasp, wanting wet, and beyond all measuring. And in the little letter something of the creep of water over land survives if only in the imagination: f is for flood.

The *fen* is the haunt of Grendel, the grim demon, and other monsters in *Beowulf*. Our word comes from the same Old English (Anglo-Saxon) *fen*, meaning marsh, dirt or mud. The word is shared across the swamp-lands of Europe with Old Frisian, Old Saxon, Middle Dutch, Old High German, Old Icelandic and Gothic: all the places where the living have liked to put the unwanted living and other, deader, bodies in bogs.

The commonality of wetness, uncertain footing, and the ordinary stuff that surrounds us but which clings unclean, can be traced still further back to both the words for marsh or mud in Sanskrit, *pánka-s* or *panka*, and Indo-European, *pen-* or *pon-*.

When it came into language, in what is now Cambridgeshire, the fen world was divided into two. Later the terms could be defined and discussed, originally they were lived as fact: there were winter grounds and there were summer grounds. Something solid was sought beneath the wet: winter grounds were places where you could stand in the winter and not drown; summer grounds were wetter places that were only dry enough during the summer months. Any map, to begin with, was thinly filled. Appearing out of the wet, parcels of land were identified when they meant something, earning a name if they could be visited to graze animals or mow hay or dig peat or cut litter (reeds and sedge and other marsh plants) before the water returned and it all became fen again. The following summer the names would come back as the drowned land rose once more, like mud- or sandbanks lifted into being as a tide falls.

Once draining began and took hold over centuries, the fens thickened with names and kept them through the year. *Fen* itself became one of the commonest suffixes to place names in Cambridgeshire. As well as Sedge, Turf, Mow and Cow Fen, there was Rushfenne, Oxefen, Hoggesfenne, Bullockes Fenne, but also Snytefen (snipe fen) and Purfenne (bittern fen). From around 1200 the word *feld* for field appears commonly on maps and documents. Fens were called fields when they were drained and brought into use. In the fens the word field doesn't have the old meaning of 'open country' – *fen* meant that. *Field* meant, as in our modern sense, a somehow 'enclosed area': Grasfeld, Pesefeld, Whetefeld, Stubbilfeld, Cleyfeld, Chalkfeld, Peetfeld, Smethefeld (smooth), Clenefeld (free of weeds), Wildefeld, Medowefeld, Falowfeld, Somerfeld, Honiefeld (sticky), Brenfeld (burned), Foxfeld, Sparwefeld (sparrow), Finechefeld, Crowfeld, Hartfeld.

Though they are all around me, I don't know any of these fields within Burwell or Adventurers' Fen by name. The fields still have them, farmers call their acres something, and there are signs on the fens where the nature reserves begin and end. But the fields that I know, I call by other names: the field where the pylons march like winter trees; the field where we saw three owls – a little, a tawny and a barn – in three quick minutes; the whinchat ditch; the badger field; the field where the car crashed into the tree; the magic field where Ade, the birdman, sees rare plovers; the fly-tip lane; the crane field.

A dun day after a thaw. The grassy fen at Burwell looked like a dead lake. Several inches of snow had covered the ground for more than a week and in that time the earth hadn't received its usual junk from above. When the melt came anything that had arrived on the snow's surface was just beginning to be incorporated into it, like a body being moved through a glacier, but now it was dumped greasily about the flattened, school-dinner grass: snapped teazels, blown straw, blue string, the body of a herring gull, and a cattle-tramped discus of ice on the hard bare earth around a gate, like a jellyfish on a beach.

Sounds travelled again. A light aeroplane fiddled. The rim of the fen bumped with gunshots. Padded jackets were going after pheasants and machines were scaring pigeons. A string of skylarks settled ahead of me, the end of the line looping close to the leader, tying a knot. Roe deer sat down on the fen once more like sandcastles. The cables sagged lower between the pylons and dripped as I walked beneath them.

On Tubney Fen, the stymied pool melted from its middle and ducks, survivors of the freeze, crowded in to talk: the soft frog pulse of teal, *whewing* wigeon, the *crick crack* of gadwall and shoveler. Around midday they fell quiet and drowsy. Across the unruffled water I watched one after another look over its shoulder and twist its head over its back and tuck it between its wings and its body. They were folding themselves away to sleep: their bills hidden, one eye buried in feathers, the other, a button flat to the sky, shutting in the warmth of the thaw.

The next day, in the inch of spring sun, the plough-pressed ridges of turned soil along the bare fields shone like fish-scale, and the water in the lodes rainbowed with clay oils: some marrow was moving again through the buttery land beneath the peat.

*   *   *

I went to Peterborough on the western side of the fen basin to inspect the reduced world of the shrunken fens, walking eastwards down the slightest of inclines to Holme Fen. Nearby, in 1851, Whittlesey Mere was drained, the last fen mere to have its plug pulled. The year before it had been one of the largest lakes in England. When its water had gone, a green-painted iron column, said to be from the Crystal Palace Exhibition hall, was sunk into the ground half a mile from the south-west margin of the mere, on the peat fen at Holme. It was hammered in until it disappeared, twenty-two feet pushed deep into the damp skin of the earth. The column's base rested on solid clay, its top was level with the surface peat.

The water was pumped from Whittlesey in a matter of days. Locals strapped planks to their feet to walk on the mud and gather the fish that were drowning in air. Eels and others were taken by the ton from the drying mere to Birmingham and Manchester. When it was fully drained the lakebed gave up a censer and an incense boat, which the last Abbot of Ramsey had lost in his watery flight from the Dissolution Commissioners of Henry VIII. The skeleton of a *grampus* (a dolphin of some species, possibly a killer whale) was also found, a leftover from more marine times. The water birds of Whittlesey went with its water. Previously, eight punt-gunners had made a living shooting its ducks. Three thousand wildfowl had been taken from the decoy on Holme Fen in one week. Eight bitterns or *butterbumps* had been shot on Whittlesey in one day.

Holme Fen now is thick with sickly looking silver birches that thin at their tops to scratchy headaches. Trains on the east coast mainline shake past, drumming the ground and making the treetops judder. The green metal column at the wood edge is surrounded by taller birches like a lamp post in an overgrown town. And, like the trees but not quite as fast, it is pulling up out of the soil. Its crown is now twelve feet clear of the earth, an iron-green stick in the birch-crowded sky.

All those who were once alive and have died since, you think, and all that rot, the corruption of what Thomas Browne called the *aftergrave*, but so much less earth to keep the bodies in: where did it all go? The column grows at Holme out of the death of the surrounding soil, revealed by the earth's loss and wastage, like a fossil tree exhumed, a bog splinter of rust, and alive only in its long dying because of the quicker death and vanishing of that which once blackly cloaked it underground. The column hasn't grown. The earth – the world, here – has shrunk.

Between the trains, the woods at Holme Fen were quiet. One great spotted woodpecker called. *Quit.* A party of tits dabbed through the sticky treetops like Christmas lights, feeble against the day. I took a last look at the post. The plug is still in but around it the cold black bath has drained away.

The first of the two books about Burwell and Adventurers' Fens was *Adventurers Fen* by E. A. R. Ennion, published in 1942. Eric Ennion was born in 1900 and grew up in Burwell. His father was the general practitioner in the village and Ennion also trained as a doctor but spent much of his adult life as a naturalist and painter of birds. His line drawings illustrate his book: he makes a perfect black-tailed godwit out of twenty strokes of a pen; his drake tufted duck, smaller than my smallest fingernail, is dense with duckishness. After the war Ennion was prominent in the founding and running of some of the first bird observatories and field-studies centres in Britain. But it is as an artist that he is remembered today. His eye comes from the fens. You would know this after a single hour on what remains of his home patch. The splash of light across flat land and the wateriness of water is everywhere in his paintings. He used watercolours almost exclusively and his pictures, especially of watery birds in watery places – ducks, waders, kingfishers, wagtails – are all fluid. Everything depicted is close to dissolving into his paper with a thin silvery wash. Nothing stands still. Each bird seen has been moving through water-lit air up until the very moment he has caught it. He can paint the nothing of the wind as well.

Ennion was a proper birdman, a seasoned looker, and one reason why his pictures still seem fresh and valuable is that he repeatedly caught the ineffable this-ness of the birds that he painted, their quintessence, instress or jizz. In 1972, when I was ten, the RSPB magazine, *Birds*, featured an interview with Ennion and a double-page colour spread of a superb painting that drenched me then and which I can still recall: a party of around twenty spotted redshanks (I'd never seen one in 1972) have just landed in a pool of clear water at Minsmere (a much desired but unvisited destination for me then) and are swimming after fish fry. Most of the birds are upending like ducks, each is angled and moving differently, many are reflected on the water and some are visible beneath the surface with their eyes intent and their beaks widening after the tiny fish. Ennion's painterly modesty – an austere palette and thin watercolours – has a remarkably strong effect, recreating the spangled sensation of surfacing after a dive into a lake. No other bird painting has gone in so deep or stayed so fresh – so *undried* – in my mind.

In Ennion's terms, Adventurers' Fen runs almost to the back gardens of Burwell. His chapters give a little history of the villages and wildlife of the parishes round about, but his book is mostly an elegy for the fen and the wet and wild decades between the First World War and the Second when what had previously been half-drained reverted to swamp. It is an elegy because, as part of the war effort, the fen was drained once again and dried and ploughed to agricultural land. Hence the second book got from these fields. *The Farm in the Fen* appeared in 1944 and is by Alan Bloom. It takes over where Ennion leaves off. Before the war, Alan Bloom had a nursery further west in Cambridgeshire (he has a perfect name for a plantsman), but he wanted more land (for plants at first and then for crops) and he felt that sodden acres of fenland languishing 'unimproved' were a crime in hungry wartime Britain.

Ennion loved the world of wet for its implacable and unownable spread, its enabling recklessness and the wild gifts that brought; Bloom needed to make a living and wanted the soil to turn for him, and the water be made useful, and only the things that he had nominated to grow (both functional and beautiful). In this way the two men were enemies, but I see them set down on the fen as one: its little acres so lovingly and humanly known, its oozy truculence so accurately and tellingly told.

I never met Alan Bloom, but I did once, aged thirteen, sit in a classroom to listen to Eric Ennion talk of turning the wetlands of his life (Adventurers' Fen, the Northumberland coastline, the water-meadows around Flatford Mill) into field sketches and watercolours. He held in his small, doctorly, hands a portfolio, and opened it in front of us to show, in one wet sheet or watery fresco after another, the fixtures he had managed, superbly, to take down in the slippery world. He propped his pictures against his chest, slipping from one saturated scene to the next, surrounded, as it now seems, by the costume or weeds of his defeat. His suit was ruddy worsted: an old ploughed field flecked with flints and the sown stars of scarlet pimpernel and bird's foot trefoil. A field of his enemy, in this way, the nurseryman Mr Bloom, who came himself, marvellously, in his later years to look like *his* opposing field: a gardener who got wilder as he got older and jumped the fence, grew his white hair until it was Crazy Horse long, and slung a brassy earring above his cheek like a gypsy moon.

The fog was everywhere but thickest on the fen, for that is the lowest ground and the air knows it – the land has been underwater before. The sky leaked. Through its emulsion, I couldn't make out much, but I heard snipe as they crisped up and away, one after another, four flushing ahead from the wet grass, two to my side, and I imagined their gimlet bills worming a hole through the day. An invisible lapwing called. The bare elder in the middle of the fen reared like branching coral. The grass at my feet pulsed. The mist and the moist earth became one. I caught again the strike of snipe wings and they burned like sedge-lamps for an instant before they faded, melding with the curtained ring of fog that kept pace with me. If just once you could reach this and part it you might find the snipe on the far side chatting amongst themselves in sunlight, loosening their upholstered tweeds, smoking.

On a rare-bird twitch one winter weekend in the late 1970s I travelled from Bristol to a field near Canterbury in Kent. It was cold. The dawn was slow to come; the day concussed with fog. My friends and I walked along a farm track between cabbages and steamed in our coats like horses. Around our moving feet the cabbages were vividly bright, those just a few yards beyond cold-cooked to grey. Somewhere beyond the beyond was a vagrant male great bustard, a refugee from central or eastern European grasslands in all probability, and, wonderfully, after an hour or so an amateurish breeze got up between a few cabbage stalks and nudged the fog just enough for the walking bird to appear, sandy brown, vast, and as improbable as a camel. There is a story that in 1801 on Salisbury Plain a man wrestled for an hour with a great bustard that was attacking his horse. Watching the looming bird stepping heavily in and out of the Kentish fog I could believe it.

What Eric Ennion calls Adventurers' Fen is now more commonly known as Burwell Fen. The names have been somewhat muddied over the last hundred years. Bloom uses both. Here, I call the grounds between Reach and Burwell Lode, Burwell Fen, and the smaller fen to the north of Burwell Lode that abuts on to Wicken Fen, Adventurers'. Most present-day maps say the same.

It is not surprising that the names of the two adjacent fens have slipped across the water and between the peat. For some decades in the last century they were farmed together; at times they were both swampy places; at other times Burwell was farmed and Adventurers' was fen. Both are now owned and managed by the National Trust. They have signs as well as names. Adventurers' Fen has been a rough grazed part-fen since Alan Bloom's attempt to farm it stopped at the end of the Second World War. It is currently fenced and is a mix of scrawny grass and reedy pools; Highland cattle graze it and snipe live in it. Burwell Fen is being newly returned, via grazing, to fenland after a longer period under the plough. It too was undertaken during the war.

To date, Burwell Fen is the most substantial expression of what the National Trust calls the 'Wicken Vision', its project for the *rewilding* of the fens. Wicken Fen was the first nature reserve to be owned by the Trust. The fen was taken into care in 1899. Now the Trust is trying to collect adjacent farm properties south from Wicken whenever possible. The plan is to buy somewhere between 10,000 and 15,000 acres of the fens towards Cambridge and take them out of arable farming and return them to wetter grounds, reducing the amount of drainage, raising the water table, and converting the fields to swampier places, thereby coaxing back the *bogbumpers*: the bitterns, the crakes, the cranes and all the rest.

From the air or on a map Burwell Fen is an isosceles triangle, like a green slice of cake narrowing west. The lodes flowing away from the villages of Reach and Burwell form its two long sides. The point of the fen triangle is made where the lodes join to flow on together towards the River Cam at Upware. At this sharp corner there is a captured pond on the fen, separate from the waters flowing on either side of it. Common terns breed on the pond and kingfishers fish. Behind it are some debauched willows at the site of an old building, long gone, called Pout Hall. Green woodpeckers and little owls like this place. The remainder of the fen back towards Reach and Burwell is a series of rough open fields, half fenced, half ditched. As well as collapsed winter grass there is some sedge, a line or two of shivering reeds, dark patches of stiff thistles and burrs and smaller stains of nettles and docks. Young beef cattle have been grazed on Burwell Fen since it was taken out of more active agricultural service in preparation for its *rewetting*. They share the grass with roe deer. A near-ruined corrugated-iron barn is sinking in the middle of the fields. The base of the triangular fen is a lesser ditch, dry at the moment, running between the lodes. Further east of that, the rough fields end and a few arable plots – rape and wheat in recent years – take over until the scrubby-wooded edges of Burwell village appear.

Perhaps nowhere in fenland truly is drained, but Burwell Fen has been particularly wet. It was a low place even in the terms of the wider low country and it functioned for hundreds of years as a kind of soak-away for the surrounding slightly higher fens. Its acres were among the very last to be drained. Wicken Fen has never been drained. The village of Wicken just to the north gets its name from *wicha*, meaning a dairy farm. It is mentioned in the Domesday Book of 1086 and reminds us that it would be wrong to think there haven't always been people *close* to the fens. Nowadays, thanks to the Adventurers and then to the farm in the fen and its wartime labours, you can drive out of Burwell to both fens (and so on to Wicken too) on a metalled dead-end lane called Factory Road (some maps call it Little Fen Drove). Along it, between the village and the fens, there is an old brick kiln, an electricity station approached by heavy swags of cabling, and a cardboard factory. There is also a hedge of wild plum trees where lesser whitethroats sing in late April, and a ditch at a field edge that seems to be a memory lane for migrant wheatears and whinchats, capturing a few of them for a day or two most springs and autumns. One December morning not long after dawn, I watched an elderly Indian man in a belted winter coat marching briskly down the road from the village, flushing dopey pheasants from the verge as he went. One hundred yards behind him, his wife (I assume) followed, her pink sari blowing tightly around her and then flapping like a flag in the licking wind as she hurried towards the fen and her husband. Both were wearing bright-yellow trainers.

Adventurers' and Burwell Fens both lie in Burwell parish. Parishes on this eastern edge of the fens are mostly shaped as long thin strips running roughly east to west. They commonly have three parts. Westernmost is the fen, once the lowest and the wettest third, a peatland of waterlogged grass and reeds, criss-crossed with waterways and flood-prone and sometimes submerged for months. It was once the way to the sea. The middle part rises slightly on chalky loam to the east and was the beach to the fen. This was the place to live and to build your churches, shops and pubs. Burwell had ten in Ennion's day, nowadays the village has four, perhaps three: one is boarded up and its wall lettering that had announced it as The Crown was reconfigured as *Whore* for a week or two by some village jokers before being removed altogether. The soil in this middle third of the parish is paler than the peat, stony and drier, but there are freshwater springs bubbling through the chalk. The easternmost part of the parish rises higher again towards Suffolk. Its sandy boulder clay once grew forest or heath. It was bustard country then. For a long time only the skirt-land around the villages beside their springs would have been laid out in fields: the fen was too wet, the heath too dry and forested.

Lodes were cut or co-opted from streams, probably by the Romans, and straightened further in the eighteenth and nineteenth centuries. They took water from the eastern uplands down on to the fens' innumerable channels, eventually feeding to rivers and so to the sea at the Wash. Before the fens were drained the villagers' lives mostly faced the water. Villages had hythes or quays on their lodes and people travelled west by boat. Paths, among them the Icknield Way linking East Anglia with the Thames valley and the Wiltshire downs, cut south-west to north-east along the parishes' eastern edges making a corridor for feet between the heath and the fen.

For most of these parishes wet feet were the norm, hence webbed feet the myth. Fen people stuffed fresh grass in their boots to cool their toes in the summer, but they still preferred them dry. In Burwell, Ennion remembered, 'most able men would live with one foot on dry land and the other aboard a boat'. Their houses echoed the shape of the parish, long and thin, boat-like, running from the dry into the wet, their east gable-end to the road, their west fen-end looking towards the water. People built barges in their back gardens and launched them from there, transforming a terrestrial animal into a marine one: 'it seemed as if some great dinosaur were being assembled . . . and slowly the gaunt frame *turned into a whale* as they nailed on the barge's thick plank skin and tarred it all over a shining black'.

After the fens were drained the villagers looked in the same direction as before – west, always west – but now their lives faced the grass. At the bottom of their gardens, as in a dry dock, their old boats rotted in the peat, while the old hythes were still visible as a 'green depression in a field'.

'The only fish that can swim backwards is an eel,' Hilaire Belloc wrote in one of his fenland essays. Perhaps this isn't true but the eel is certainly the best fen fish for the sometimes salt, sometimes sweet waters; for the once dry land now drowned now dry again; for wet grass turned elver; for Ely, island of eels. Aristotle thought eels grew out of the mud. Izaak Walton, writing from the wet heart of the fen-fixing seventeenth century, wasn't so sure and kept his options slippery: the 'putrefaction of the earth' might breed them or 'divers other ways'. Eels have skin not scales and the very largest ever caught in the fens (which weighed twenty-five pounds) was not hooked but *shot*. In cold winters they were thought to clamber from the water into soft earth to sleep. In the severest weather they were known to climb into a stack of hay in a meadow on dry ground and bed themselves there. Turf cutters wore eel-skin garters to fend off rheumatism. At one time in Ely, eels were a destination, a punishment for the wicked: St Dunstan, who re-established the monastery there in 970, insisted on the celibacy of his priests and 'all those who disobeyed the order of the saint were, with their wives and children, transformed into eels'. In other times eels were a crop. They fed the people. Eel-cake, Walton said, was eaten 'like as bread'. And being valuable they were transformed into money. In the medieval fens there was a currency in *fish-silver*, also called *phisshe-silver*. Debts, rentals and tithes were paid in *eel-stickes* (twenty-five eels per stick). These bundles, in their vain suggestion of the straightening of the sinuous, are paradigmatic tokens of man's efforts in the fens. As if you could clasp an eel. Or keep one in your purse.

A dull near-colourless midwinter day hung with badges of the times. A day for a Flat Earth Society. Ely Cathedral, a gunmetal tanker run aground across the fens, was the only bright thing in the ring of grey. Because it is taller than anything else, the body of the church pulled the sun from further away, capturing the weather that was over the horizon, living longer in the little light. In Burwell old dogs wobbled in tight green coats. The posh horses in Reach were saddled in blankets. At the row of houses along Factory Road people had driven their cars right up to their living-room windows and wrapped them in black tarpaulins. At Upware handwritten signs offered 'Horse Carrots' and 'Home Grown Vegetables' between garish roadside shrines: a failed bonfire of MDF and Formica; the seaweed mess of discarded clothes spilling from split carriers; and dog turds picked up and bagged in blue, but tossed and hanging as scrotal ornaments in a bald blackthorn. The two streets of fen bungalows looked like Atlantis inland, sunken castles, moated and overgrown by their firs and flags, with dark hedges of leylandii and the snapping cross of St George periscoping above.

Few people lived out on the fen proper. Even today, despite the pumps and the drains, the nuzzling drone of machines and the straight dug lines, there are not many houses at sea level or below it. The parish shape still applies and it has sunk into the mind of the place even if it is no longer necessary to live by it in order to keep floodwater from lapping at your bed. If you plan to stop on the fens it remains best to be ready to move on quickly. You must either fortify your house with fir trees and barking dogs or live in something with wheels. Nowhere in the flatlands is fixed and the area feels *gypsy* to this day. *Pikeys*, they call them in Burwell from the token security of the village's one or two brown contour lines lifting it out of the wet, though at the moment the gypsies are likely to be Polish or Lithuanian. At the field edge next to some leeks near Tubney Fen, five mouldy white caravans were parked like great skulls dug from the black peat around them. On the east edge of Burwell Fen a kind of wagon train outspanned on the soggy prairie with huts and trucks pulled into a forlorn circle. I watched a man struggling over the grass towards the camp with a fridge somehow tied to the back of his bicycle. Piebald and skewbald ponies are tethered nearby, horsepower under the pylons. A recycled advertising banner for Benetton clothes of a girl's face looking skywards had been lashed as a roof of sorts to one of the huts. I saw gulls jink to one side of it as they looked down when flying over the thirty-foot lipstick pout.

Towards dusk the sky crowded with air-minded birds. For grey weeks in winter the whole day is tilted towards its end, and the sky always promises more life than the land. As the light fails, everything appears to be heading home. Twelve waxwings hurried over Upware in a flying brown diamond looking for last berries in the hedges. Nine magpies pranged into a single ash tree. Buzzards clenched on fence posts like dark fists. Gulls planed sensibly overhead. A great assembly of rooks and jackdaws was noisily underway on the fen, restive and festive before their roost; a cormorant steered through the tumbling corvids like their lizard king. A raven, a fen rarity, croaked once along the sky edge, its black hammered far away in some ancient smithy and still cooling. Below it, lapwings plotted a ploughed field, heads into the wind, crested like isobars. When I got too close the birds rose as soft black smuts.

Their round wings looked like feathered hooves pushing at the sky. As they climbed I noticed golden plovers among them, slighter and paler, cutting their own channels in the air. And strings of starlings flew between both waders, twisting through the flock, dotting and dashing it like punctuation. They had been mixed haphazardly across the field, but each species took to the sky at the moment its own blood did, regardless of what its immediate neighbours were up to. The golden plovers went first, then the lapwings, last the starlings, and the field was cleared like a game of pelmanism, the spaces where each species had stood opening around the remaining birds until eventually they all left and the field was emptied.

I don't know any sexier lines in literature than the sequence in Book VII of Milton's *Paradise Lost* that describes the sixth and last day of creation when animals crawl out of the soil into life. Among other things, the poem explains how Adam was made out of dust, how the human race fell into farming and scrabbling around in the dirt (for both a living and as a place to keep our dead), and how we will all end up down there. But its most sensational lines – writing you feel as well as read – are about the earth turning and its birthing of cattle, lions, leopards, lynx, tigers, deer and an elephant. It is amazingly done: ductile and mimetic of movement in a rather woozy half-awake tense that perfectly captures a coming into the light as, with the strange and oddly erotic sense of a film being run backwards, the decay and rot of things to dust and dirt is played in reverse. Life shakes free of the dark and creatures are disinterred before us as the earth quakes alive:

> . . . out of the ground uprose
> As from his lair the wild beast where he wons
> In forest wild, in thicket, brake, or den;
> Among the trees in pairs they rose, they walked:
> The cattle in the fields and meadows green:
> Those rare and solitary, these in flocks
> Pasturing at once, and in broad herds upsprung.
> The grassy clods now calved; now half appeared

The tawny lion, pawing to get free
His hinder parts, then springs as broke from bonds,
And rampant shakes his brinded mane; the ounce,
The libbard and the tiger, as the mole
Rising, the crumbled earth above them threw
In hillocks; the swift stag from under ground
Bore up his branching head: scarce from his mould
Behemoth biggest born of earth upheaved
His vastness: fleeced the flocks and bleating rose,
As plants: ambiguous between sea and land
The river horse and scaly crocodile.

There is a fen poem in here as well. Every animal comes as a vivid impression, like a field note, of how seen things look, of how creatures stand up and move through grass as much as how they might grow out of its soil: cattle getting to their feet, a stag lifting its head into view, and blind Milton imagining or remembering how a lion rises. The lines also evoke for me all that primal fen traffic of becoming and disappearing, of wet and dry, soil and water, winter and summer, of everything (not only the river horse and the scaly crocodile) being uncertain and ambiguous between sea and land.

I like to think of Wordsworth remembering these lines in his sonnet 'London, 1802' and recalling that Milton, like him a sometime Cambridge resident, detected the fens north of the city: 'Milton! thou should'st be living at this hour: / England hath need of thee: she is a fen / Of stagnant waters . . .'

Neither Milton nor Wordsworth saw the value of pilgrimages to the wet flats but, whatever Wordsworth was remembering, Milton is cast in his poem as a dynamic operator, the sort who might coax flesh and blood from the soil, a moral and emotional dowser for natural flowing life. 'Thou hadst a voice', Wordsworth says, 'whose sound was like the sea.'

On the fen, lapwings marked their patch, mopping at the wet sky, something in their heads making them window-clean the same spot over and over. Golden plovers are differently nervous. At any one time a stipple of them through the field was fretting with doleful calls that piped softly through the big-eyed flock, their wings flexing open in panic as if they'd seen a ghost. Alarm parties went up on short flights but they were wary of rising or angling their bodies too obviously above the skyline. There were peregrines over the fields: even I sensed them, like a bee down my shirt the moment before it stings; and here was one now throwing down the grey anvil of itself through its prey, lowering all of the sky as it arrived, squeezing time into a tight ball and tripping up the light. Only then, but then obviously, did I see the meat in front of me. Thirty woodpigeons, just now stolid on the green, were smashed apart and directed hellwards, shell-shocked mad men grabbing at their dressing gowns as they rose in panic in their day room, pushing their chairs from under them in a clatter, always too slow and stupefied by the peregrine's unavoidable terms and conditions. The falcon turned, looking as ever casual and at ease, and moved, an intensifier of the air, spinning the globe beneath it, from the grass field to the bare soil where the nervous golden plovers were now due their terror. The pigeons had splattered into the sky, as if hit from above, and dispersed; the plovers coalesced, pulled in on themselves, wanting a herd and wanting to be in its heart, and they turned over as one, like fish pulled in a net, their tightening quicksilver making the hunting peregrine for the first time look lame. It rampaged on, freaking out a crow and a hare as it went. Through binoculars I could see the pigeons a mile off, collapsing into a wood. The lapwings, far and away the most visible edible things, had escaped, and they lifted into the sky again, crosspatch and cleaning it once more.

Attempts to drain Burwell Fen continued over many hundreds of years. The Romans, as well as building the lodes, may well have tried to drain the fen around the channels they were digging. Ennion believes they did. In the medieval period before 1300, villagers from Burwell enclosed and drained the fenland that was near their houses. Ennion thinks Bishop Morton of Ely, one of the succession of wealthy and powerful local clerics (although possibly half-eel beneath his vestments), also had a go at the wider fen in the fifteenth century. But the most concerted and most successful drainage, for a time at least, was undertaken in the seventeenth century when the Adventurers were active. The 'rigid grid' of field shapes on the fen is evidence, the landscape historian Christopher Taylor wrote, of 'massive drainage and reclamation'. In the mid 1600s, the Adventurers were allotted 2,600 acres of fen in four blocks from Burwell south towards the village of Lode. A drain was cut connecting the blocks south to north and by the early eighteenth century the majority of the fenland in Burwell parish was enclosed and drained as best it could be. But the peat shrank and the fen surface lowered and water turned sluggish and hard to shift. A drainage commission was proposed in 1766 but by then the landowners of Burwell didn't want their fen drained any more. The still-deep peat was too valuable as a fuel resource and they thought drainage would destroy it. Landowners to the south were keener on drier fields and the villages henceforth split and went their own ways.

Over the next hundred years various new drains were dug, wind was co-opted to help, and pumps set running so that the flow of the water across the wider area was manually changed about. The Romans had started this by turning the natural south-west to north-east drainage through right angles by digging the lodes, the Adventurers corrected this with their purpose-built drain, but then in the eighteenth and nineteenth centuries wind-pumps on the banks of the Cam pulled the water at right angles again from its original flow.

Burwell Fen had got wetter, and despite its value for peat cutting the landowners woke up in the nineteenth century and decided they wanted it drained. But they were too late and the adjacent waters on the neighbouring fens were already being whipped into shape in ways that couldn't help Burwell, so the Burwell drainage commission, set up in 1841, had to cut a new drain – called the Engine – following the line of Burwell Lode to their own steam pump at Upware: 'this proved to be', Christopher Taylor says, 'a serious mistake, for they were in effect trying to make water run uphill'. It didn't work and most of the fen was waterlogged by the time Eric Ennion moved to Burwell as a four-year-old boy in 1904. When he first knew the fen a few years later the

Adventurers' field shapes were more than part-hidden, there were flooded turf pits, peat-shrouded bog oaks crumpled the surface, and the place was sodden: it looked like it might have done in the fifteenth century before the great drainage years began.

Though it was a swamp it was alive with people. The locals had long known how to use its wet. Before he gets to the birds in his book, Ennion describes a productive and busy fen, a part-wild part-farmed place crowded in a way that is inconceivable nowadays. There were always people in every field and on every fen. Even with today's caravans of vegetable pickers and the travellers' stalled wagon train on Burwell Fen, it is hard to picture the place moving with working people: reeds and sedge scythed for thatching; ducks and fish trapped for food; peat dug for fuel; litter or what Ennion calls the 'welter' of marsh plants cut for coarse hay. As a boy Ennion was on the fen so often that he was on personal terms with some of its fish. He could tell one chub from another by the slight variations in their shape and by the differing patches of white fungus on their scales. There were eels, tench, perch, roach and bream too and also the mysterious (and now extinct throughout Britain) eel-pout or burbot, a kind of freshwater cod, with three long feelers stroking its face, one over each eye and one under its chin.

Peat or turf was dug from the fen in spring, the pits growing to about six turves or three feet wide, and about three beckets (turf-spades) or four and a half feet deep. When floods came the pits filled readily. Reeds grew on the wetter part of the fen. After winter frosts stripped them of their flags, old stems of four years or more were cut for roofing and younger stems were mixed with litter for fodder. If the bottom of the reed was dry or glazed with ice it could be cut with a scythe; if wet, a reed hook – a short, toothed sickle – was used. Coopers sought the bulrushes on the fen, their long round stems were dried and placed between barrel staves where, on contact with beer or whatever else filled the barrels, the stems would swell and keep the joints watertight. Sedge was cut in the autumn by scythe and brought home by a broad-beamed boat, haystacks of it pulled up the lodes across the fen on a 'float'. The navigable lodes were kept clear by a reeve and other men who were employed to *rode* the waterways. Two men on either bank of the lode, dragging back and forth a jagged chain fixed with knives, cut waterweed and emergent vegetation. They were mowing underwater so that another crop could sail on the surface. The sedge was used for cattle bedding and as an alternative thatching material. It could last for forty or fifty years and was more durable than reeds. At the end of the summer any uncut litter died down to add itself to a future layer of peat, which could build up, Ennion said, 'by a foot every twenty years'. Osiers from willows on the fen were cut for baskets, eel traps and faggot binds; thicker branches made good scythe handles. To keep the stick swollen and the fastenings firm between harvests scythes would be stored under the fen water, like moon-slivers of rusting silver. The blade was easily rubbed clean when needed once more. The tool wanted to be wet. 'During dinner hour scythes were kept out of the sun', Ennion wrote, 'the fittings might work loose if the stick got dry. They were laid in the ditch border or heaped with an armful of litter.'

There are fen emblems and parables too of swampy metamorphoses in this: the way water goes into and out of things and breeds by itself, the parthenogenesis of wet. A bulrush in the barrel holds wetness in by its wetness, and shows how waterproofing can be done by water, an osmotic soak being best for brokering edges. A scythe stick is sent underwater having been cut from the wet fen and kept damp on the same ground under a rick of vegetation that it itself has helped to cut.

Molecatchers also had a use for willows. The soft fen earth swam with moles. Their tunnelling business made work for men. The moles' 'scribbling' was so successful at undermining banks and putting holes in dykes that each and every expert floodsman was sought out and killed. A four-foot stick of willow or elder was cut for the spring device in an underground mole trap. The stick was replanted in the buried trap and its angle at the fen surface told the moleman when the trap had sprung. The mole, caught and killed with 'a tap on the snout', was often strung up by its feet on the stick, which was replanted for a second time in the fen as a sort of combined gibbet and sandwich board for the moleman, a warning to others and an advertisement of success. John Clare, on the western edge of the fens, wrote of moles being 'hung . . . for traitors' and 'sweeing to the wind / On the only aged

43

willow that in all the field remains'. The mole-stick often rooted and lived on: a new tree growing with a mole-fruit rotting in its crown. In Arthur Randell's deep-dug autobiography from 1970, *Fenland Molecatcher*, we find this and more: 'there were, in time, quite a number of willow trees growing in Magdalen Fen which had been "planted" in this way, and I still know, today, where there are three willows and two elders which began as mole sticks'. Thirty-five years on, I have an explanation for what I once saw on the bank of a Norfolk river on the eastern fen edge: four separate whittled branches stuck in the soil three feet apart, and on them four beaten-up furry black flags, four pairs of front feet rowing at the air like tiny human hands, with fingernails and creased palms, and four fleshy but dry pink noses pointing to the peat.

There were more days of ice before the winter was over. Thin hours of bruised sunlight, the skate scratches of contrails on the cold sky otherwise scoured of cloud, and a canine wind that blued my bent knuckles, even in their gloves. The parching air burned and the saturated ground stiffened. Mud foundered iron-hard, or 'frawn' as Eric Ennion remembered it on his winter doctor's round walking from Burwell towards Upware and the 'lonely yellow square' of a single lit window of a house on the fen. Crossing the same fields, frozen peat rattled at my feet like clinker and there were carrots scattered in the black like severed fingers. The ducks disappeared and the deer hobbled. To stop my legs slipping from under me, even on this flatness, I had to shuffle as if chained at the ankles. Everywhere the ice spoke glassily of its conquests: in reedy ditches the water froze muddy brown, in grassy ditches it was khaki, puddles on the fen solidified to bones, on the lode the wind had blown the freeze to a skin of chopped ginger. As the water thickened there, moorhens were forced out of it and up the banks, where their cumbersome reed-green legs and giant clammy feet looked like some hauled-up deep-sea by-catch. On the frozen bank otter prints crossed with hares' and both circled stone-hard molehills. The jewelled toolkit of a kingfisher flew along the lode, plumbed still to the iced trench and seeking a way through the thick vitrine that kept it from its bullheads and minnows.

Now, in the frost, the grass died to the colour of a mistle thrush's back: dead brown. Chaffinches gathered at the beet-clamp by the cattle pen on the edge of the fen, drawn there by the grains still lodged in the straw bales that walled the beets. They were hungry and, forced by hunger to shed their fear, they moved close to my feet. Like workers allowed back into the remains of a crop, they hovered at the straw, gleaning.

Around 1910 the business on Ennion's Adventurers' Fen shifted as demand for its natural produce declined. A decade of agriculture followed. Coal was preferred to turf for fuel, new roofs were tiled not thatched: 'the reedbeds stood unwanted in the fen and no one cut the sedge'. Previously the water on the fen had been part-baled by the engine at Upware and two creaky and inefficient wind-pumps on the fen edge. Now the wet was more fully banished. A new drain was dug and a tractor-driven pump installed. The fen dried out sufficiently to be planted. Its sedge was ploughed in and its deeper clay married with the top peat to 'lighten the one and stop the other blowing away'. A row of cottages called New Zealand – because they were so far from anywhere – was built, tucked in against Reach Lode on the south side of the fen. Wheat, barley, mustard, potatoes and beets followed.

The First World War was hungry but the farmed fen was short-lived. The wheat did well for a few years on the new turned soil but not for long: the peat was too light and began to blow away, it hadn't been ploughed deep enough to mix with the clay beneath it, and because of the dry surface the wheat couldn't be rolled and therefore properly bedded. Wind and rain bashed about the top-heavy stalks. And then 'the Bailiff of Bedfordshire' – floods from the Bedfordshire watershed – was always a likely visitor and, as Ennion said, 'he was to come yet again'. Daniel Defoe making his *Tour* labelled the fens 'the sink of no less than thirteen Counties', and much of central England's river water exits the country through them. The Bailiff duly called in 1920. The following decade was one of agricultural recession: after only a few seasons under the plough the fen sank back into itself, the pump wore out, winter floods took longer to drain, harvests were spoiled, cut wheat wasn't even collected and 'many a sheaf lay sprouting on the sodden ground'.

By 1930 only a hundred acres of the fen (at its corner nearest the village) was still arable land. From then until the start of the Second World War, nature reasserted itself and wildlife came back. Swallowtail butterflies reappeared. And during what remained of the harvest turtle-doves came 'in their hundreds to feast on the seeds and cool their pink toes in the mud at the sides of the drain'. The 1930s was the last decade of part-wild original swamp and part-worked man-made fenland: probably the best recent environment for nature. The National Trust might have those unloved years in its mind's eye as a model for its rewilding plans. I have never seen a swallowtail on the fens. They are extinct now. One recent September I did see two turtledoves cooling their toes just as Ennion described it, but I haven't seen more than two at any time since the 1980s.

In the winter of 1936–7 a great flood rolled from bank to bank of the fen and topped up its ground-water. Reeds began to spread, fields became reedbeds, divided only by open ditches of water that were too deep for them to grow in. The hollies that had been planted at New Zealand drowned, and the cottages there were abandoned. Their wooden floors were 'smashed by horses wandering through downstairs rooms'. Little owls took over the lease – they, at least, are still there in the patch of scrub that New Zealand now is (or was; the National Trust has recently cut the scrubby copse to the ground). The owls nested in the ruins and spat out pellets containing the beaks and crushed skulls of starlings.

Ennion says he knew every inch of the new fen and he records – and draws – Montagu's harriers and hen harriers, a vagrant lesser yellowlegs from North America, and he sees a water rail swimming (I have seen this once – it is like being privy to some secret ceremony that brings the skulking bird not only out of the reeds but into the water to swim like a high-class passenger on the Titanic, proud and hopeless). A colony of black-headed gulls painted the fen with white squawks; bitterns returned to breed like swaying reeds gathered into a stook. In 1938 black-necked grebes nested, and Ennion describes pushing his punt out on to the fen and lying all day under its canvas cover to sketch them. Spring waders passed through on migration, joining the fen to other flashes, marshes, rivers, seas and oceans, flying from Africa to Siberia and landing en route only where their feet might be covered with water. He watched and sketched, beautifully, a party of bar-tailed godwits:'As if overtired they couldn't settle comfortably: waders always fidget when they sleep. Later they rose and circled to gain height. They flew steadily north till my glasses could find them no longer. Where were they bound? The Yenesi? Whence had they come? The Nile?'

The godwits disappear and the book ends abruptly soon after: one sentence, there is a brilliant observation (the stare of a kingfisher), and the next, a goodbye. The fen has been drained and dug to farmland once again. 'Nature cannot let sentiment usurp her laws: that is for us to feel. Adventurers Fen in all its loveliness has gone but nature goes on elsewhere.'

Ennion's old fen at Burwell is a good place now for owls. In the willed abandonment of the fields here the crops have gone and for some years rough grass has grown on Burwell Fen. More water is expected soon but for several winters the fallow has fed many things. I counted seventy roe deer on one afternoon scan. Barn owls have bred in the ruined buildings at the centre of the fen, and it is rare to walk the banks around it and not see at least one. Most winters, migrant short-eared owls from further north and east join the resident barn owls adding a sheaf of sedge to their straw. One December day thirteen were seen working the fen.

The pallor and intent of hunting barn owls configure them as winter's thing even in the heavy hum of summer evenings. They are paler than everything else around them. Outside they are all sangfroid, within they seem to burn with heat, and their eyes are like portholes on to an oven. Tawny owls – darker and more severely nocturnal – are leafed and summery by comparison; they are brown bags of soft air, bark and foliage made feathers, hewn from the woods. Barn owls, in the middle of the day, in the hovering ghost dance of their mothy obviousness, are like a moon in the sky at noon, a lantern by which to see the night, even in daylight. In their scull and swoop above the dead grass, they fly as if their wings were stiff-wired and subject to some force from below that meets and matches their hollow-boned lift. They hunt by a kind of laying-on of wings, crossing and recrossing the fen until the hidden contents of the grass are shown to them.

Short-eared owls also quarter and dive in a crash into the grass after voles. Their yellow jelly eyes burn bright. The warmth of their brown back and wings flushes like a heart above the cold fen. Their flying is easier, longer and looser winged than the barn owls', less intense, less hungry perhaps. I watched two jousting in flight, weaving around one another, their legs dangling like thick socks come out of wellingtons. Another was harried right at the edge of daylight by a late-flying kestrel and both birds towered high into the sky, the owl yapping in distress at the fluster, escaping higher, odd and gawky.

Soon enough the night comes to meet the birds. The winter sky lifts and abandons the earth to darkness. One short afternoon on the fen I felt the light being taken as the owls became part of the dusk. A short-eared owl's hare-brown back and upper wings turned to grass; nearby a barn owl's burnt cream float became the mist that rose out of the grass. As the light thickened, the dark crept along the ground, just where the owls flew. At the fen edge it was darkest of all. This middle distance, the rim of the near, is the first to declare for night.

I turned for home. A little egret appeared from nowhere and circled overhead, a nervous white towel. Looking for somewhere to sleep, it lowered its black legs towards a ditch of black water and its dangling yellow feet flashed suddenly above my head like a bunch of bananas. Two hidden nearby pheasants called their ko-kocks and I felt their invisible horse-shudder of wings. Lapwings lifted from the field and tumbled along, hugging close to its surface, hurrying to resettle. Last flights after lights out seem panic-stricken for all. All except for the crows, rooks and jackdaws that sail on blackly into the black, flying their history as it seems, knowing where they're going.

*   *   *

Nowadays the fens are hard to love. Love, rather, is difficult for what we have made of them. Though it has owls, Burwell Fen is a straight-sided, flat and unmistakably man-made place. At the moment it doesn't really qualify as a fen. It is just some fields. Its neighbour, the nature reserve at Wicken Fen where no Adventurers ever set foot, is a shaggy place by comparison, with large reedbeds, bold mosquitoes, booming bitterns, but also a problem. It is turning into a wood. Being the only undrained place for miles around is not easy. Its peat was deep – sixteen to eighteen feet thick in places – and protected, but when the adjacent fens were drained Wicken suffered as well. It wasn't big enough to make its own rules. The fens share a common wetness and when all those around you are sucked dry you do not escape.

Wicken proves that nowhere in crowded, man-altered, southern Britain can natural processes create and sustain a natural landscape. How then could we best live with the fens in the future? Might we redefine our tenancy over that which we have subjugated? To this end something new has crept out of the drying earth – an almost posthumous chapter in nature-conservation thinking. Our tangle with the place is to be declared – how we made the fens, altered them, ruined them even; and then, demonstrating that we have finally understood this, some knowing and kindly repairs will be proposed. The new ethos extols prefixes and is another film running backwards: rewetting, rewilding, unfarming, the undoing of doing, the managed retreat from management, the letting go via legislation of what we once ruled. And all of it will be offered with a curious half-devoted half-nervous face put forward to show how we might still love this place.

This floats all sorts of questions about projected or imagined environments. How does land management, even managed retreat, live with a dynamic landscape? Who sets the year for the climax of creation? If trees have to be felled to maintain the fen, then in what way is the fen now anything other than a farmed place? In any case, for some, dry might be better than wet. Nightingales and woodcock have liked the trees at Wicken. And I liked them both. But I also thrilled to an invisible spotted crake cracking its unworldly whiplash in a new patch of reeds through several June nights one year. Whatever we do, whether we drain or we wet, we remain thoroughly and forever implicated. To return is always as difficult as to go on.

Some of the first notions of what an ecosystem might mean – how lives work by being meshed with other lives, life alongside life – were teased out at Wicken Fen by the botanists Arthur Tansley and Harry Godwin in the early 1920s. The fen then was still naturally reedy and wet, or at least still living the long losing of its nature. Now neighbouring Burwell Fen will get wetter once again. But to replicate nature – to build an ecosystem – involves a lot of pipes. I've seen them on the fen. Taps must be turned on in order that the big field might shine its sheet of winter water once more.

Sometimes I don't mind this thought, sometimes I do. There are days when the fen feels continuous with the thronged banality of southern England: a supermarket mind, a bird list that stops at pheasants and woodpigeons, local radio news, and eventless rain. Trying to come up for air through this weather, the projected fen-future sounds like cant and looks like spin, the nonce words alerting us to the sleight of hand: *rewilding* will be a trick involving no less human interference and delivering no wilder life. And – warming my bile – isn't there something oddly self-regarding and tonally superior about the leaving of the scene as it is proposed: the bowing and scraping and walking backwards that draws more attention to the departed than to the empty stage? And isn't that a nonsense anyway? There can be no true leaving. We cannot just stop and clear off. Instead, some sort of facility is being made and, though the public noise is all about access and community benefits, what is being offered can sound, even with value-adding booming bitterns, like a reduced version of the place. In substantial part this is because wisdom about the land and any feeling for it – contact or occupancy of any kind – is being siphoned off as the sole province of experts and managers. What the former dairy farmers of Wicken know will no longer be admissible; new landowners have decided that their ecosystem was the wrong one. Rewilding will not then return the remade fens to the farmers or indeed to anyone; we have all forfeited our rights to be in them in any way that isn't mediated. Ordinariness will be banished along with muddy feet. A new sort of alienation has already been devised: the tristesse of the birdwatching hide. I can feel it now in the strange log cabin that has been erected on Tubney Fen. Nothing seen from its shelter seems as real as it does when seen from under the sky.

On sunnier days I've had still blacker thoughts. Thinking of that emptying stage, it can seem that the corporatized language boostering a one-hundred-year vision for thousands of acres has released something unexpectedly metaphysical on to the fen: an idea of life after us and life without us. Curiously, for all the positive-sounding future and for all the management needed to get there, what is proposed is a description of our profound separation from the fens and the fields, a terminal version of pastoral. Behind the new picnic tables and the bike racks an exclusion zone is being conjured, an enclosure beyond enclosure, the darkest arcadia. I could put that differently. And on good days, on and off the fen, I do. Let the water come, but let us be allowed to step into it as well, as we surely have and must for it all – wet and dry – to mean anything.

Winter is long but the end of summer and the beginning of spring press at it from both sides. In the village churchyard in mid November I had watched a red admiral sunning itself as it clung to the lettering cut into the slate gravestone of Edwin Muir, the sometime worker in a bone factory, translator of Kafka, and great poet of horses, the describer of 'that long-lost, archaic companionship' between humans and other animals. Then, the day after the midwinter solstice, from the middle of a blackthorn in the lane beyond the gravestones, a blackbird was whispering subsong, like a message sent on ahead from the coming spring. In the haunch of winter, as Shakespeare had it, the summer bird is singing the lifting up of day. June's ghost talked through the silver of finch calls and the tinsel of a dunnock. Near the blackbird a great tit sang for the first time in its life. The sun had warmed the hedge enough and the bird within it. A handle turned in its throat, its biddable brain was stoked, and the extra spoonful of light after the shortest day pulled its beak apart. After three cranks its squeak was tuned into sawing song as if it had never been silent.

Rooks, too, are early starters. Along the eastern edge of the fens where taller trees thrive in the villages, there are rookeries. Like a photographic negative of seabirds, whites for blacks, the rooks crowd their high sea-cliff trees and sail out over the waters of the fen like black gannets. At Burwell, there are three rookeries, or perhaps a single exploded one, scattered in the churchyard and in trees nearby. In Bottisham, there is a rookery in beeches at Bottisham Hall, near where Leonard Blomefield lived in the early nineteenth century and kept his *Naturalist's Calendar*. Blomefield records his rooks returning to their nest trees to roost after they have raised their young on a mean date of 2 July. Their spring starts then. They pair up in the early autumn. Every day through the winter they visit their old nests and sit beside them as they might at a bedside. On dull days you can often mistake the nest in the tall trees for the bird and the bird for the nest, until they get up to front the wind above the trees with their smoky paddle of wings, before returning to their vigil, warming their black stick bundle through the season.

An oil-painted day came after weeks of watercolour. A wet and greasy sun fingered into the western sky in a broadside of light. Mildness bowled about. Insects appeared. The hedges steamed, and the dung heap at the field edge next to the fen smoked thickly and, doing so, seemed old, an inexplicable and happy survival from some ancient world. I walked home through the fields like a bird scarer, flushing woodpigeons and pushing them ahead of me, out from the field I was in and on to the next. Pale fire was coming into the willows along the fly-tipping lane. A roebuck sprang up in front of me with new velveted antlers like gloved hands. I passed an old orchard, and I stopped because I had seen that there were fresh leaves like mouse-ears on the apple trees. And then, news out of Africa: a wheatear leapt up from the sheep's grass at the dyke's end, its white rump an invitation card, bouncing away like nothing that had lived in the fields or on the fen through the winter.

HONEYGUIDE

I grew up with no sense of what a farm in Africa meant. I didn't know there were any. I think most of the people around me would have thought the same. Karen Blixen's opening words to *Out of Africa* drew attention to this common misperception by, exotically, stating its opposite: 'I had a farm in Africa.' In my childhood, butter and lamb came from New Zealand, bacon and wheat from Canada, but nothing as far as I knew was from Zambia. From Kenya there was just ground and bitter coffee. A crushed bean from a bush didn't suggest a farm to me. It came in vacuum-sealed tins that hissed when you opened them. We had it on special occasions and I didn't like it. I remember the palaver of the percolator. Otherwise, I knew the Masai kept cattle and secured them in thorn kraals each night against predators. They drank their cows' blood, tapped from the living animals, and I used to wonder whether it tasted more like a nosebleed or black pudding. Those humped cows and their vampire masters seemed the extent of African farming to me. This was dumb even for a seven-year-old – a continent of people mostly existing at subsistence levels means there must be more farming by more people in Africa than anywhere else in the world. But those ordinary farmers were absent from any accounts I knew, and my wider confusion about what farms could be ran deep.

The first time I flew from London to Cape Town, I looked down and saw how fields, such as I thought them, barely made it across the Mediterranean. The sand of the Maghreb and then the bones of the mountains dust them out of existence. The swaddle of equatorial forests smothers the ground, permitting only rare clearings. Further south is a steaming tangle of vegetation and swamp. Only into coastal southern

Africa, the strip of temperate Africa beyond Africa, do anything like regular recognisable fields return. As I was born in Europe, a child of enclosure and settlement, a farm still means to me something other than the farming of Africa that happens between the Atlas Mountains and the Cederberg – its scratched livings, unfenced cattle, children minding goats, and tiny stands of maize next to simple one-room houses. There are big farms now of course, and rich local farmers as well as international business interests busily growing profits as they feed the world from the soil of the poorest places, but Africa still farms and feeds itself as it has done for thousands of years – those children around the goats, forever. Put it this way: throughout most of Africa the word *countryside* remains meaningless. Habitats are being degraded, forests are cut to nothing, lakes fouled, fetid shanties grow as large as cities, but the whole continent is still living *in* nature. In Africa there is only *bush*. And it runs, scratchily real and as a landscape of the mind, for 7,500 miles from north to south.

Everything here is under the sun. We'd left the fields and were almost home when we heard the call. A dirt track snaking back to the farm-house had put us on the edge of an old tobacco plot. The call came again, *chakka chakka chakka chakka*, loud over the toil of the four-wheel drive. We stopped. Once more the bird shouted against the judder of the switch off. It had come closer, and this time Lazaro, who works in the fields of the farm and knew what he was hearing, was already out of the car and answering it, his mouth full of whistling and tutting and Tonga chatter. We're coming, *kacheka kacheka*, he said. Lazaro had seen the *kacheka*, as well. Fumbling with binoculars I had managed a glimpse of a brown flycatcher-sized bird with pale undersides, far smaller than its stone-sieving call would suggest. It dropped from a high branch towards us through the air in a mock fall, fanning its tail to show white outer feathers and twisting upon itself. Having successfully caught our eyes as well as our ears, it flew on ahead. We were hooked.

A bird calls with some news for someone who is passing. Across Africa, south of the Sahara, the same bird has called to people for thousands of years for the same reason. The hunter coming home, the herdsman driving his goats, the woman carrying water from a well, her son walking back from school – all of them at one time or another have looked up to listen, and knowing what the honeyguide's call meant, they moved towards the bird and followed it. Because they have done this, the bird has kept calling and will call to you if you pass, as it called to me. It knows us for what we are. Sweet-toothed.

The honeyguide's chatter is good news. Sweet news. It has found a wild bees' nest, a hive of honey, with a combed stack running slowly with its sweet warm sap. But the prize is locked in the dark of a hollow tree. The bird has seen the bees going in and out of their hole; it knows what that means and, remembering how things are, it has gone in search of help. It loves to eat beeswax but it is not a woodpecker. Instead, the honeyguide employs us as its tool. A chimpanzee will strip the leaves from a fine twig and poke it into a narrow hole from where termites run, before sliding the stick and the insects it has disturbed through its lips. We are to play the part of the stick for the honeyguide. It will hunt, we will gather. And, as he walked towards the bird, answering its call, because he knew the deal, Lazaro had an axe in his hand.

The field edge here in southern Zambia was no longer clearly an edge at all. The field might be a field no more. Spindly but confident saplings were already advancing across it, breaking from the thirty-foot-wide wooded corridor that doubled as field edge and track-way. The bush is coming back. The new trees reached towards four old termite mounds, wooded islands rising from the tall yellow grass, never taken into the field when it grew tobacco. Pythons thicken there beneath knotted dark-leaved trees and the honeyguide calls from the canopy. Unless someone cuts at the trunks, old and new, the clearing will soon disappear, its open green eye shutting to something darker, older and shaded. Today, the honeyguide doesn't mind. People are still passing, but what will happen if Lazaro is no longer available to listen?

Perhaps humans are not essential to honeyguide happiness; perhaps there are other ways to wax. Can't they do it without us, as they must have done when we were otherwise occupied and only good for putting twigs in termite holes? No evidence exists but some have speculated that honeyguides once used honey badgers as their field labourers. It might be that the birds sacked the badgers when it became clear that people had learned, presumably by watching the badgers and the birds, and had rapidly become better at the job. It's hard to know because it is hard to watch a honeyguide without it watching you. And if we are watched and there is honey to be had, we are to be pressed into service.

For now, Lazaro was talking back to the bird. He said, in words I found myself assuming the honeyguide understood: show us what you have found. The bird obliged, thinking we were obliging it. Lazaro stepped into the field barefoot from the car, and moved his axe from his hand and slid it down his neck inside the back of his shirt until its shaft lay straight along his spine and its head faced out from above his collar. This was in preparation for tree climbing, but it also allowed him to roll and light a cigarette as he walked towards the bird. His paper was a scrap of old newspaper; his tobacco – flakes and filaments of brown crumbled leaf and stem – came from the next field. Last year's crop, planted, tended, cut and dried – all on the farm in the fields about us. His lit cigarette sent up thick grey smoke, like a smouldering bonfire of damp leaves and grass, and for a moment his faun-face was lost in a cloud. He looked out on the same scene as me but as if from another country.

After each call the honeyguide flew on 200 yards or more, sometimes straight, sometimes zigzagging, through the field trees and hedge until it reached the more continuous miombo woodland at the back of the farm. As we caught up with it there, instead of flying on, it came closer to us, buzzing about the treetops, swooping down nearer to the ground. 'One honeyguide', Lazaro said, 'showed me four hives; one hive then another then another; and sometimes, because it is interested, it showed us other things as well, a snake or a dead animal in the bush.'

Climbing wasn't necessary. The bees' nest this honeyguide had found, and brought us to, was at the foot of a *muyongolo* or snake-bean tree. Lazaro gathered twigs and a few strands of dry grass, fire was set, and smoke made to coil round the trunk. I saw the soles of his bare feet as he knelt; they looked like the cracked earth. He dug a little in the sandy soil to expose the base of the tree and hacked at it.

Smoking grass was held to the gash. Bees started seething at two exit holes higher up the trunk, driven from their comb by the smoke rising, through their nest, up the chimney of the tree. Swirled in smoke himself, with half-stunned half-furious bees crawling over his head, Lazaro reached his hand into the hole he had made and pulled out the *buchi*, the wild honey. The comb came twisting like snakeskin. It was eighteen inches long and three inches wide, a dripping tongue. He pulled at it, laughing and breaking it apart. A rope of honey ran from the chunk in his left hand to that in his right. It stretched, glooped, broke, and spilled to the ground. Something precious and potent was being desecrated so that we might eat. Lazaro passed me a piece of the chambered wafer. I felt its tug back from where I was taking it. On my palm it looked like a block of flats at sunset. There is a similar building, Soviet-style, in the centre of Lusaka. The comb itself was the colour of our fingernails, but the honey that drained from it was a uniform and clear golden-brown varnish that coated everything it flowed over. I sucked it from my fingers: the sun itself had been distilled, the forest and the field captured and concentrated. Something beyond sweetness caught at the back of my tongue and throat and burned there with the rasp of pollen or a balm that stung. I picked off two bees glued to the comb by their own honey and drowned in it in the chaos of excavation, and bit into three stories of the apartment block. In my mouth the comb was all texture. I pressed the sweetness from its gum and what was left was too chewy to swallow. I spat it out as Lazaro stuffed more dripping mess into his mouth. He ate it all. Today was a quick opportunistic feast for him, a raid on a sweet shop; on other occasions he puts the comb on a plate of bark and carries it home for his family. Now, he placed one piece back into the hollow tree, so that the bees might return, sealed the smoke hole he had made with a wedge of bark, and on the ground placed a last lump of comb for the honeyguide. In our honey lust we had lost sight of the honey bird. It had stopped calling, but sat silently in a tree a few yards away, watching us doing its bidding.

We walked back towards the car, out through the wood and across two fields. One was scrubby, the other dry and near bald; every green thing had been scorched back into the earth. It was hot. The blue of the sky was the colour of sensation, not of contemplation. It did not calm the eyes so much as stretch and drain them. The air sizzled. Birdsong was heat-flattened to weary purrs and static pulses. Drops of honey, trapped in the stubble on my chin, dried to scabs. Flies moved to any damp creases at my nostrils, lips and eyes. Underfoot the old rind of the earth crackled, like metal swarf, with a scrunch of seedpods and the foil-scuff of dead leaves. Poachers had burned all the grass to encourage new lawns which might lure antelope. The baked soil crumbled at the surface and chinked. It was impossible to imagine the stuff of honey being made in this dead field.

All things look blasted and ruined in the dry season but on the Major's farm it was worse. The Englishman had died and his Zambian widow was sick. The farm had failed. The Major had run out of cash some years back and no crops had been planted in the last season. A stoical orchard of guavas produced a few fruit but that was all. There was one prepared but unplanted field on the farm. It took eighty litres of tractor fuel to plough, and used the last of the money; there was nothing left for seedlings. There would be no tobacco that year or perhaps ever again. Royce, the dying widow, had spoken to the workers; they were free to go as they hadn't been paid since May and it was now November. It was remarkable that they were still there, that they had survived on so little, but the uncertainties of upheaval had kept most families in the compound. Lazaro, who had lived there all his forty-two years, and the other tied-hands (their homes, such as they were, came with the job) eked out a living as best they could from their one-room huts in the shadow of the idle tobacco barns. Lazaro and his family lived off *nshima*, maize-flour porridge, garnished with an occasional rat, optimistically known as 'relish'. His cigarette, as rare a treat as honey, was built from tiny threads of leftover tobacco salvaged from the barn.

Walking back, we came across a lorry pulled off the track into the trees. A gang of men around it fell quiet and looked up in surprise as we crossed their path. They were wearing town clothes and were cutting at the thicket with axes and saws, throwing branches on to the flatbed. The wood was leaving the farm, though not in order to keep the fields alive.

Perhaps we should have confronted the wood thieves. But the farm seemed beyond rescue. No one was working in its fields any longer. The farmhouse wasn't a home. The building where the Major had lived was a near-empty shell, blown of life. His fabulous egg collection and bird skins had been boxed up and shipped out and the house had been stripped. Any remaining furniture had been pushed to the room edges. On the walls, the framed family trees had been taken down, leaving stains and ghost outlines where the pictures once hung. Outside, the tractor's wheels had been stolen. It sat on its axles like a stone lion. The Major's museum for his dead birds and their dead eggs was never finished and its doors were open, the heat and dust of days bowling into the sanctuary like any other abandoned outbuilding. Old charcoal ash blew into the grass in grey drifts from the four iron ovens at the base of the tobacco-drying barn. Inside the building, green tobacco was once cured by being hung on a vaulted lattice of wooden slats and struts six shelves high. Hot air smoked and rose through the indoor forest. The cure took a week; the leaves like a sort of cud in the barn's gut, drying in the body of the building. Stepping through the low door and looking up now was like finding yourself in the skeleton of a huge extinct animal among a gantry of its bones. The smell of cooked grass was all that remained.

In the orchard, the guavas dropped from the trees and baked in their skins in the grass below. Waiting, without hope, the workers were mostly too nervous to gather the fruit themselves. Back at the farm we ate peanut-butter sandwiches that Claire had made. She was employing Lazaro as a nest-finder for her scientific fieldwork on honeyguides, studying not their honeyguiding skills but their co-evolution with the host birds they parasitise. They live, like cuckoos, by laying their eggs in other birds' nests and leaving the rearing of their young to other parents.

At the Major's, the honeyguides' wet-nurses were mostly little bee-eaters. The nest-finders call them 'John Deeres' because they are the same green and yellow as the tractors. In Tonga they are called *hatwili*

– the ones who follow the small flies. They feed on the bees that make the wax the honeyguide loves. They breed in the fields or their remnants, digging tunnels in the sandy soil, hollowing out a nest chamber two or three feet down a narrow passageway. Often they will dig into an aardvark's hole, excavating their tunnel within the roof of the ready-made burrow.

We walked back through the fields to examine a nest for signs of honeyguides. Lazaro had spotted adult bee-eaters going in and out of a hole earlier in the week. He picked a long thin stem of yellowing grass from the ground, stripped it of its seed head by passing it through his closed fist, and crouched at the entrance of the aardvark hole where a much smaller dark circle opened off it. He pushed the grass into this hole, feeling with it until, three feet in, it reached a wall of sand and could go no further. He pulled the stem out and laid it like a thin tawny arrow on the bare surface of the field above the hole. With a mattock, he dug at the earth a foot back from where the grass marker ended, scooping up palmfuls of sandy soil, slowing his actions the deeper he got, until eight inches down, the sand began to drain beneath his hands and he knew he had reached the nest chamber. He tamped the walls of the shaft he had dug and carefully picked his way towards the floor of the nest, clearing any sand that had fallen into it. There was no built structure under his hand. The female little bee-eater, having dug out the chamber, simply lays her eggs beneath her in the scrape she makes in the dust of the hole.

Hot light beat in on the nest for the first time. We peered over the rim, but seemed to have come to the wrong place, pushed at a door we were not supposed to, opened it on to the aftermath of a battle. There were two dead bodies, bald, blind bee-eater chicks, each an inch long, splayed headlong and limp in the sand, little gobs of meat, half pink, half yellow. They were bruised on the head, neck, thighs and back. In the middle of the scrape, a boxer in a ring, a cock in its pit, panting in the heat and from its exertions, was a living chick, bald, blind but bigger, a honeyguide. Grains of sand armoured the black blisters where its eyes were pushing through its skin, its bill hung to one side, and at the end of it, under the bright smash of sunlight, I could see a needle-fine

61

hook pointing down from the tip of its upper mandible. A dinosaur tooth. It is the only tool of its own a greater honeyguide ever needs. Just a day or so old, still blind and, in any case, in the total darkness of the burrow, the chick had sensed movement alongside itself or heard the begging calls of the fresh-hatched bee-eaters. Then, with this sharp weapon at the centre of its being, the honeyguide pursued its foster-siblings in a frenzy of killing, puncturing their bodies, dragging them from side to side, clinging to them over and over in order to dash them down again and again, until their blood ran beneath their skin. The attacks continue until each chick is dead.

Something about the way we broke in on this scene, the bird's sweet communitarian name, and the minute severity of the hook on the tip of its bill took me somewhere else altogether: some other trespassing; a witnessed moment of the arrival into a safe round world of a sharp point from outside. Around his fourth month in the womb, there were worries for Lucian, my second son. An amniocentesis was arranged and while his mother lay on her back, a doctor inserted a needle, guided first by his experience and then, when the needle's tip broke through the wall of her womb, by its image on a screen at the bedside. Some amniotic fluid would be drawn for examination and testing. As I watched the needle in the womb on the screen, thinking how straight it was in a world of curves, our baby's newt hand, creamy fingers and thumb, came slowly swimming out from the dark and reached – with what looked like generous curiosity – towards the new pointed arrival in its cave world.

In the hole in the field were the corpses of the little bee-eaters, forgotten now, tiny sandbags pushed beyond the edge of a dug-out. We stared at the victor, an inch and a half long, a bald, blind king, exposed in the chamber of its horrors and triumph, whose first action on hatching was to seek warmth and life by reaching for whatever was adjacent and killing it. The chick must have been doing this as, earlier, we walked a foot above it across the ashy earth, led on by a promise of sweetness, sung by an adult honeyguide, calling its call, speaking of the reasonableness of shared enterprise, making us feel at home in the fields.

Looking up, I saw one of the parent little bee-eaters sitting quietly on a branch of a tree, beyond the circle of the old field, in much the same way as the adult honeyguide looked on as we plundered the honey. The bee-eater seemed to be waiting for us to finish so it could return to its nest and the young it thought it had. Lazaro carefully repaired the roof of the nest chamber and we stood up and moved away. The bee-eater called a quiet *chip chip* as it left its perch and flew above us, circling its hole in the ground.

There are more ways to farm than we might think. The honeyguide isn't interested in snakes and dead animals in the same way as we might be. But its attention to the fields and the trees, their bees and their bee-eaters, and its fruitful and violent diligence in those places, enlarges the meaning of the farm. We can know the fields through the magnifying lens the honeyguide gives us, if we grasp how to use it and choose to do so. There is now no ploughing at the Major's, yet the soil there is being turned constantly.

At one unmarked point, as we headed home, we crossed a boundary and strayed on to another property. Behind a rampant hedge was a house, netted with creepers and vines. A farmer lived there; he was old and didn't come out as we approached. Lazaro knows him as Mr Kandondo, the white man who loves black women. I asked what his English name was but Lazaro couldn't remember. It was not needed and had got lost in the bush somewhere.

We neared the Major's house and passed a large shaggy termite mound with, at its base, a bare hummock of new-turned reddish earth like a snout of moraine. It was the Major's grave. He lies at the edge of a field on his farm. Lazaro and the other farm workers who dug his burial hole also cut at termite mounds to use their soil for bricks. The fields of the farm are not totally abandoned. The mounds are valuable. Termites are extraordinary fieldworkers themselves: farmers, engineers, industrial experts as well as geniuses of demolition. Their mounds are hardened compost heaps made from chewed wood and other vegetation. Seeing what termites have built, human farm workers have learned to make homes from the termites' house. They shave slices from the mound, cutting it open like a peat bog. The termite chew is mixed with water, poured into a wooden frame, and baked to bricks in a kiln itself built from cooked termite chew. The finished bricks make houses that look like harder, darker boxes of the original mound. Rain wears away at the bricks and eventually it will return them to where they came from, but for now Lazaro lives in a house made by termites, and both he and his late employer lie beneath the soil of the farm.

Claire and I headed down the dirt road towards another farm. Bruce, our host, a white farmer on the property west of the Major's, said he would drive us to look at the dam and the reservoir at the edge of his land. His car was an old station wagon, grumpy about starting. The front windscreen was cracked in four places and shuddered as we went. The hazard lights flashed on and off as they wished. Four dogs came with us. Two huge brown beasts that would not stay in the boot of the car and blundered over to the back seat, peering from Bruce's shoulders, dribbling on to his shirt. And two Jack Russell terriers that sat on his lap, resting their heads on his arm. In order to avoid disturbing them, he steered as if taking his driving test, his hands at ten-to-two on the wheel.

On the way to the dam, Bruce showed us some of his fields. He talked as he drove. Farming is hard. His poly-tunnels for bringing on tobacco seedlings had to be abandoned because of a mystery disease. Many young plants in the fields were struggling. They were flowering too soon and were feeble. The night before, 700 older tobacco plants had been cut, slashed and ruined. Two men were tracked by Bruce's workers but their trail went cold in some woodland. Most likely they were attacking Bruce's crop because the pension scheme he devised for his workers had partly gone wrong. The authorities had supported him but his labour force had been left resentful and many wanted out of the scheme but couldn't get at their money. A ring-tail Montagu's harrier drifted over a wheat field, silencing us for a moment. The wheat hadn't done well and the world price fell as Bruce was planting. He hadn't planted further acres. A neighbouring field was burnt. That was a mistake. A cattle herders' campfire got out of control. Bruce has bought movable electric fences for his cattle, believing Africa is 'overgrazed but under-stocked' and wanting cattle to be encouraged to eat all the available fodder by being confined rather than roaming in bigger fields where they can pick and choose the most palatable grasses. He'd been trying this for two years, but hadn't yet got the system right. He wasn't a cattle specialist. He now thought he needed more manure on his farm, but didn't have enough manuring animals. Too much scrub had grown up. Goats might have been the answer. He'd have liked the Kalahari red variety, as they would be easy to spot if they were rustled. Fifty would have been good but he could only afford fifteen. There again, the goats he already had hadn't eaten much scrub. Now he needed sheepdogs to keep the goats on the move and to stop them eating the cows' grass.

We arrived at the dam and the dogs burst from the car along the banks of the reservoir. Bruce walked and talked. The village chief and headman took a lot of persuading about the wisdom of the dam, though Bruce was paying for the pump and the irrigation scheme. Relations were still strained; the benefits slow to show. As we got to the edge of the village on the shore, the big dogs went berserk, hurtling off like terrifying tubular robots, running down the local scrawny mongrels. Bruce shouted. Floris and Demi charged on.

The village side of the reservoir had hardly any large trees. Because the villagers on the chief's land remain tenants and do not own their trees, they cut down any they can. 'If your village owns a wood, you learn the value of the wood. If you are on your own, you know only the value of a single tree as fuel for cooking and firewood.' Bruce urged the chief to give land to the people, but the chief was reluctant. Not enough African farmers have experience of farming at increasing densities of population. The common practice has been to move on having exhausted the land, but now 'Africa has been used up'. A balloon would help. Bruce was building one. It would be twenty feet in diameter and fly a mile high over his farm and his neighbours'. The plan was for a camera slung beneath it to take photographs, showing the villagers how many trees they have and what their land looks like from the air, in the hope that they might attend to its survival.

It was dark now, I couldn't see more than a few steps in front of me and I tripped over my feet in the long grass. A million night insects were scratching at the damp and the dew around the water. We stopped talking and finally the dogs returned to Bruce's side, frothing with the bliss of their exertion. They love him.

It is hard not to. Bruce walking back along his dam against the skyline and jouncing with his dogs was tall, energetic, intense and indefatigable: a young Tolstoy on his estate. Walking through the ruins of the Major's farm just an hour before, I'd thought how loveless it seemed, how its fields had failed through a lack of care, as its poor owner became mired in bitter thoughts, locked in his terminal illness, cheered only by his harvest of blown birds' eggs and dead birds' skins, and by his scrutiny of the decay of avian and human genealogies, the end of lines. On Bruce's farm it's the opposite; there is, perhaps, too much love and a farmer who is trapped by the sweetness of his ideas. On my last visit to the Major before he died, at his request, I had brought him a jar of Olde English marmalade and sticks of sealing wax for his will; on this trip to see Bruce I had carried a hundred yards of ultra-light balloon fabric from Britain. Three different packages, assorted tools for assorted lift-offs.

Everywhere in the wild grass of the Masai Mara in southern Kenya, the shortest route is found between the earth and the mouth. The answer is always grass. Six elephants walked through tall yellow grass that reached to the bellies of the smaller animals, to the knees of the larger. Their haunches rocking, they paced as if they had an appointment at the end of the world, as Karen Blixen said. And they reaped as they went, their tusks like pitchforks, and the rest of their bodies like various loaves of bread. Three miles away, a line of giraffe necks appeared from the grass, all else was hidden. Five canted masts. Ten yards away a female cheetah and her two cubs, with rouged cheeks and whiskers, fed on a Thomson's gazelle, the meat of its exposed muscles drying from crimson to rust as we watched. The downy ridge of hairs along one cub's spine waved in the light just as the grass next to it did. Two barn swallows dipped to nip at the flies the kill had brought out. A baboon sat and ate, picking hand over hand at fresh grass stems; it wiped its face with one palm, its other fist wrapped round a hank of grass, pausing midway towards its mouth. A shining hippopotamus, tagged on its flanks with emerald reed-stalk calligraphy, wobbled from one wet patch of grass to another. Grant's gazelles and topi looked up from their cropping, jaws sliding, top over bottom, bottom under top; quern mouths.

Arriving in the Mara is to enter a grassed universe. The plain widens in the Rift until you are nowhere other than simply here, in the middle of the grassiest place you've ever been. The earth stretches generously over its equatorial miles. I have never seen so many blades of grass in one *field of view*. Like all the flat places, the plains, the fens, the steppe, it works on your eyes first with a scene so wide it pulls at their corners and a view so deep it furrows the brow.

Let the Mara then *be* one field. The sun splashed down between great cakes of cloud on to countless communities of grass-life: spread acres of tall grass and of short, herd after herd of mixed animals, browns and blacks and fawns, scattered trees and their tethered shadows. Every yellow, every green, every brown surrounded me, running from my feet to the edge of the world. Beneath the grass the land rises and falls; it is worn in places where rock pushes through and cut in others where rivers channel wet across it; but overall the business of what is beneath is muted and what prevails is the surface. Over all: the grass which covers everything is not just superficial – it becomes the Earth as well as growing from it, for the movement and shape of the land rhymes with the movement and shape of its outgrowth; the grass is both the world's body and its gesture. Mara in Maa, the Masai language, means dotted or spotted, patchy or chequered. It is also the word for cheetah, leopard and giraffe. It suggests the entire view and its contents.

In the grass were corpses. Thousands beyond counting. So many in one place that, there and then, the plain effected a revision of everything I knew about death. Almost all were wildebeest. Dead young and dead old, alike. They hadn't come here to die, but since they were here, they would die here and because they live here in hundreds of thousands, the dead gathered at the feet of the living. In places, for every standing animal, there was a shadow at its hooves, a skeleton, a skull, a mummified body, brown bags of bones, old overcoats shed in the heat. I didn't see anything die but I have never seen so many dead. The new dead steamed as vultures stoked at open ribcages. The old dead liquefied under the sun in a meltdown to meaty molasses. Bones blurred in a hymn of flies. Grass grew livid from beneath, through bleached bone houses. Grass grew livid from within, pulling up from ruptured guts; a last meal germinated, juiced into life by rot. A wildebeest grazed on the grass that sprouted from the stomach of a wildebeest.

The same sun blared evenly down over everything. The air above the grass was either rancid or chalky. There were meals of bone to be had and there were dead eyes to be drunk. The vultures were fat. Hyenas too. Where the grass was long, sometimes only a rib or a horn was visible above it, the ruins of a city lost in a jungle; where it was short, whitewashed collapses of bones daubed the plain with tents of spines and skulls like an abandoned camp. Death's organising genius is to be disorganised, to make a shambles everywhere. The very scatter of bodies was frightening. A skull where all else had gone; a complete skeleton without a skull; three legs arranged like the spokes of a cart-wheel; a splay of yellow teeth rolled like dice across baize; the skin and hair of a wildebeest looking as good as new, its interior a hollowed cave of gore; a new corpse plaited through an older one; a skull resting within a ribcage. And, all the time, the grass growing all about, and the living stepping through the dead to eat it.

What is it that pulls the herd of living and dead together? What moves the congress across the plain? Grass, exhausted, trampled and cropped beneath hooves. Grass, longer, fresher, greener, ahead. The smell of grass beyond the smell of the dead. The smell of green beyond the brown river. A glimpse of lions, yellow in the yellow grass. The push of teeth at the heels of the herbivores. Like a rising flood, a blunt front of wildebeest reached us; the advancing line, half a mile deep, billowed into the grass of the plain. Behind it, a solid scrum, a continuous, interlocked shunt of 50,000 parts. The earth raised by five feet for miles into a moving brown crust. The first animals flushed yellow-throated longclaws from the grass that flew up above and tried to settle again but could find no space to land between the wildebeest. I couldn't see where the herd ended. The horizon was made of animals.

The beards at their chins are the colour of the grass that strokes them. Nose to tail, flank to flank, walking, eating, walking and eating. Nothing prepared me for the epic ordinariness of the herd, the mind-wipe of its pedestrian repetitiveness, the same again and again in front of me, moving from right to left, passing and passing, plain as the plain itself, like wind through grass and made from both and becoming both. The wildebeest moved in a cloud of audible near-quiet, with only an occasional husky *gnu*, or adenoidal cough, marking their progress and showing the bigger silence of the others, while behind everything, and making its wildtrack and weather, was the breathing of the herd and their steps through the grass.

The grass was no greener on the southern side of the Mara River, but animals were beginning to gather on its northern bank. As they did, so did we, slotting our car between the other tourist vehicles on the south side. To overlook the herd, we had taken a clattering iron bridge thirty miles downstream and driven back to the river edge. To arrive in the same place, the wildebeest must get wet. The southbound crossings of the Mara begin in August and end in October and through those months in every recent year 1.5 million wildebeest have swum 200 yards from one bank to the other. Most of them will have already swum north in June or July. They come then, with their calves of the year, in pursuit of grass, up from the Serengeti in Tanzania. *Serengit* in Maa means *endless plain*. The same grass continues across the border; the Masai Mara is simply the northern field of the Serengeti.

Shifting weather, above all the movement of rain across this vast area, draws grass up from the ground at different times. The wildebeest and other herbivores follow the rain and eat. The sun dries the plain around them from salad to hay. By August the Mara is looking wan, by October it is time to return south where the rains have revived the stubble the animals left behind in June or July. They track towards green and away from yellow, moving under a circling smear of cloud as it blows hundreds of miles over the savannah. Old pastures are swapped for new, hooves and mouths making those grasses old in turn. The herd scent moisture in the air, they can smell rain from thirty miles away. They walk towards the weather they want and the grass that the rain is making.

They walk, except for the 200 yards of the Mara River where the earth falls away beneath them and they pluck at muddy water with their thin legs, trying to gallop over it, finding themselves ploughing through it. The river, on the day we watched it, was deep and fast and iron red. It had been raining further upstream. Clouds were milking the sky to the north. But the time had come for the herd opposite. Further back, across the plain, were lines of wildebeest, pencilled through the grass. Their hooves had trodden a delta of paths that gathered, as at the neck of an hourglass that is as narrow-waisted as the wildebeest themselves, to drain into the water at the crossing.

When they move towards the river the wildebeest tie themselves into a thread often only one animal thick, a single file of one-track minds, nose to tail. Behind them, grazing animals spread out in loose ruminant meanders. It is hard to see how and when the graze turns into the trek. Feet apart, as if different species, some continue to eat while others are set on passage. The lines coming to the bank picked up speed into a rocking-horse canter with apparent resolve, but a parallel pathway opened of animals running from the river with the same sense of purpose. Had they given up? Would they cross later, or elsewhere? The oncoming wildebeest reached the top of the gently shelving slope that led down to the beach. The riverside was empty, but many had already crossed and the bare sandy soil was pockmarked with hoof prints right to the water's edge. On our side of the river twenty wildebeest, a mixture of adults and young, having heard the animals arrive opposite, ran past us, returning to the top of the bank, which is steeper here, like a low sand cliff. They looked back over the water they had crossed at those who were to follow and mooed. The sound – encouragement or the pain of separation – didn't bridge the river. The animals that must cross had stalled. Having hurried to the edge they stopped, as if waking from a trance. How did we get here? Why did we come?

All of a wildebeest lives in its ugly nervy head, its long goatish face, boxer's nose, lawnmower mouth, flattened grey horns and thickset heavy shoulders slung with a straight black cumbrous mane lying over a brindled neck. At its rear, the animal is something else, petite and unfinished and edible. Those nearest the river tossed their heads, turned and moved away from the water. No thanks. The rank behind them – the file had thickened at the waterside to the width of about twenty animals – walked down to the river and did the same, spinning round and moving back up the bank, causing a jam. A startle spread through the herd and they all turned and moved up the slope. But more arrivals were pushing through the reluctant animals and, four times, individuals broke from the front of the herd and stepped right to the water's edge before wheeling back, their decision rippling through the animals behind and prompting all to retreat. Another line made it down the slope to the river. They all turned except for a calf, still brown where all around were grey. It moved to the edge, dithered for a moment, and then launched into the water with a skittish lunge of splayed legs, bared teeth and flaring eyes. The tap was opened. Previously cautious animals streamed back to the edge and jumped in, one after another at first and then in a broader line of divers along the riverside.

The crossing was terrifying to watch. Each wildebeest takes twenty seconds to cover the yards but, in that time, they look far from home. Entering the slapping river they seem stripped naked, forced to endure a swimming lesson by an instructor who, for all his severities and cruelties, sits nowhere but in their own heads. Within two plunges they are sodden and out of their depth, broadsided by the brown swirling current, blinded by spray and the splashes of panicking neighbours. Midstream the lives of the animals seem wrenched from themselves and violently transformed. Their faces, accustomed to look down, made for living downwards, must now strain up, marked with struggle and anxiety, to keep clear of the water. As we watched, one swimmer turned round and went back headlong into those behind it. Freaked by this spin, they all turned and the chain was broken.

The last animal ahead of the recusant reached the bank beneath us. It clambered shakily up the crumbling sandy wall. The moaning encouragers had moved off and the last swimmer tried to pick up speed to follow, dripping water, its loose hair darkened and plastered to its grey body and dribbling the last of the river from it. It looked shattered but it must keep going, for just there, ten yards away, between our trucks and the wildebeest, were four lions standing around like Nazi SS officers.

After the first yards of trampled mud at the bank a beautiful corridor of grass ran away from the river, curving around a low domed hill and opening beyond to a broad plain dotted with acacias. Having crossed the Mara, the wildebeest head towards the grass, to spread in the bulb of its hourglass, and resume their chewing. But the grass road is fringed on either side by a natural hedge of longer tangled stems. Here there were more lions, all females, and they tussled with one another as, in a catty mixture of animus and apathy, they took up positions in the hedge. The day was heating up and they had already eaten. Sleep kept on creeping over them but meat kept on passing as well. The wildebeest must run to avoid being taken to one side and pulled down into the grass by hot sharp mouths.

The last swimmer was alone and a crouching lion in a gap in the hedge pulled her head below her tensed shoulders and dropped her lower jaw. The wildebeest might or might not have seen the lion but it hurried on, picking up speed, trying to catch the tails of the animals in front of it. The moment passed and its taut specifics slackened. The swimmer reached the other wildebeest and re-entered the herd; the lion loosened her muscles and lay down in the grass, flattening a yellow bed of straw.

The dead hadn't finished with us. We drove back to the bridge over the Mara and this time we stopped. The bridge is just south of a bend in the river, and a succession of wildebeest bodies that had drowned in their crossing attempt had spun from the turbid flow and eddied at the shore into a gruesome flotilla. There were more than a hundred corpses along fifty yards of bank. In death they had arrived on the side of the river they died trying to get to. The uncrossable crossed. At the shore the corpses bumped into one another, nuzzling tenderly in whirlpools, like calves to mothers. The sugar-slime smell of decay was so thick it seemed animated; particulates furred my tongue, I tasted sweetmeats on the air. In the water, some bodies were still supple and flowing and seemed to manoeuvre as the river buffeted them; others were stiff and bloated, like dirty anchored buoys. Some were still recognisably mammal; others were ballooning hairless haggis-bags. Any visible eyes looked iced with green cataracts. Any anuses bulged with a pink plug of distended rectum. On the beach there were bones from earlier tides; midstream was one skull washed clean by the swirl and rot of the river, its body behind still apparently ready for life if only it could be untangled from the rocks that had snagged it.

Negotiating the pontoon of glutted bodies were two monitor lizards, walking from haunch to haunch, licking their lips, and tasting the cooking smells. Marabous waded through the shallows of ox-tail soup, digging deep into submerged bodies, pulling up skin, gristle, and viscera that they juggled into the best position with their huge canoe-bills before swallowing. White-backed and Rüppell's griffon vultures were more squeamish about the water, and gripped on to hairy corpses in order to dig lusciously into more ruined animals after drowned lights, their heads coming out shining red with wet blood. A common sandpiper surfed on the back of a slow drifting corpse, daintily picking at the insects that crawled over its drying skin. A vast crocodile – Francis, the man who guards the bridge with a 1930s Enfield rifle, knew him as Solomon – gorged on wildebeest, lay half out of the water, one yellowing canine poking up at the front of its yard-long head, anchoring him to the bank.

Further out into the centre of the river there were many bodies still riding the rapids and bucking through the breaking water. Seventeen went past in ten minutes and, if that is typical, 2,500 therefore each day. A couple embraced, locked together by entangled legs. One sailed past on its back, its feet curving stiffly upwards like an ornate table. Another was steered into a whirlpool by the useless rudder of its horns. New ways to be dead came past every minute. The corpse of a hippopotamus floated round the bend, an incidental casualty among the failed swimmers; some vast continent of death, the biggest uncooked sausage ever made.

*   *   *

I dreamed about the river that night, my face pushed into roiling water with monstrous bodies coming at me like malign bumper cars, tumbling in free-fall but torqued and glutinous. I woke: hot, knotted and twisted into my sleeping bag. Months later, on the other side of Africa, at Ameib in the Erongo Mountains in central Namibia, I re-ran the dream in a drier place, at the edge of another wild field, this time counting falling elephants.

I fell asleep in a cave. I'd climbed over hot rocks on a day stunned by the sun and lay down to rest on a smooth tongue of granite at the shaded mouth of Phillips cave. As my eyes adjusted to the dim, I could make out a train of creatures walking across the stone ceiling over my head: a chalky white elephant coming through the straw-lemon rock, and next to it another with, in its belly, a red antelope, then a line of ochre human stick-figures, a dark oryx with elongated horns emerging from a rust streak, an ostrich, a giraffe's neck crossing another line of people. I tracked the parade back and forth and as I did I could feel my eyelids pebbling with tiredness and the cosset of the warm stone beneath me. In a minute I was gone, the cave slid over me, its elephants the last things I saw.

When I woke the animals swam on into focus, floating out from the rock, crystallised from its grits and sparkle. It seemed they came *through* the roof of the cave, as if the painter had seen the living things surging from their own centre to surface on the stone. As my eyes got used to the light, the animals drifted, walking without anything beneath their feet, and overlapping one another, a projection of depth without space, a herd moving and adding animals as it passed without leaving any behind, elephants, oryx, people all together, the draught of life still in their steps.

Stone tools found in the cave date to the southern African Late Stone Age, probably around 5,400–5,700 years ago, but no one has conclusively aged the Bushmen paintings nor said what they were for. Looking up at them is to see the stony logic of the illogicality of dreams; to see truths and the uses to which those truths have been put; to see facts (the species are readily identifiable and depicted moving as their living counterparts move in the valley below the cave) but also beliefs; to see tricks of the eye and tricks of the light, but also tricks of the mind; to take in the observed and its setting but also the observer. The pictographs are accounts of how nature writes itself – an antelope's stride, the curl of an elephant's trunk – but also of how people write it, and of how different that is; they are shockingly man-made things in a stone room amidst miles of wild. I imagine the Bushmen painters making the frieze of images, aware of the gulf between those they painted and those they saw, driven by wanting to articulate the gap and interested in trying to close it. They are indoor versions of outdoor things whose shadows are cast, as in Plato's cave, on a stone wall, but which are cast here not by the sun but by human minds. The painted elephants, the antelope, the oryx are more than food; the pictures more than a shopping list or a propitiatory offering. This is not just the hunting and gathering of the wild, but an enclosing of it within an idea, a human settlement among and around nature, and evidence that farming began in the mind before it started in the fields.

The elephants seemed to be ambling above me, floating in their rippling sea of rock. I noticed, for the first time, a small red one as well as the two white, and wondered at the difference. I imagined the painters falling asleep under their paintings like me and then waking to see the cave roof like a night sky, with animals instead of stars. I thought of a Chagall picture with people and animals lifted from the earth and blown, without harm, through space. The cave is a refuge overlooking a vast spread of bush and weather. By comparison it seems an intimate place, not so different from the inside of a head, and good for storing things, including ideas. Lying there, looking up, I could see how it might have been the same for the painters too. The very concept of mind might have evolved from living in caves, their interiority allowing for internal life. It was calm and still there and quieter than outside as well as cooler. Sound changed – the cave's room acoustic, its chambered feel, allowed for indoors talking and softer human utterance. Bushmen clicks would work especially well, their echoes encouraging conversation. Cave talk is like night talk, dimmed but close.

Under the eaves, I sat up and looked out at the ends of the day.

Ameib, the outward side of the mountains here, means The Green Face. The inward run of the Erongo range is all rock and it gathered below me to a wide amphitheatre of granite known as the Bull's Party. It is named for the huge balls of weathered stone that perch on plinths of the same rock, like vast worn skulls or giant dislocated ball-joints, a stone bone-yard three miles across. There are dozens of boulders and thousands of smaller round rocks. On one, below the cave, was a Damara rockrunner, a stone-specialist bird, endemic to Namibia, looking like a large, brightly patterned rufous and rust wren and, here, like a ball of hot rock hurrying over the cooler, older domes. It flew to a closer stone and scattered lizards on a boulder at the cave mouth. On the ceiling, near the paintings, rock martins had slung two mud hammocks. Beneath their nests was a spatter of droppings. Further along, dassie or rock hyrax urine had chalked the stone in a similar colour to the white elephants. There is more than one way to paint a cave.

Just below, back out in the sun, was a tiny front garden. The granite is smooth but not totally flat, and rainwater – and perhaps urine too – had gathered in depressions and hollows and rubbed at the rock until it flaked and gritted. Seeds had found moisture and minerals and purchase. Long-stemmed green grass sprouted from one coffin-shaped gouge. Its feathered heads trapped the dipping sunlight, making a small lanterned meadow. Beyond it and far below, the great swatch of plain ran from the foot of the mountains like carpet from a wall, implacable, unfenced, open miles of mottled bare earth and grasses and scrub. I could see zebras and giraffes through my binoculars. The slanting sun picked at the breath of dust, sprinkling its smoke with pinpricks of brilliance, sharpening the view rather than misting it. Every moving thing was revealed and caught in the last of the lowering light. Every animal threw a lengthening dark shadow across the earth but also a bright corona that snagged in the air. At the very moment the sun, lighting the view and its contents, showed the separation of things, singling out animals moving far apart across wide spaces, the same light spilled and streamed everything together. At six-fifteen in the evening, I could see fifteen giraffes, at least five miles away, with their necks above the thorn scrub holding the sun in warm orange bars. Nearer, two mountain zebras grazed in the shadows, their white stripes seeming to move more than their black ones. To my side, dark slack shapes of granite-dusted dassies had emerged from their hiding cracks to sing their sundown songs like sad hens.

As the sun dropped it pushed shadows further and further, until the mountain's shadow, the shadow from the cave, reached the giraffes, and then the Earth's shadow, night, reached the horizon in its daily dreamy ambush, collecting everything together, sifting everything into dark. I lowered my binoculars and could see nothing with my naked eye. The animals were lost from view. I knew they were still there but the dark had folded them into its corral. As I watched, the images of the elephants and the antelopes on the cave wall came again to me, floating out of the rock.

By the time we had walked back to our tent the full night was upon us. Its sky so crowded with stars it took me close to tears. The seeming emptiness of Namibia invites you to think about these things: the night being no lonelier than the day; the plain no more open than the cave.

For two weeks in the desert I slept at snake-level, on the ground, knapping the corners of my body, my shoulders, elbows, hips and ankles, making arrowheads of my bones. Beneath my thin camping mat, there was always some worn aggregate of sand or grit. If stray strands of grass were caught under the tent, by the morning they were flattened into zigzags like lightning strikes or broken stems of dry spaghetti.

We drove one day for three hours along a hundred miles of one desert road and saw neither a single car nor a building. Where else is there so little soil or vegetation, where else so much exposed rock? Where else is so apparently field-less, so man-less? When we asked an old Afrikaner in a shop for a corkscrew he waited long seconds before he answered, looking far over my shoulder deep into the dusted distance of his store. The whole country looks back at you in the same way.

The sea is a few dozen miles to the west but the place has dried up. An ocean has been baulked. The land seems ancient, on the far side of the green rush of life, long finished with all that oozes. It is too hot to move, too hot to stand still. Mica and quartz dazzle you from below but to look up would be madness. You must walk to create your own breeze, but strides breed sweat. Every step is hamstrung. I felt the fat melting from me. To expose a liquid in this heat is to kill it. Our wine dregs dried to cave-paint rust. I stepped away from pissing in the sand and, as my shadow cleared the wet patch beneath me, it disappeared as quickly as breath from a mirror. On a dirt track was a dead puff adder squashed to a slack S of amber dust, a last glisten of wet at its open jaw. In the dry grass Ludwig's bustards panted, their pink mouths quivering in the heat. From the hot sand lizards raised their feet one at a time against the sun's battering monologue.

We travelled through the country, winded by its scale, drunk on its level, blinded by its light. The surface of the Earth has been reduced and salted, rubbed away to a worn-out old cloth drained of colour. The soil is thin; the grass is thinner. Everything is pulled gaunt against bone, stretched at a heel or knee or elbow or brow. It seems tired; reverted in its withered collapse to some simplified dried shape. It is like looking at the stone a lithograph has been cut from – not at the print, but at the printer. Here, just into Lüderitz province, all the hills from which the valleys run are at the same height, flat topped, like army haircuts. The hillsides and the valley floors are uniformly empty all the way down. A dead-straight road rolled over the lip of what seemed to be the floor of a valley, the lowest part of the outside of the Earth, but which, as we descended, was revealed to be part of a plateau. What I thought was down was up. At its parched mouth, a valley broadened and opened into an impossibly wide plain, dipping lower, blurring into sand, sky, and invisibility, all one in the heat. I could see ostriches miles away like black weather balloons trembling in the haze. I was never in an emptier place, never felt so obviously on a ball of stone rolling through space.

There were no surface rocks in this valley. The distribution of loose stones in Namibia is magically or madly mysterious. In places there are so many, in others so few. The summoning and banishment, the gatherings and clearings of talus and scree, of rocks piled neatly in peaks, of dust dusted and of naturally swept fields suggests a strict and particular plan beyond our comprehension, a plan that is legible but unintelligible. There are porcupine cairns of a million un-climbable fragments, and, just 300 yards away across open grass, huge single boulders like slumbering giant tortoises. The valley floor here is made of sand. Grass grows over it in snaking lines, following the ripple of wind and dune. The sand settles in the valley like a filled bath, its surface calming after the taps have been switched off. Except here they never are. Mountains dry-rot to sand, and the sand returns to bury its shrunken, stooped parents. Dunes are mountains made from the ruins of mountains. In the next valley the countless stones on the hard earth look planted, as if they were sown yesterday; nothing hides their freshness, but perhaps they have been lying there for thousands or millions of years, incubated under the sun and kindled by the wind and dust to shine like dark coal-stars.

Only in the short dawns or dusks can you lift your eyes and see. Much remains hidden. Invisible, a Rüppell's korhaan, a small bustard the colour of dry grass, dribbled its liquid croak. A sundowner: a cork eased from the neck of a bottle and followed by a glug. A common tit-babbler stowed in its bundle of mimicry the sound of water droplets, an almost-cure for drought. As I walked, lark after lark brushed up grasshopper-dry ahead of me, a thread of tattered browns through a desert of brown scrub, brown grass, brown rock, brown sand. There being so many larks in the desert, everything moves towards the condition of lark. Each bird is a slight and dusted survivor, a desert father or niche farmer, occupying subtly different landscapes and living in what they know: a karoo lark, then a black-eared sparrow-lark, a karoo long-billed lark, a grey-backed sparrow-lark, a lark-like bunting, a spike-heeled lark, a Stark's lark, and, just before dark, a dune lark, its back the same colour as the red sand it had walked on, lifting like thrown sand from the dune into its song flight, a shower from an open beak that scratched like grass, carried easily through the dry air, hooked to it like a seed head, then dried itself before reaching the ground. The desert given wings.

In half an hour the sun hurried behind the dunes. The mountains and the plain softened briefly, pastel-rubbed like sea-washed glass, and then disappeared into the dark; the skyline along the west held an ember-rift of orange, but it thinned from overhead, and the black from above descended the sides of the sky's dome to join the black from below. For minutes it seemed very dark and then the starlight came. Nothing is more beautiful. A field, in the fieldless place, growing at night. The entire sky was stuffed with stars like spectral pollen. They lay thick and deep and ran down to the ground: the Milky Way arching its voluptuous leash. After the lone tyrant sun of the day, barging all over, came the democracy of night, ancient lights, a myriad silver pin-suns. Their waltzing spangle said you are there and we are here, here and there and everywhere; a concert of stars spun through space, distant, open-mouthed, silent yet shouting; now is yesterday, here was tomorrow. The shock comes, once again, at the demonstration of so much *other*, a star for every lark, a star for every grain of sand. And once again, the oldness of the view, the way looking up shreds your life, strips it back, joins you to all those who have looked up, millennia of watchers, a star for every gazer.

You could, it seemed, step from one to another along the warming crowded stretch overhead, where the stars flowed and swam together and turned from jewellery into cloth. It seemed so, yet the stars teach only rock-like cold-blood. There is no human kindness in the Milky Way and no stride long enough to tread the star chamber. We might be at a party, but we weren't invited. I looked down at the sand at my feet. I had been walking around our tent looking up. There was a puff adder squeezing under a fence, alive this time, chunky and muscled, just beyond the end of my flip-flops. It looked like a businessman's tie thrown on the floor of a hotel bedroom. Brown sand against brown sand. I could see far-away stars reflected in its green-gold chips of eyes. Perhaps it could see the same in mine.

The next night we stayed at an old farmstead called Stellarine. We had the bliss of a bed, and slept under a roof, keeping the stars from us. Though we were seventy miles inland from the Atlantic there was probably no one sleeping between the sea and us. It is all sand. The desert runs out of the ocean up the cold and misted beach, shrugging off the sharks and fur seals in the waves and the wrecked ships driven on to the shore. The beach rises and dries and becomes desert. A great buckled blowing, hundreds of miles long, a hundred miles wide, with flat feet and flyaway skin, accumulating and drifting, rising and plunging like nothing but itself. It is, in all sorts of ways, an unsettling place. Movement is its life. En route through it, as the Bushmen always were, a living might be possible. En route, the European would-be settlers could temporarily outspan or remove the yoke or harness from their animals and sleep. En route was one thing; to root was harder. Farming is and always has been tough here. South of the South African border with Namibia you pass a sign to a place called Douse-the-Glim. There doesn't seem to be anywhere down the dirt road to which the sign points. As it says, put out the light and give up hope. Nearby is Moedverloor, or loss of heart.

The dunes begin at the back of the house at Stellarine. This was once the furthest into the desert, the nearest to the ocean, that it was possible to farm, but the sand has won and pushed its warm rust east into the fields. It heaps at the low walls surrounding the house. There had been a farm on this site since the turn of the twentieth century. Jacob van Lill was the original farmer. His wife was Stella. The farm was named for her not the night sky. They had six children. The van Lills grazed sheep for their skins and wool. In the early 1960s a good fleece from Stellarine was worth two pounds and five shillings. The sheep were fat-tailed central Asian karakuls. Their name carries the promise of water. They share it with an oasis in Uzbekistan and two lakes in Tajikistan. Karakul wool, or rather the pelt of newborn lambs, makes astrakhan collars and hats. For a time the farm worked, but low rainfall meant livestock rearing was always hard. When nearby water supplies dried up, bore holes to aquifers had to be dug further and further out west into the desert. The sheep were pushed into an oven. Wrapped in their greasy fleeces they boiled in the sun, while over-grazing led to a drastic deterioration of the land. In the early 1980s a severe drought finished the farming off.

Now oryx and springbok come to the old water-troughs, trekking across the plain to drink at the back gate of the farm. I woke in the morning and watched them from my bed. The oryx is all frump and resignation. Its progress to and from the water is a definition of weary stubbornness. They make you think of the farmers in their overcoats arriving here with their ox-carts. Hot and heavy and trying hard to conceal their anxieties on a great trek that never ends. Yes, I am going over there; yes, I know the sun is boiling the plain; yes, it smacks at my skull; yes, I am wearing an unwieldy crown of horns too long for my head; but, yes, I will doggedly cross this thinning grass; why, I don't know, but I must. Through the broken heavy plod of oryx came springbok, moving like a corps de ballet, light on their feet, frisky in their stotting and pronking, never too hot to jump, cooling themselves as they went.

On the verandah of the old farmhouse a familiar chat came looking for insects. I love this bird for its colour, its name and for the reason it got its name. It came, familiarly, around us as it has come around people in caves and on farms for thousands of years, moving into spaces we had taken as our own. It is intensely drab, soft dusty brown throughout, except for a warmer brown tail, the part of itself that it does not see. As it landed its wings flicked and every few hops it made them flick again. Sunlight passed through the bird's raised feathers and scattered in the same way it shone through the grass heads nodding in the hot wind. The chat flicks its wings as a card player shuffles a pack: beneath his fingers but beyond his mind. It flicks its wings, as a starling paddles its when it sings or a redstart quivers its tail, unthinkingly and yet with an action that defines it.

In Afrikaans the familiar chat is a *spekvreter* or bacon-eater. It came around the trekkers and ate the ox fat they used to grease their cartwheels. The van Lills would have known it. On the verandah of their farm we ate local salami for breakfast and I tossed scraps to the chat. Even in the shade, the dabs of fat liquefied and ran through the meat. Grease sweats away here without a *spekvreter*. This is the land of biltong and rusk, a place where things cook dry rather than rot.

In the oven-warm wind, I walked from under the verandah towards the oryx and springbok. My shoes filled like flowerpots with the sand's soft sift. Beneath a camel thorn was a mummified orphan, a springbok calf, its dead tongue withered in its skull, its stiff and juiceless board of skin lying propped on the sand. Some bones had escaped from the manila file of its body and fallen to its feet like kindling. Running across the sand between the dead springbok and the tree trunk was a black dung beetle. It carried its dry turd ball, a springbok pellet, towards its desert sewage farm. The ball was clasped between the beetle's back legs; it ran using only its front legs, and the dung ploughed a little furrow behind it as it went towards its burrow.

Hoisted up into the far side, the desert side, of the tree was a hayrick. A vast communal nest of sociable weavers. The farm no longer has human sounds but it chatters and scratches with farming life. The birds, patterned in desert camouflage of greys, browns and blacks, have lifted a mighty forkful of grass twenty feet into the air, weaving it brilliantly into the thorns. They carried the grass stem-by-stem, one blade at a time, each held in their beaks like a single whisker. I have watched them gather it and begin starter homes in other trees and on telephone poles. Here the nest was old, its upperside a dome of greying grass twenty feet across, and its underside, brighter, less bleached grass with dozens of tunnels plaited into the thatch. All the straws at each tunnel mouth were woven to splay centrifugally outwards at the same angle like a flash photograph of a fiery wheel. Like rookeries, the communal nesting places seem to be raised mostly in sight of neighbours. I could see a further three weaver townships across the plain along the edge of the dunes. At dawn and dusk the ricks glow like low suns, a solar system of floating grass.

For their nests, the sociable weavers harvest only the stems of the Bushmen grass. Below the birds' nest live tiny ants, no longer and no thicker than a dash. Cutters and harvesters, a colony of *Messor denticornis*, they snip Bushmen grass heads from their stems for food and carry them one by one underground to thresh and store in granaries they have built. The chambers are kept dry so the hulled seeds don't germinate. The chaff is taken back to the surface and dumped carefully along the rim of a growing ruff of husks that rings each nest entrance hole.

These mounds with their single dark eyes in their centre are scattered through the short grass like cushions. They are crisp at their outer rims and pale and fading like the sociable weavers' nest, the colour gone to the universal non-colour of dust and old grass. Bushmen and others once knew how to steal the stored seeds from the ants, to make porridge from them, or beer, or a stronger liquor called *poka*.

At Palmwag, 370 miles north of Stellarine, there was less sand and more scrub but there were still plenty of harvester ants. There were bigger ruminants too. We rounded a corner of a dirt road and arrived mid stand-off in a war over cud between a cow and a small herd of elephants. All had been intent on their browse, the elephants curling their trunks round great hanks of grass and gathering it tightly from the earth, the cow dribbling with pleasure at the same stand of lush green, until it looked up and started bellowing at the knees of the elephants. They stopped their harvest to retaliate with blasts from their trumpets. One dropped a tube of hay bricks behind it as it moved off. It rolled towards us and I could see within it the same stems of grass a harvester ant would cut or a sociable weaver select for its nest.

The empty quarter isn't. It only seems that way. There are arrowheads and axes scattered through the plain, man-made things on their slow journey back to the condition from where they started. And the land is farmed; the plain is a field. But because there is apparently so little in the foreground, our eyes are always being drawn further and wider. The plain proposes a kind of nomadism of looking. As we drove towards the coast we startled an oryx. It is continually surprising how large animals can remain unseen in acres of flat and treeless country until you are almost upon them. In its panic it ran alongside the car, outstripping us but heaving with terror and unable to flee because there was a fence at the roadside as there had been for much of a hundred miles. I hadn't noticed it, until the oryx, which also hadn't, ran up against it. Snorting, with flared nostrils and streaming eyes, it turned and breasted the fence, stumbling into a crash of horns and legs and dust; a galloping nomad unable to see the wire, unable to believe a fence would stop it. The Bushmen cave painters in Namibia abandoned painting around the time a different people, herders who were more farmers than hunter-gatherers and more settled, arrived on the plains. Various fences, real and understood, stopped the animals coming through the rock. In 1985 one of the last recorded phrases of the /Xam Bushmen language, as remembered by an old gardener called Hendrik Goud on a South African farm near Gifvlei, were interpreted as /hu kwa koa se: /ke / / a. This was translated as, 'Here come the Boer, we must hurry away', or better still: 'Run, here come the farmers.'

In June 2011, in Zambia, Lazaro killed Stanley Munkombwe with his axe. Stanley was a fellow farm worker and honeyguide follower and nest finder. Lazaro attacked him in an argument about thievery in a field of maize that both men were guarding. He was sentenced to five years' hard labour. Claire, who visits him in gaol, reports that he still talks of the fields on the old farm by name: R4 and R3, Number 12, and Shangwondo and Mubanga.

SPRING FEN

New weather redecorates the room. You go to bed, as Hardy has it in *Under the Greenwood Tree*, among nearly naked branches and wake next morning among green ones. Rise and put on your foliage, is Robert Herrick's less pyjama'd version of the same transformation. Spring grows on the world.

First the light changes. A lid lifts. In the black poplar on the fen a mistle thrush sang, throwing out everything it had saved through the winter. Fen skies are wider and open higher in March than in February and they are bluer and whiter. The angle of the Earth's orbit of the sun does it, but the effect is felt overhead in the species of sky. I watched clouds at odds with each other barge together above the fen, seasons in battle. Mizzling curtains of rain messed with wedding cakes of cumulus. The motor of the year turns in this.

Looking out for swallows from the bank of Reach Lode, I was about the same height as the first fields that rose away to the east where the fen ends. But in the low sun streaming from behind me the grass plots there on the rising ground seemed to lift and tilt. Because these fields are hedged rather than ditched, they looked like framed paintings of soft rumpled green hung on the edge of the day. It is in this light and during these spring weeks that the lines and dips of old ridges and furrows appear through the grass, all gentle and snowy, and the new green reveals the farmers and the farming that lie behind it.

One of these floating fields at the end of the Devil's Dyke lures migrant wheatears every spring and, sensing or sharing the draw, I hurried there to see three bright males working the short grass. Close up, all the snowy folding had gone, and the green was still wintery thin, with chalk obvious beneath it. The light had played a trick and yet the birds had come back, or another generation of them had found the same inducements in the same field. I wondered if these birds (old timers or newcomers) had travelled with something like a *feeling* for this grass, and if so whether a sense-memory was being topped up? And what happens when they leave? They printed their feet into its late-winter turf but maybe they fly north carrying something other than its first spring insects with them: some fold-away version of the field, its essence or co-ordinates, its value or its taste, its reason? In this way, the wheatear would *be* the field at the end of the Devil's Dyke wherever it was, and the field (and every other field the bird stopped in) would get out and about and travel the world. If the light was right, it might even be possible for those of us grounded below the birds to catch the traces walked by their little feet into the thin March grass, year after year, like those ghost-ridges and furrows from the old days that appear in the early spring.

The wheatears faced north with their black eye-stripes like compass needles all looking the same way. Cold air did fierce battle with the warming evening light and four swallows came flying low in a black line over the wheatears, my first of the year. They pushed into the wind, their heads drawn down to their shoulders like polar explorers; the birds cowed and roped as Wilson, Bowers, Oates and Evans, a different magnet to the wheatears' drawing them on, keeping them from dropping down to the grass, seeding their minds with home.

I turned south to the village and the shelter of its still-bare trees and the jam of blackbird song came warm as I walked towards it. The cumulus rafted on overhead, piling themselves upon themselves. For days in early spring these clouds mass before the leaves burst below them. The sky tutors the earth in this way, showing the shapes of summer trees, the towering black poplars, skulled willows, keyed ashes, shaggy oaks. When the trees open and fill at last, any clouded sky looks suddenly old, grey haired beyond the green, and it stays this way throughout the summer, getting older still.

In 1980 I went to university in Cambridge believing that incest was more prevalent in the fens than anywhere else in the country. The epicentre of consanguineal sex was the village of Soham. Or so it lodged in my mind. I had never been there or stopped for any length of time anywhere else in the fens and I am not sure where I had picked up the notion. I wasn't, however, alone in my delusion. For hundreds of years Cambridge had lived *under* the fens. In the summer, wind dry-choked with pollen and thrips blew the flatlands into town and, in the winter, wet fog coming off the shadow-swamps seemed to drip-feed all sorts of myths and fantasies, stories of webbed feet and incest.

Another version of the same impulse – the simultaneous capturing and holding-off of a place, believed close enough to mark the place you were in – could be heard ten times a day some winters in Cambridge. It still can. I learned it in my first weeks in the city. The wind in Cambridge was cold, it was said, because it blew directly from the Urals. This was almost but not quite a joke. The wind did often blow wolfish from the east but no one in the city could really say where it came from. Nor did anyone in the Urals think they were breathing on Cambridge. What was designated as an import was actually invented in situ. In a flat place it is hard to believe in mountains but, as a remote opposite of Cambridge, the Urals sounded plausible, and they took on an imaginary truth that made them and their wind more than an almost-joke and raised them, fantastically, into local life. The mountains became, in this way, a hinterland of the city.

I arrived in Cambridge already bogged with fen baggage no less nonsensical. I knew the people of the fens couldn't have webbed feet – I was a birdwatcher and strong on my ducks – but unconsciously I had given headroom to a mishmash of other prejudices and received ideas. Fen people, the wind and the fog said, were the last peasants of England, trapped throwbacks like gypsies who couldn't move. The isolated population was genetically raddled. Ignorance and poverty had condoned father-and-daughter sex and other too-close-to-the-bone breeding liaisons. Shaking with marsh-ague or poleaxed by opium taken to alleviate their pains, the runtish people crouched under dwarfing skies. In the summer the wind blew them around a dust bowl. In the winter the same soil, now glutinous mud, clung to their short legs and sucked them in.

This gallery of grotesques was nothing more than the local encore of a yokel pantomime, a situation-comedy done in broad Mummerset. Versions of it arise everywhere. The neighbours just across the fields are always the strangest of people. We are too much alike to permit any other truth. But it is striking how strong and how shared these fen caricatures were. Why should that be? I think the place itself is the substantial reason, particularly its apparent emptiness. It was the place, or rather the lack of it, in my mind's eye, not its villagers, that had allowed Soham to be the incest capital. The village barely occurs between the peat and the sky. The fens all around it look like an open stage asking for some scenery. Their unemphatic mundanity makes them (still, as it always has) into a place where a kind of negative capability of landscape operates. Where less becomes more. Where the landscape itself is thin but the weather is wide. Where the prospects are so low that small things loom tall. Where you might mistake a windmill for a giant. Where things are so boring they become interesting.

There is energy in all this. At a first glance the fens might seem surrendered and banal. They are flat and farmed. Their drained soil is turned to our advantage. Every inch of them represents a human victory over the wet. Look a little longer though and you can see how unfinished they are and how they declare it themselves. The ghost of water is everywhere – its presence, its absence, its removal and its defiance – and it wetly mirrors everything dry. Fen flatness is not beautiful. Man and nature have wrestled and their business has resulted in a curiously abrasive and uncouth emptiness: an ordinariness that refuses to be just tame. The eradication of wild detail in so worked and so low a place gives off the opposite of familiarity. Each field, even the dreariest square, has the smack of itself. That they are all man-made redoubles their power to disconcert. They cannot be left alone if we want them to remain as they are; yet they cannot be subjugated no matter how much we lean on them. Though they are edged and boxed and rolled, they will not stop where we would have them stop. And the people living in the fens, even the commuters of today who shuttle its A-roads, are still under the fen regime. In the space here, between how we would configure them and how they will be, in the contrary weirdness of the deeply human but deeply resistant land, a kind of fen pastoral has taken root and grown up. And so: webbed feet and the fishing in your own family's pond.

Every student day I walked through a reduced or playground version of the fens. Fen fields and ditches ran almost to the centre of Cambridge. On either side of the straightened River Cam, the college gardens and grounds of The Backs were reclaimed and drained swamp just like the fens to the north. That cod with the book in its belly had arrived not far from here. The autumn mist that hung above the conduits and culverts, and which seemed able to detect or remember where old water had once flowed, came with the fen. Even the punts on the river began life as fishing boats for shallow water and as a way of lying down on that water in order to steal up on ducks.

Severed from their source yet still ghosting the world they were born in, the micro-fens of the city are diagrams of nature mastered; 'enclosed within the garden's square / A dead and standing pool of air' (as Marvell's 'The Mower against Gardens' has it). The Backs are a double-dream of connection and control brought into a half-life and laid out in lawns and flowerbeds. And, mastered also at the expense and exclusion of people. At King's College, cattle are still often to be seen on the grazing meadow just over the river from the college buildings, looking like bovine extras with walk-on parts in that same fen pantomime. No cowherd walks among them at King's and the trailer that brings the animals to the field doesn't hang around getting in the way of the view. Instead, it was possible, when I was a student, to see either Raymond Williams or John Barrell, two great critics of the comforts and deceits of artistic arcadias, passing the field of lowing kine as they walked to the University Library where they were doing their best to reframe the old georgics and bucolics of literature, and to revise our understanding of them by – broadly – putting people back into the picture.

I came, like almost anyone born in Britain in the last hundred years, to the peasantry through books. It began romantically. I was beguiled by Levin among his serf haymakers in *Anna Karenina* and enjoyed the photograph of Tolstoy in his peasant smock, fashion model for all hay writers. Long before university I had cherished a child's-size fisherman's smock of orange canvas that my parents had bought for me on a family holiday to Cornwall – it had deep pockets in the front and I'd imagined stuffing twitching mackerel into them even though I was always frightened of the sea and had never caught a fish. It was similar with hay. It made me sneeze. At university, I also loved John Berger's *Pig Earth*, new then, with its stories of the haymakers of the Savoie and the photograph of Berger – such a good pastoral name too – in a hay field. If that shepherd had started a commune I would have joined the flock. But I only had to walk through Cambridge market, 500 steps from the cows at King's, and thronged then with people from fen villages shopping and selling vegetables, leeks and celery stuck with black peat, to know that Tolstoy's or Berger's truth, if that is what it was, couldn't apply around me any longer. Likewise, nor could that more ugly version of the fantasy fens that I had somehow imbibed en route to living on the edge of them. The woman who cleaned my room in college took the bus in from Manea in the fens every day. Her husband gardened the college grounds. I didn't enquire after their sex life but she seemed thoroughly ordinary and, for weeks, kindly overlooked my stowaway girlfriend. Between my bedder, Raymond Williams, and later a stone curlew, I eventually woke up to where I was.

I took a train to Ely and walked east to Soham and then caught a bus back. No signs of incest, but the bus made the tallest thing for miles; even the people at the bus stop craned over the fields. I knew little of the history of those fields but, unlike so much of the rest of Britain, they seemed new. The ground had been settled with squares of wheat and rape and fenced by ditches of water. More water was being carried in straight channels raised, improbably, above the roads and as high as the bus. Following the hemmed flow even the gulls were forced to turn chicanes or right angles in the sky. All this was unlikeable as much as unlikely but I couldn't pass it by.

Along the eastern miles of the fens, among carrot fields at Lakenheath, there was a square-edged poplar plantation being grown for matchsticks. Above it the sky shook with planes ferrying cruise missiles between the nearby British and American airbases. Nesting in the box of matches were golden orioles, the only ones breeding in Britain. They belled my name, *dee-o*, and burned like yellow candles with black wicks among the green leaves. Stone curlews lived a few fields away, on an old rabbit warren rising from the fen. They walked about like slow lizards in the haze, their goat eyes yellow and bulbous as if myxi-sick.

Nothing seemed quite wild, yet nothing was fully tamed either. The soil was special pitch-black like the stuff you got in grow-bags from garden centres, except it was everywhere and almost greedy, running up over the grass as if it hadn't sanctioned its growing. Raindrops bounced little chits of it up the legs and over the back of feeding lapwings, like black fur. The rain thickened to a summer storm and I was caught out in it and felt like a tree. How stupid to be so tall and obvious, lost in the flat and shown up by it at the same time. I scrambled down a bank and hid in some reeds, underneath thunder and shrunken in the wash.

On Remembrance Sunday, in the autumn of the same student year, I cycled from Cambridge to Ely through Swaffham Bulbeck, Burwell and Soham, accidentally tracking war memorial ceremonies in the villages as I rode. There were church bells, wreathes and old soldiers wearing berets and medals and talking and smoking and standing about in the brittle light. In Burwell, one man, who must have been in his late eighties, wore a black furry jerkin. His medals, pinned to it, shone out from the fur like eyes. Slowly, he walked to the memorial and stood in front of it, with his feet apart, his stiff legs and mole-fur waistcoat redolent of a time when farm workers from the fens went to fight in the fields of France: digging for shelter as they had dug peat or ploughed furrows; eyeing what Isaac Rosenberg called the 'sleeping green' between the opposing trenches; feeding horses as they had at home; living, as they knew how, in the open air and close to the ground, in sodden hedgeless fields under the same astonishing expanse of sky; and keeping company for a while with those who would be mown down under that sky, like 'autumn corn before the cutter' as a witness to the first day of the Somme described what he had seen. Mole-men out in the light.

On 4 November 1914, Franz Kafka recorded in his diary some of the experiences of a brother-in-law (a soldier for Austro-Hungary) newly returned from the eastern front: 'Story about the mole burrowing under him in the trenches which he looked upon as a warning from heaven to leave that spot. He had just got away when a bullet struck a soldier crawling after him at the moment he was over the mole.' Six weeks before he was killed, Edward Thomas wrote in his war diary from northern France on 25 February 1917: 'Does a mole ever get hit by a shell?' Sixty-nine didn't come back to Burwell and their names are recorded in little carved trenches on the village war memorial. At the end of his play, when they have met on the beach at Dover, broken Lear says to blinded Gloucester: 'You see how this world goes.' Gloucester replies: 'I see it feelingly.'

All those I saw are dead now. Much has changed in thirty years. Another generation of ordinariness has arrived in the fens. There are newer soldier deaths to remember; the villages are dormitories for bigger towns; the volume of traffic makes cycling off designated tracks dangerous; in the fen nearest to where I live, migrant workers pick most of the leeks, gathering around what looks like a slow-moving portable office block suspended above the field. But the flatness and its thin potency remain: the determining sky ('chief organ of sentiment', as John Constable called it not so many fields away) and the equally striking refusal of the place beneath to be fixed. To fix the fens – to perform repairs thought of as necessary and thereby to bring them towards some solid state – has been the desire of people forever who have lived in or dreamed of its villages and fields, their grass, soil and water. In some ways this is functional and familiar – we might call it farming – in others it is strange, idealised or hopeless. It has made an unbeautiful human place from acres of ground that will not ultimately settle. There again, their not settling has been the making of the fens, keeping the most turned-over and dug-out place inviolably itself.

In early spring just before the green wheat came in the ploughed field, the opened soil folding along the surface of the earth looked like the crust of a loaf of bread. The furrows were like ribs scored in dough that crack open from below as the bread rises. Ploughmen and bakers must have noticed this many times. In the same field woodpigeons, fat already, moved with the heaviness of tanks up and down each ridge and trench. The spring-bright birds have a white neck-plate with a turnip-green patch above and, as they waddled, the feathers of the plate split and glistened also like the turned soil, magnesium bright at the surface, dark and unlit in the cracks. Some trapped charged air gathers there; the same warm spring static that comes in the purr of a catkin or the humming spark of the bumblebee's bum.

The next day a blue sheet dried in the western wind over the whole of the fens. On the chalky fields behind the village a green flush opened like mould on an old bone. The wheatears had longer grass at their feet. The nap that comes gentle at the sharp edges of the trees fuzzed tenderly at the air, warm and quick. Everything that was and will be wood was furred. The brightness of midday polished the bone-axe beaks of the rooks walking the fens and turned the sheen on their wings from black to glassy white. Songs rose from the fields like a freshet or a spring: skylarks mirroring the bright sky, the simple washed tune of a chaffinch in the hedge unfolding like young water making its way downhill.

There followed a week of air warm enough to feel continuous with skin and blood. But then the wind moved hard into the north-east and slapped down a dish-cloth sky. The birds stopped singing. It rained and made a sodden silence of the fields. Tree trunks, black with wet, were papered with leaves that had fallen after only days of life. Grass blades were bent awry by watery lenses. Cattle lay down, as if defeated, in the cold air of the fen field. Overnight, ruined blossom dropped along the hedges. The demolition of the year began before swifts had arrived into its skies.

It has always been like this and always will be. But other birds had started and couldn't stop. Through the rain a cuckoo flew along the lode with what must have been a reed warbler's egg jammed in its beak, its head wobbling as if surprised by what it had done; a second cuckoo crossed the first, calling its tongue-swallowing yelp as if another egg was gagging its throat. This bird, in its long-winged whickering flight, was chased by chaffinches, pulled out of the farmhouse trees by the *gowk* charmer, a wolf in a skirt, like a folk tale being flown across the fen.

* * *

The fens have been cast forever as a place needing repairs. Their story might have gone a different way in the middle of the great fen-fixing seventeenth century had Charles I built Charlemont, his projected Venice or St Petersburg-like city with a Versailles-like palace near Manea, and thereby come to rule the country from a flat fen. When Cornelius Vermuyden's first attempt to drain the Great Level with spades, wheelbarrows and horses had failed, and the Adventurers under Francis, Fourth Earl of Bedford, were near ruined, Charles declared himself the Sole Undertaker and plans were made for 'an eminent town in the midst of the Level', a fen city, 'the design whereof he drew himself'. It never happened. In the Civil War the captured king was bundled across the fens to prison in a hunting box or lodge in Newmarket, in a richly inverted ballet of power and pursuit. Later, Charles the would-be undertaker was beheaded. Charlemont Drive is now a cul-de-sac near the railway station on the edge of Manea. But in the imagined fixing Charlemont offered – the planting of the centre of the nation in a bog (the *mont* being all of fifteen feet above sea level) – we have another epigrammatic definition of all fen projects, Canute-moments in the tides of men, from the earliest dryings to the proposed rewettings of today.

Adventurers in the fens have repeatedly dreamed of combining one sort or another of moated castle (safety underwritten by wet) with the wholesomeness of drainage (swapping webbed feet for dry socks). That this combination is irreconcilable is a further fen truth. That Manea was also the site for a utopian commune inspired by Robert Owen is a fen joke. Robert made a little more progress than Charles. In 1838 at Colony Farm on Manea Fen, a follower of Owen started a 150-acre commune for between 100 and 200 colonists. Money was abolished, a windmill, cottages and a school were built, the communitarians wrote and read a newspaper called *The Working Bee* and dressed in suits of Lincoln Green. It didn't work. After a couple of years the Cambridgeshire Community Number One was abandoned.

*   *   *

From my bed at five in the morning I could hear the jackdaws trying their flint-knapping calls around the church towers in the village, testing whether yesterday's echo will be today's as well. At the front door the new air tasted unbreathed, birdsong alone had taken possession of it. But by the time I was properly out, the sun was already rubbing its white burn into the sky over the chalk hills at the edge of the fen. The incoming day had almost finished its work. The shadows running west from the village and its trees shrank back as the sun rose. Its splash turned up the birdsong and with that came the sensation of the day waking, the covers of night falling from the shoulder of the Earth as it rolled eastwards into the sunrise.

Dawn song through the northern hemisphere is continuous in the spring – it being always dawn somewhere, at every minute of every day, in May. If we could travel with those first splashes of sunlight we would hear the waking music of the whole of the top of the world beginning again and again and on and on for a month. As the sun touches each new yard of earth, song unfurls from it and sings it into life: the eastern thrushes at the Great Wall and through the taiga; the redwings and the fieldfares that ate and rested in the fens in the winter, now back in their birches; the bluethroats in the reed-lines around Moscow; the redstart in a tree in the centre of Yalta below which the Tatars come to sell honey; the thrush nightingale in a ditch outside Tallinn; the collared flycatchers of the Buda Hills; and here a common nightingale in the scrim of a hawthorn brake near the end of the Devil's Dyke – the relay of the day held for a moment in the water droplets and fabric-tears of its music.

From the shrinking pool on Baker's Fen at Wicken at six in the morning, twenty-three bar-tailed godwits clambered up into the air, a mixture of old-shirt grey and old-brick red, winter and summer plumage – the ratio changing each day as they make their passage from the Atlantic coast of Africa to the tundra of Russia. As if they were picking up the thread they had stitched to get them to Wicken, they wheeled as they climbed to the point from where I had seen them drop ten minutes earlier to the shallow dish of wet. Sky-hooked once again they moved confidently, flying with the whole of their bodies and heading urgently into the wind, determinedly north-north-east, seeking their tether, and following the same airway as Eric Ennion's birds nearly a hundred years ago. In the same sky, homing airforce planes, sand brown, mud grey, dead green, banked over the fen into the sun stream, turning into the wind as they descended towards the American bases, seeking their earth over the county border.

This was the story of the day: the necessary and sought tie to the world at a time of flight. In a square of ploughland a pair of lapwings had settled. Their winter flocks have broken apart and each bare acre has tugged two birds to its soil. In this the lapwings are ahead of the golden plovers, which, like the godwits, are still away from home. The same fingered-flights of plovers that were gloved with lapwings until just a month ago now swirl around the black and white breeding pair. The two species have become strangers to one another. *Wypes*, lapwings used to be called on the fens. And in their territorial agitation the birds cast their short-stringed kite flights above the furrows, tilting the earth to them and away, writing with their rounded wings a hurried looping script above the fen. Somewhere below them are their eggs: 'dingy dirty green', John Clare called them, 'deep blotched with plashy spots of jockolate stain'. The golden plover flocks will split up themselves when they reach their hilltops and tundra breeding grounds. Already some are carried north by their plumage. Most are still tan-coloured above and silvery-grey below, but a few have stepped on into their summer suits, with their neck, throat, breast and belly feathers new moulted to a peat-black bulbed flask painted down their fronts, and their backs prickling with a stone-top graphic of orange and green lichen. The season is stretching into its various clocks.

Yesterday it hadn't been here, today it was: a male whitethroat had arrived from the 10 million umbrella thorn trees of the northern Sahel to find one hawthorn on the fen edge. The bird settled to its summer anchor and the place grew up around it. The arrow-flight of its lengthy linear journey bent into tiny circular display sallies made once a minute through every day for six weeks. It had flown 5,000 miles in order to fly fifteen feet. On its song flights it launched from its thorn perch over domed-planets of cow parsley, but each time it was pulled back to its tree, the cursive script of its journey matching the length of its scratchy tune. The next tree along the ditch was an elder and it held another singing male whitethroat. Because it must, this bird adventured out towards the other but was pulled back by its tether. Between the white-throats a reed warbler, also not long installed, sang alone in its stand. Its song made a crowd out of its chopped and fretted mimicry, the sound of the world as it might be known from a summer cage of reeds.

Above the fen, twelve snipe chased one another in a dispute over women and living space. They flew like swifts, horizontal and furious, and then broke apart to work up their own wooing speeches and aggro gestures. Each male described his ambition in the air, drumming above his territory on the fen and marking its borders upwards. In the spring, tugged by the sun, these swamp-loving hunkered birds transform themselves into little horses and ride the sky. The males dance and bleat, calling *chip chip chip chip* on and on as if they are loosening something tight, their beaks screwdriving up, their whole bodies rocking from side to side. Moor-lambs, snipe were called in the Lincolnshire fens; the goat of the air is what *Gabhar-athair*, one of their many Gaelic names, means. They climb until their calls thin to the edge of the audible back on the earth or when their twisting bodies become too small to see and then they turn downwards and fall sideways back through the sky. As they do they fan their tails and part the outermost feathers so that, in their headlong dive, the rushing air rippling over their wings sounds through their spread plumage and their bodies sing. The sky then drums with a woolly thrum like a slow mosquito at your ear. The horseplay gallops on through spring moonlit nights. Drumming is among the very best sounds of the fens; a shaking of one of its membranes, like a bittern's boom ('his bump', John Skelton called it), that is heard in your chest and which vibrates there like the heart's foghorn.

One man went to mow. And let him stand for all men, that is for all those who sought thinking through haymaking and harvesting, sparing those poor anonymous millions who more simply, more exhaustingly, just had to *do* it, to mow in order to live. Since the first poems of Greece, Western writing has been drawn to lines of mowers strung across a field and, among the cutting men, there have been those who went to mow seeking something other than a swath of aromatic drying grass. Pastoral literature grew up in these fields. It cut two paths out of them. Some pastoral is an account of the fall of man (farming wasn't needed in Eden or during the Golden Age) and the repeated and commonplace repairs that can be made around that fall (wholesome good lives, grass that grows again, wool that can be cut without killing a sheep). Some pastoral writes a darker arcadia, a place or a mood that can only be known at the point of severance from it, that can only be lost even at the moment of its apparent possession (death is a condition of life no matter how sweet the roses smell).

The pastoral in William Empson's far-sighted formulation in *Some Versions of Pastoral* is characterised as being an intellectual or emotional position or cast of mind as well as a literary trope. It is a way of thinking and of feeling. A pastoral scene – imagined, written, dreamed, painted, sung – first of all is a description of separation that takes in both sides. A poet looks at a mower or a shepherd and thinks, 'I am in one way better, in another not so good.' We like scything peasants because we imagine their life makes a shape in the world that we desire but at the same time we are glad we don't have to cut grass in order to live. What Nietzsche called the 'pathos of distance' is at the heart of pastoral. The mower seems like the *echt man* or the *ur-man*, living a life of *soft* primitivism, organic and sustainable. But he is also stuck outdoors with straw in his hair and mud on his feet, struggling with *hard* primitivism. Empson goes on to say that his definition of pastoral 'may well recognize a permanent truth about the aesthetic situation'. In the fens, and in the fields more widely, I think it goes further still, beyond the aesthetic and deep into life. 'I am in one way better, in another not so good' speaks of our current relationship with everything natural that isn't us, with modernity, urban living, nature craving and with our estrangement from much of the planet, and with the drained world that we have dug for ourselves, north of Cambridge and south of the Wash.

Here is our mower – now looking impossibly old – Hilaire Belloc, wing-collared, high Catholic, advocate of conservative agrarianism and friend of the fens, arriving at his field (not in the fens) with his scythe in 1906. '[M]y own field', he says, 'my scythe'. Possession was important for him, though not essential for others. Some hay writers or turf accountants have been landlords determined to divest themselves of what they owned (Tolstoy). Some have been willing tourists into indentured labour (John Stewart Collis – who wrote on Tolstoy as well as on the plough and its pleasures). Some have scythed as young men or as holiday workers and recalled it later as writers (D. H. Lawrence: 'you could have seen me high on the load, or higher on the stack, like a long mushroom in my felt hat, sweating with my shirt neck open'; and John Fowles in the memorably blazing opening chapter of *Daniel Martin*). Some have less directly but no less intently walked and watched fields into meaning, making grassy versions of Philip Sidney's (the poet of *Arcadia*) poetic curriculum vitae that said '[m]y sheep are thoughts' (Richard Jefferies, Thomas Hardy). One, John Clare (and a handful of less well-known others too), cut hay to live at times, so to put food on the table of his crowded cottage, but also made a version of hay in words to try to communicate how he lived, and to hold on to what he knew he was losing – a way of life but also, in his case, his mind.

Belloc is certain he has no such doubts. Perhaps he protests too much about the healthiness of what he is doing. His field is an unidentified secret place, locked in a valley in southern England, 'remote from ambition and from fear'. It is hidden and he further hides it, as he must, for hand-mowing was already moribund when 'The Mowing of a Field' was published in 1921 (a year before T. S. Eliot's *The Waste Land*). A scythe swinging through time and sickles hissing through wheat – the ancient pastoral verities were losing their anchorage in the real world. The cutting, gathering and carrying of grass and grain were being mechanised and therefore the metaphorical gleam that the blade and the severed stems laid into the human mind was dimming. Our once common tools for the alteration of the earth, our harrows, sickles and scythes, had fashioned a sharp-pointed armoury for our imaginations, but without a real scythe, why should we fear the reaper?

Scything had only a decade or so left in Britain, but Belloc's anxiety about its disappearance is literary rather than agricultural. Even a few years earlier when Edward Thomas wrote about a ploughman (in 'As the team's head-brass'), he was separate from the scene: he sat and watched the man and his horses; he didn't need to (nor could he any longer legitimately or literarily) grab hold of the reins. But Belloc's sense of arriving in a fifth and final act, and catching the last trembling shimmer of halcyon, old world days, is a recurring given in hay writing. The land of cockayne is always slipping with the sun behind the hill in Samuel Palmer colours, and with it the shepherd and his fold, the goodly crop, the hare hiding in the last sheaf, the sweep of the scythe.

Anxieties about these sunsets come as often as the sun falls. There are no arcadias that are deathless. The very first cave paintings of animals would have flickered into life around the leaping shadows of a burning torch in the midst of a black hole. The pictures weren't how the animals looked in the light of day outside. From Hesiod and Theocritus onwards, from the invention of poetic fieldsman, hard on the goat heels of the birth of farming itself, part and parcel of pastoral is the impossibility of recovering any unblemished arcadia, or Golden Age, or Eden. Already in Virgil is the endless fact that a joined world with simple abundant treasure, the natural giving of the earth, is no longer ours to be had. The shepherd cannot pipe until his flock is folded. Fields without fieldwork don't work. Virgil's *Eclogues* and the *Georgics*, like Hesiod's *Works and Days* and Theocritus's *Idylls*, were new but they told old stories.

While all the poems were being written, generation after generation were working in the fields, of course. No matter how little the poems meant to the fieldworkers, through this adjacency, the poetry of the imagined communion was repeatedly vivified by the life going on outside, by real contact with harvests, animals, weather, the earth. Even fantastical pastoral poetry can read like valuable documentary realism in this way. William Langland's agricultural parable-making worked for the fifteenth century but also speaks through the years to us: the poor ploughman hanging on his plough, wearing knobby shoes and clothes slobbered in mire, his wife at his side, wrapped in a winnowing sheet, barefoot, and three tiny children in rags at the edge of the field, crying. D. H. Lawrence's pastoral, the farm so brilliantly created in *The Rainbow*, comes from farms he knew in the Midlands a couple of counties away from Langland's fields. It doesn't seem odd to me that both speak to my memory of reading *Farmers Weekly* in the 1970s. I was naïve in many ways and romantic in others, but the endless truths of mud and grass, of seeds and milk, of work and death remain. 'Nature is never journalistic,' the poet W. S. Graham said – a warped and wonderful fringe-pastoralist himself – and its not being newsy has allowed the pastoral to keep it company. The specifics of pastoral will change from age to age, even a decade-old copy of magazines like *Country Living* or *Resurgence* (two contrary but not unconnected contemporary catalogues of pastoral dreams) seem dated and ancient but the bigger picture persists. Pastoral lives on, powered now as before by being not just about the good old days (although it often lives there) and not just about losing touch with the earth (though it likes to garden both with bare hands and in gloves). Its spark-plug energy, as Empson discovered, comes from being always about the gaps between things: the town and the country, the rich and poor, the sick and the healthy, the cerebral and the manual, the viewer and the participant. It is further charged by being nearly always invoked at the moment of its leaving or its loss. The green flash at sundown is how the pastoral has worked for 2,500 years: blink and you'll miss it, but it was once all fields around here.

We might write the rules of hay pastoral. The field to be mowed is as close to Eden as we are permitted to get. The acres must be old but recalled vividly from childhood or other impressionable days. Belloc's field is being revisited from an 'exile', he says, that was dirtied by life and the world – 'cities and armies . . . a confusion of books . . . and horrible great breadths of sea'.

The grass must be ready for the scythe and the writer-mower must show that he (I don't know of a woman haymaker) knows this himself: 'it is just before, or during, or at the very end of that [spring week of] rain – but not later – that grass should be cut for hay'. Hocus-pocus of this kind is required proof of earth-knowledge, with nods and silent obeisance paid to Thomas Tusser and other almanacs of farm lore as well as to Hesiod and Virgil. You can catch an echo of this today when you hear the 'Agricultural Story Editor' being credited at the end of an episode of *The Archers* on BBC Radio 4. What is that? Another name for God?

Having asserted the (pseudo) facts the usufruct can be enjoyed: without wasting the substance of the harvest, ancient metaphorical truths are stooked before us, as at an agricultural show: 'what we get when we store our grass is not a harvest of something ripe, but a thing just caught in its prime before maturity: as witness that our corn and straw are best yellow, but our hay is best green. So also Death should be represented with a scythe and Time with a sickle; for Time can take only what is ripe, but Death comes always too soon.'

After any dalliance with capitalised concepts, practicalities must be underlined; tools are holy objects and are to be venerated as well as well-kept: 'there is an art also in the sharpening of a scythe, and it is worth describing carefully'. The hay essayist builds an icon in words, smitten with the hard matter to hand: half a page on whetting, another half on listening to your scythe in order to know when it is blunt.

The morals of mowing must be delineated: bad mowing is clumsy, formless and isolating; good mowing is a stepping through the now into an ancient but continuing rhythmic and balanced embrace: 'the scythe [will] mow for you if you treat it honourably and in a manner that makes it recognize its service'. But don't – despite the details here detailed – think too much. Indeed, you must unthink yourself in the field in order to mow well. Tolstoy struggled with this and beautifully and honestly recorded his difficulties in his diary and made Levin falter in the same way in *Anna Karenina*. Belloc gives us an unthinker who is rather more homiletic and pleased with himself: 'be thinking of anything at all but your mowing, and be anxious only when there seems some interruption to the monotony of the sound. In this mowing should be like one's prayers – all of a sort and always the same . . .'

Honour the hayseeds, 'the permanent root of all England' or wher-ever, the first farmers, the taciturn but wise natural-men. Capture them by taking down their noises ('Ar') but let them laugh at you and your smockery, your *nostalgie de la boue*, your Marie Antoinetting with the scythe so that you both play 'the comedy that we [are] free men'. Mention, if necessary, Cobbett and Bottom ('Methinks I have a great desire to a bottle of hay: good hay, sweet hay, hath no fellow').

Mow from the outside to the middle of the field, listen for the whisper of the stems as they are scythed, then, under the dipping sun, pause when at last there is 'nothing left but a small square of grass, standing like a square of linesmen who keep their formation, tall and unbroken, with all the dead lying around them when a battle is over and done'. Wipe your brow. Drink cider from cool earthenware flagons, drink ale, drink kvass. Pick up the corpses of corncrake chicks sliced in two by your mowing. Set your dog on the hare in the last stand and run the fleeing animal down in the stubble. Rake what you have cut into cocks. Sling your scythe on your shoulder and walk through the windrows and the aftermath to follow the farm track home in the red dust of the harvest sunset.

In 1847, at the age of nineteen, Tolstoy inherited Yasnaya Polyana, the estate where he had been born, near Tula, south of Moscow. The 5,400 acres of woods and fields came with 330 male serfs and their families. Long before he put on peasants' clothes (the *tolstovka* is still the name for the rather fancy loose smock-like shirt that he made famous), or started making his own shoes (offering them to his literary friends, much to their horror), or became a vegetarian (his lonely soup tureen for his special meatless meals is the saddest thing you can see at the museum of his Moscow town house), Tolstoy had grappled with what best to do for his fields and his fieldworkers and how to make his estate into a complete and happily, wholesomely, answering world. First he took up beekeeping and planted apple trees. At Yasnaya Polyana, after I watched a party of schoolchildren and their teachers blithely scrumping armfuls of apples from the orchards, I stole one myself, an Antonovka, from a basket of them, filled outside the stables in preparation for the horses' dinner on their return from the fields (the last clover hay was still being mown when I was there in September, and it was brought back to the farm by horse and cart). It tasted unripe and sour and not at all great, but I was told that, as a cooker, it transforms borscht and is perfect for stuffing a goose. The linen-coloured honey, set hard in a plastic yoghurt pot, that I bought from the beekeeper in the wooden greenhouse at the side of the old Tolstoy home was much nicer: a grown-up taste of a sweetness that didn't cloy, smoked through with the toasted smell of late summer.

For a time, Tolstoy was interested in technology, and attempted to modernise the farming on his estate with agro-gadgets and scientific growing. He tried raising cabbages on an industrial scale, built a distillery, diversified with sheep, and imported fashionable breeds of Japanese pigs. He designed a mechanical threshing machine and had one built to his own specifications. It made a big noise in the fields but threshed nothing. 'Master, our young master!', Henri Troyat, the first biographer of Tolstoy that I read, imagined the peasants respectfully saying, 'and when his back was turned they called him a madman'.

Frustrated, deflated and already (and characteristically) bored, Tolstoy moved on from machines to minds. He started a kind of hedge-school at Yasnaya Polyana, teaching the children of his peasants by devising things for them to read. He researched and began to publish an ABC, illustrated with huge simple copyable letters and woodblock prints. Typically for Tolstoy, though, the project was abandoned before he got, in effect, to the end of the alphabet. He was always hurrying on to the next thing, except when he stopped in the fields.

Trying to simplify himself in all departments, Tolstoy gave up wearing socks and invented a one-piece romper suit that he could climb into and button up from within. His wife, Sofya, was not impressed by peasant chic and continued to embroider L. T. in red letters in his underwear. But, incognito in his body bag, Tolstoy was able to eavesdrop on his peasants out on the estate and it was thus that he overheard them talking of their hatred for the nobility. In his earlier days, when more heavily dressed, he had once tried to impress some young ladies by diving fully clothed into a lake. Bogged down, he got into difficulties and had to be rescued by some peasant women who were haymaking nearby and who dragged him to the shore with their rakes. Everything Tolstoy did seems to have turned into a parable along the way.

Sex with his serfs (he had a son called Timofey with one) and scything with them were what survived longest in Tolstoy's pastoral. He was addicted to both: the contact with the skin of the earth. To begin with the master was seigneurial about his rights and it was no accident that he could install himself at the heart of the simple, hard won, hard worn, physical world that he championed. He wanted to learn from the peasants, but then he wanted to teach them what they already knew. He wanted to scythe but he wanted always to watch himself scythe, even as he declared the bliss of the loss of his selfhood. He was a permanent *thinker* even though he knew thinking could be oppressive; he was always, as he put it, 'thinking that he was thinking about what he was thinking about'. To be lost in action was what he wanted, to be lost in thought was where he was; once, thinking, he reached for a piece of bread when fishing and ate instead a handful of worms, his bait.

But as he grew, even though his ideas got less orthodox, he became subtler, cleverer, and more self-aware. Tolstoy, the master and the boss-farmer, might not have directly heard his peasants laughing at him, and he rushed from fad to fad and tried on different shirts for different personalities – but increasingly Tolstoy, the more private man and writer, returned candidly upon himself, and was harder on his own failings than anyone else could have been. In his diary he shows a far deeper self-knowledge than any of his peasant play-acting would suggest, even if sometimes the self-treatments he proposed eluded him. In his fiction he made his characters, above all Levin in *Anna Karenina* (almost a match for Tolstoy's own Lev with just a couple of extra letters), inhabit a world so fully realised that all their external actions and internal thoughts were lit by the comedy of truth. Sensing, even as he stumbled with his scythe, something of what his peasants were thinking of him, enables Levin to grow and to harvest or mow *himself* and, thereby, know himself better. And through this he (both Levin and Lev) saw the yearning for selfless belonging for what it was – a selfish dream.

'The gentleman must be mowed,' the old harvest song has it, and among Tolstoy's best diary entries are his field notes, his honest mappings of the passage of his life and mind across various open places, a weathered mix of bright noticing and clouded judgement, of moving forwards and backwards, in time and out of step, into and out of the grass:

20 April 1858: 'the grass is pushing through'; 10–13 May: 'drooping bird cherry in the workers' calloused hands . . . Caught a glimpse of Aksinya . . . Her neck is red from the sun . . . I'm in love as never before'; 14 June: 'All day in the fields. A wonderful night. A dewy white mist. Trees in the mist. The moon behind the birch trees and a corncrake; no more nightingales'; 15–16 June 'Had Aksinya . . . but I'm repelled by her;' 15 June–19 July: 'I'm not writing, not reading, and not thinking. I'm wholly absorbed in the estate. The battle is still in full swing. The peasants are trying it on and putting up a fight;' 20–22 July: 'Mowing . . . The idea occurs to me of describing this summer. What form would it take?'

At the house at Yasnaya Polyana, one of the small downstairs rooms with a low cellar-like curved ceiling served as a study for Tolstoy and also as his dressing room for scything. Rooms decorated in the folksy 'Russian style' were fashionable in the late nineteenth century. Olga Ivanovna, the narcissistic and wannabe artist in Chekhov's story 'The Grasshopper' (she is jumpy like a grasshopper) has peasant woodcuts, bark-shoes and sickles on the wall of her dining room with a scythe and a rake standing in one corner. She entertains her art-celebrity friends surrounded by these tools. Tolstoy did actually play with his toys. In a display case in his room there is a copy of two small blue ink sketches of the Count at his labours. They look like a page torn from a Brueghel notebook. In the same case is a totem, a scythe blade, one that Tolstoy used, displayed like the cursive stroke of one of the giant letters from his ABC, or the long metal flight feather, a primary, of a huge bird, a crane or a bustard or an eagle: escape tools of one sort or another here boxed and half-buried in the cellared room.

Imagine being a child of Tolstoy, woken in your bedroom at Yasnaya Polyana every morning by the sound of your father harnessing himself to a sledge outside the back door so that he – rather than any animal or any servant – might drag a barrel to the well, fill it with water for the household, and drag it back again. Imagine hearing how your embarrassing dad attended a party in town but was mistaken for an old peasant in sheepskins and told to wait outside. Imagine having a father, who didn't believe in using reins when in philosophical conversation, and who went for a ride in a cart with a holy fool of a follower, who didn't believe in using the whip. The recovery of the overturned cart from the ditch and the extrication of the thinkers took some doing. But then the same thinker also kept what was called the *Letter Box* at Yasnaya Polyana, where moans or boasts, confessions or apologies, jokes and news from all the family were encouraged and posted and which, every Sunday, would be read aloud by those in residence. Imagine, then, hearing your father read one note that he had written headed 'Bulletin of the Patients of the Yasnaya Polyana Lunatic Asylum' which reported of himself: 'His hallucinations consist in thinking that you can change other people's lives by words. General symptoms: discontent with the whole existing order of things, condemnation of everyone except himself, and irritable garrulity quite irrespective of his audience; frequent transitions from fury and vexation to an unnatural and lachrymose sentimentality. Special symptoms: busying himself with unsuitable occupations, such as cleaning and making boots, mowing hay, etc. Treatment: complete indifference of all surrounding the patient to what he says . . .'

There were years when Tolstoy didn't mow but the cutting comes around and, despite his posted confession, the harvests and the people in the fields operate on him repeatedly as a steadying corrective to his wayward self, while also (and also repeatedly) setting running some marvellous imaginative motor that never stopped, even during his last decades of fiction-hatred and self-castigation. One day, on a visit to Yasnaya Polyana, Turgenev saw him carrying bales of straw on his back and concluded he was 'lost to literature', but that was not true:

11 August 1893: A blue haze; the dew seems to be sewn on to the grass, bushes and trees to the height of a *sazhen* [seven feet]. Apple trees are bowed beneath their weight. From a log cabin comes the fragrant smoke of fresh brushwood. And over there, in a bright-yellow field, the dew is already drying out on the fine oat stubble and work has begun, binding, carting, scything and, in a violet-coloured field, ploughing. Everywhere along the roads and caught in the branches of the trees are torn off broken ears of corn. Gaily dressed young girls are weeding a dewy flowerbed and quietly singing, and man-servants in aprons are bustling about. A lap dog is warming itself in the sun. The gentlemen haven't got up yet.

As the years went on, outdoors life at Yasnaya Polyana remained similar; a little more hay and a little less love in the haystacks, but otherwise much the same, hay being good where life, especially indoors life, was mostly bad. A walk through a field, laying waste to it, came for Tolstoy to represent the opposite of all the mess and chaos of humans, a way of putting to one side the sex and women and drinking and gambling and art-making that derailed him and, beyond that, the wider curse of wealth and grand families and, wider still, the deluded vanities of the church and the state and almost every other person, as it came to seem, that lived, or had, or would:

4 June 1884: I'll do some mowing and stitch some boots. Tomorrow I'll get up at 5. But I don't yet undertake not to smoke. Mowed for a long time. We had dinner. Then I went to stitch boots until late in the evening. Didn't smoke. Around me the same parasitic life goes on. June: Recapitulation. I've been trying to change my habits. I've been getting up early. Doing more physical work . . . I don't drink any wine at all, don't put sugar in my tea and don't eat meat. I'm still smoking, but not so much; 25 June: Got up early. Was five rows behind the peasants but did my stint. Worked all day. Had no dinner; 30 June: I don't notice how I sleep and eat, and I'm strong and am composed spiritually. But at night there

are sensual temptations; 3 July: Got up at six. They had already done four rows each. I mowed with a terrible effort.

6 July 1890: In the evening I'll go and cut the rye. In the morning I argued again with Helbig about art ... Harvested the hay. Then the Zinovyevs came. I feel depressed with dead people; 10 July: Went for a bathe. Came back; the table was set for thirty people. The Ofrosimovs and Figners. Then music and singing. Terrible, pointless, it got on my nerves. Two pathetic machines and trumpets – people eating and making a nasty smell.

Tolstoy knew, nonetheless, that he made his own smell just as pungently as his houseguests. By 1889 he had already begun to worry that mowing had become, like his cigarettes, an addictive, almost masochistic, luxury. The more he mowed, the more he wanted from it, until either no cut was enough or every cut was self-lacerating. It was as if he knew he had ruined scything by taking part in it. And the mowers around him came to seem like fallen people, the prisoners of modernity. So the inklings of a further escape rose up in him, a dream of open country that would take him both backwards and beyond farming:

27 July 1889: Agriculture, which is replacing the nomadic conditions I experienced in Samara, is the first step towards wealth, luxury, dissipation and suffering ... We must make a conscious effort to return to the simple tastes of that time.

When he finally left Yasnaya Polyana in 1910 on his half-mad, half-wretched escape attempt, he started on foot towards the more open east. That he ended up falling ill on a train and then dying next to a railway station is one of the many indignities that the world outside Yasnaya Polyana seemed to have ready for Tolstoy whenever he left the two round towers at the park gate and joined the public road.

I had to make a spring journey by train on a fine day from Edinburgh Haymarket to Bristol Temple Meads. All the way down the country, there were fields being cut for the first haying of the year. In places the grass had already been lifted from the fields and hurried away in black plastic, as if it were evidence of something wrong; in others it lay drying in lines and the windrows or swaths rendered its late home an old picture, no matter what machines and geometries had constructed it. All the good green had gone in one mowing and the fields were ridged with the fallen. An old world was laid before me. For the first hour after the mowing, the tented grass is what you see, but quickly the aftermath, the fog of living grass coming through the cut, begins its work. The mown stems shrink and silver and sink. The beheaded but vigorous shoots rally and pull up through the dead, as green as they can.

Somewhere in the Midlands one tiny field had been spared or overlooked. Last year it had grown a single tubular bale of hay that had sat uncollected in the middle of its half-acre. This year new grass had grown vigorously at the bale's base and some cut stems in its top had seeded and sprouted. The grey face of the dead head now had shaggy green hair as well as a luxuriant green-knight ruff growing and spreading out from beneath it. That one field alone had escaped. But brambles were already fingering from its hedges. It might have only one more year left as runaway grass before the scrub closed it down. Everywhere else the hay fields were shorn and their grass surrendered. And like that they were half-lovely and half-not. My year falters hereabouts. I die a little more now than at any other season. The best has come so quickly and is taken so fast. And I cannot see those fields without thinking of my children's first haircuts, the plank on the chair in the barber's and the clippers and the scissors coming at their grown-out soft blond fur.

Back at home I went out to cut the lawn. The clatter of the wonky old mower struggled against thick and juicy stems, its rusty grasshopper mouth straining in a toothless chew. Every ten pushes or so it gave up, having tangled itself to a halt, knotted with the grass blades that it sought to cut. I knelt to the mess, unpicking the grass from the mower, and my hands came up dyed green and sweet-scented with sap. For the rest of the day, I had grass stains on my palms, and for the rest of the week, I had green cuticles.

Near the back door I dumped a heap of the longer stems of the drying cut grass on its way to the compost. A female blackbird found it and wanted it for her nest. Over the afternoon while I pottered down the garden she made repeated purposeful journeys to and from the pile every five minutes or so. On each visit she selected grass strands that were eight inches long or more. I could see her looking and choosing. She pulled at the pile and she gathered the stems she wanted with her beak. She worked fast but with care. It was beautiful to watch. She had to hold on to each strand as she plucked the next. It looked a little like shepherding peas on a fork. In the time that I watched her she got better at the task. Either that or I watched her less closely once I knew what she was about. When she had a beakful – sometimes fifteen strands were enough, once she took twenty-two – she flew down the garden towards her nest, jinking past me with her new whiskers trailing below her. In the time she was away, she tedded and turned the strands and stems until she could plait and weave them into her nest, making a wheel of hay which she would curve round her incubating body like a grass skirt. Then she came again to the heap.

A marvellous day opened on the fen, the greenest of the year, and foaming with tender brightness. It ran on and on, hot and cloudless for sixteen hours, but softened by the wind from the east and by the air filling with willow down and poplar seeds, mayflies and birds. The fields were full and working. The shaking leaves on the trees appeared to taste the air in the wind. Butterflies tumbled in the lower sky like stamps from an album. All of the wet of the rainy spring was held in the lush green that had raised the surface of the fen by a foot or more. The blue above surged but was not so harsh that I couldn't look up into it. And much was happening there. Above the lode that runs between Wicken and Burwell Fens there were ten or more hobbies hawking for insects, their sleek wings and long tails printing trident-shaped cut-outs all over the sky. In their yellow claws hanging from their red trousers they caught dragonflies, and other insects too small to see from the ground. And then, like all the best birds, they stopped in the air, pulling up into it and breaking from their stream-lines as they bent their heads forward between their wings to pass their prey from their feet to their bill in an exquisitely athletic gourmet action. To watch this treading of the air is almost as good as seeing swifts mate on the wing: the loved world made lovelier still.

There were other bright things below the hobbies. At the pond at Pout Hall the common terns had come back to breed. The bird incubating on the little gravel island was hot under the sun and panted, opening its red bill like a pair of bloody pliers. A kingfisher flying like a giant blue bee steered straight towards the dark foliage of the huge black poplar on the bank of the lode and disappeared, apparently taken inside the tree. Cuckoos called all across the fen, deepening the place, summoning the curve of the Earth in their deep-throated song. And on the flat turf fields at the fen edge four yellow wagtails ran after insects and, doing so, disturbed orange-tip butterflies and both yolk-bright things leaped into the blue, embossing the sky.

Around the fen, blossom thickly dressed from the thorns. Whitethroats and lesser whitethroats scratched and rattled in relay from the bushes like burrs snagged in underwear. Rape pollen gathered in the corners of my eyes, sticky as moth dust. On the pool at Tubney Fen two pairs of avocets had managed four chicks between them thus far. Four other young had already disappeared into the compost of the season since I last visited. On land the surviving babies looked like melting dirty snow-balls. When the field of cows arrived through the evening mist of butter-cups to drink at the waterhole, the young avocets floated away from the huge animals like thistledown hovercraft. The cows sank up to their knees on the shore. As each began to drink it pissed in a great split carrier-bag wallop. The hot plunge drilled into the mud. A coot scuttled from its nearby nest, assembling its seaweed legs from the twisted wreath of green reeds. As the cows drank, their calves latched on to their bagpipe udders. A drake shoveler paddled close to the cows' legs, dabbled and then surfaced, its spatula bill running with water, like the baleen of a whale.

*   *   *

The lapwing knows, and the eel must too, but no human, resident or stranger, quite grasps how to get into the fens or what that would mean. Are they geology or mindset? The outside looking in or the inside looking out? A room, or weather? A draining board, or a granary? A dustbowl, or a floodplain? A delta of catchments, or the sea deferred? They fall between. In books they often turn up at the end, beyond systematics and topologies, overlooked and under-loved, half-lands and etceterative places. 'Sunk' as Defoe says, in his *Tour*, of Ancaster, the Roman village on the Lincolnshire fen edge, 'out of knowledge'. In the 1950s, after writing of its few acres, Eric Ennion and Alan Bloom – the two rivals for the projected fixings of Adventurers' Fen – both attempted panoptic accounts. Ennion wrote *Cambridgeshire* (1951) for a series called 'The County Books' and Bloom, for 'The Regional Books', wrote *The Fens* (1953). Ennion ends his book lamenting the disappearance of wild fenland lost to farmland, Bloom lamenting that drained and farmable fens will without 'constant vigilance' return to 'wild nature'.

'I had almost forgotten *Marsh-Earths*,' John Evelyn writes in his *Terra: A Philosophical Discourse of Earth*, a book written in 1676 from the centre of the open-horizon century, 'which though of all other, seemingly, the most churlish, a little after 'tis first dug, and dryed (when it soon grows hard, and chaps,) may with labour, and convenient exposure, be brought to an excellent temper; for being the product of rich Slime, and the sediment of Land-Waters, and Inundations, which are usually fat, as also the rotting of Sedge, yea, and frequently of prostrated Trees, formerly growing in or near them, and in process of time rotted (at least the spray of them) and now converted into mould, becomes very profitable Land: But whether I may reckon this among the natural Earths, I do not contend.'

Up until its last paragraph, John Henry Gurney's book *Early Annals of Ornithology* (1921) painstakingly attempts to lasso scientifically the flightiest of histories (birds seen by poets rather than through binoculars, Homer's eagles, quails in the Bible, the meaning of 'gannet'). The final words are about Thomas Pennant (the naturalist and traveller and Gilbert White's correspondent) and a heronry in the Lincolnshire fens at 'Cressi Hall', six miles from Spalding (and twenty-five from Defoe's Ancaster). They are telling words, even in their retreat into the wet unknown. The truth must be out there but where? Gurney, elsewhere oftentimes number-cruncher, mapper, and fly-poster of facts, admits defeat. And so the herons disappear into the fens: 'On less competent authority so many as eighty nests on one oak tree would hardly have been accepted as credible, nor has Pennant's counting met with a modern parallel in England. Lincolnshire heronries appear to have been larger than at the present day, but it is hardly likely that the birds themselves were more numerous. Pishey Thompson, a local historian, writes of a very large tree at Leake, in the same neighbourhood, which was literally covered with Heron's nests, but he does not tell us how many, or whether anybody counted them.'

BUFFALO

For one summer day, outside the little town of Interior (population: 94), in the Badlands of South Dakota, I walked along animal trails through dry grass and the scratch of low scrub. Meadowlarks kept me company. Until you get to an edge here you feel you are on the floor of the Earth, flat and low. Then the ground gives way and, beyond gulches and canyons of bare earth, the busy washing away of the world, are dropped and sunken miles of more grass blowing into the distance. Through binoculars I could see a small herd of buffalo moving a mile below me and three miles out, their backs rippling through the silvery-green. They looked like surfacing whales shiny with brine, watched from a cliff top, and swimming far out to sea.

In the early evening storm clouds put a lid over the plain. A line of bikers passed me on the road on their way to a rally at Sturgis, their engines panting like tired horses with loose lips, the last riders of a late cavalry. In the end of the light I went down to the buffalo. There were twenty pushing up against the fence of the national park. Their dark eyes wept with dirty pollen and their dark brown fur, old pipe tobacco at their heads and shoulders, was deep-scored with the tattoo of the barbed wire. They had open acres behind them in which to roam but they had all gathered tightly together into a wheel of hot dusty wool and sniffed at the thick air beyond their enclosure. On the other side of the fence were five black cows avoiding their eyes. Next to the buffalo, they looked modern, compact and close-shaved, but also rather gormless. In another field, three brown horses stood and stared, shifting their weight from hoof to hoof.

A single fence, a line across the land, means that nowhere is truly unfenced any longer in North America. One fence is all it took. I walked to my car through a run of grass, between the fields, keeping my eye out for rattlesnakes and pushing legions of grasshoppers ahead of me. Prairie dogs whistled from the open mouths of their sandy burrows. Rain spotted the earth just as I got back to the road near a sign that said: 'Caution – Prairie Dogs Have Plague! Keep People and Pets in Vehicles.' Someone had used the yellow square for a rifle target.

I camped nearby that night. A thin bar of electric light spilled from the toilet block but everywhere else was very dark. Once for a few moments the clouds opened, and a shooting star and a hunting night-hawk moved in quick succession across the gap above me. Then the rain came and I hid in my tent, the sky flashing on and off with lightning and then pile-driving with thunder, a riot that kept me awake for an hour and made the horses whinny in the Indian rodeo field next door.

I lay there and imagined the undoing of it all. First the lightning leaping back into the sky, the clouds sucked into the dark blue night. Then, across the plain below and stretching ever wider, the United States united, unfenced and unfarmed; wire twanging from its staples, posts returned to pine trunks; hay sprung from its bale and replanted as grass, the juice coming again into it. Earth in the ploughed fields tamping back its own furrows, the glister of wet soil gone; seeds springing up into a sower's hand; the crust of the badlands made good without a scar; grass touching grass across thousands of miles into a single spread. Barn swallows, before barns, coursing the lawns for insects; a grasshopper that never stopped; and across this open land, flapping flags of skin and fur rushing at mounds of meat and wrapping them, the buffalo kneeling up from the ground and moving away through the grass. Smoke drawn back into the barrels of rifles, arrows taken to sticks, feathers and flints. The railway tidied into reversing boxcars; other buffalo pulled up a cliff like a smoking waterfall; wheels rolled from the skeletons of carts; the continent remembering the drum of unshod hooves. An Indian climbing down from the bare back of a horse; animals in the grass losing the smell of people in their noses, the Europeans at sea losing the green smell of the new world and sailing backwards over the horizon.

I stirred in the early morning and, as I turned over, a half-squashed grasshopper crept stunned from my side.

Later the same day, in midsummer haze, piebald and skewbald Crow ponies swam as they grazed next to the Little Bighorn battlefield in Montana. In the hot wind, bowling from all around, their colours slid from them, and their long manes and tails rippled in concert with the grass. They stepped towards the wire that kept them from the stone markers indicating where fighters from both sides fell in the battle that killed Custer in June 1876. Around the markers were visitors, with guides (Crow in their National Parks uniforms and others) explaining what happened here. At every step the ponies flushed dozens of grass-hoppers that leapt up like dusty spray in all directions, some sailing through the wire fence, others falling back into the grass on the horses' side of the hill.

What happened, in the end, *was* the wire. The Plains Indians, who forced Custer from his horse and held him here, the Sioux and others who won the battle to secure their way of life, the Crow who had fought with Custer, all of them lost everything within a few short years. Fields came from the east and with them fences. 'We use nails to stir the tea,' wrote Wallace Stevens, poet and unlikely dude-rancher, on his western adventure in 1903. The blowing prairie was wired, its herds hobbled and its nomads stalled. The settlement and farming that followed, the opening of the West, marked an end not a beginning. At the very moment it was taken into white possession the space closed.

Many of the Sioux's battles throughout their history had been about grass. Two of the three Sioux groups, the Yankton and the Teton (also called Lakota), were agriculturalists. Pushed south into the Great Plains by the Santee Sioux (themselves fleeing war with the Ojibwa around Lake Superior), all three Sioux groups, acquiring horses and surrounded by buffalo, abandoned farming and moved through the grass. They traded buffalo products for maize with farming Indians ('dust scatterers' they derisively called them – the Hidatsa, Mandan, Arikara, and

Pawnee) but they raided these tribes too, eventually driving them into alliances with the US military.

The Sioux's conflict with the United States was similarly centred on farming and fencing. The First Treaty of Fort Laramie in 1851, negotiated between the Plains Indians and the US government, restricted the Santee to reservations and encouraged them to take up agriculture. They didn't like it and in 1862 starvation threatened their reservation in what is now Minnesota (it remains a reservation and the site of the state's first casino). A white trader, Andrew Myrick, refused the Sioux credit saying, 'Let them eat grass.' His remark (as well as his name, perhaps) was one of the inciting factors in what became known as the Sioux Uprising. He was killed. His killers stuffed hanks of grass into his mouth and his opened stomach.

On 1 August 1867 near Fort C. F. Smith, forty-five miles south-west of the Little Bighorn, between 500 and 800 Lakota Sioux and Cheyenne warriors attacked six settlers cutting hay. Almost all battles have been in fields; this was a fight explicitly about what was in the field. Twenty-one soldiers from the Fort assisted the settlers and were able to defeat the Indians with the help of new breech-loading rifles and a howitzer. The engagement, part of Red Cloud's War, is known as The Hayfield Fight.

In 1870 Red Cloud, the Lakota Sioux leader, met President Grant in Washington, DC, and spoke. 'The white people have surrounded me and left me nothing but an island. When we first had this land we were strong. Now we are melting like snow on the hillside while you are growing like spring grass.'

In 1875 Red Cloud spoke again to a United States senate commission who had arrived in the Black Hills. Gold had been found during the previous year: Custer, sent after it, had said the hills were filled with gold 'from the grass roots down'. The government wanted to negotiate a lease of the area from the Sioux or buy the hills outright for 6 million dollars. Red Cloud said he would not accept payment of less than 70 million dollars and beef herds to last seven generations. 'I want a sow and a boar, and a cow and a bull, and a hen and a cock, for each family. I am Indian and you want to make a white man out of me . . . Maybe you white people think that I ask too much . . . but I think those hills extend clear to the sky, and that is the reason I ask so much . . . I have been in to white people's houses and I have seen nice black bedsteads and chairs and I want that kind of furniture . . . and a sawmill . . . a mower and a scythe.'

These abrupt and violent passages from grass as a universal given to the man-made farm, from the grazed to the scythed, from bending stems to wire fences, from the mobile to the settled, are all evidence of a people forcibly estranged from what had been their familiar place. The Sioux encounter with white America effected, for them, an alienation at home. In large part this was externally dictated – the Indians were basically caged – but it was also internally grown. I don't mean the Sioux were complicit with their own destruction, but it is hard not to feel their deep shock over meeting this new and devastatingly successful way of being on the land. Nature was being bundled into stooks and ricks; wild things were given hard edges and turned into money. Industrial metals were driven into the ground like weapons: tethers, posts and ploughs. The grass was suddenly greener. But there was a fence where there hadn't been one before.

Grass still covers the battlefield at the Little Bighorn and stretches as far as you can see. Its green persistence makes it hard to mourn a prairie. To my lazy eye it still looks *good*. Green and watered coulees meander through buttery hills under a bone-yellow sky. There seems more than enough grass to go round. Yet that is what the battle was about. Grass and its fencing. The conjuring of proleptic fields. Today, despite the green and despite what the plains grow, the world here is curtailed and depleted, and in many places speaks only of the end of things. Standing in the battlefield makes you look into the distance and eventually something arrives through the heat shimmer and grass gloss of July. Nowhere else that I know has the enclosing of wild grass seemed so humanly germane (summer in Montana is beautifully, humanly made) yet so precisely terminal (to know anything of this place's past is to know how much death lies just below its surface). Or, perhaps, nowhere else other than these Elysian fields and those in Las

Vegas – Las Vegas, that is, which means *the meadows*, las vegas, that is, that aren't.

For some it was like this two hundred years ago in England. The closing off of the wild drew attention to a world that had been lost, not just fenced. The quarried ground at Swordy Well in Northamptonshire, a broken place on its knees, answered back through John Clare's poem from the 1830s. 'And me they turned inside out / For sand and grit and stones / And turned my old green hills about / And pickt my very bones.' But it is different in Montana. Much of England had already been harrowed by 1800 and most enclosure was of already man-made open fields. Those who were fenced out were among the millions who crossed the Atlantic. Forty-four per cent of the 839 men of the 7th Cavalry at the Little Bighorn were foreign-born. Among them two were born 'at sea', two in Hungary, one in Russia, 128 in Ireland, and fifty-three in the United Kingdom. Smith 1st, Smith 2nd, Smith 3rd, reads the roll call of the dead. None of the white dead were born within 200 miles of the battlefield. A closer parallel with Montana would be the time in Britain when the old woods were cut for the first plough, but that was long ago, the raw materials were different and the land itself hardly remembers. In North America the old world lived until my grandfather's time. In Montana wild grass grew recently enough for us all to feel its passing. And the fences still operate today, putting a brake on a land that seems – despite its posthumous atmosphere – not reconciled to stopping.

Custer didn't want to dismount. Prairie riding was a delicious species of bliss. Another plains sailor, James Silk Buckingham, described the waving green as 'the bosom of a new Atlantic'. Westering through interior seas of grass to the rim of the world, Custer liked the way the wind through his hair cooled his neck, the way the land flowed away from the saddle, the way his buckskin joined the world-skin. He titled his autobiography *My Life on the Plains*. He travelled in a laughing and festive mood with his friends and family as well as his own cook, a sixteen-man band, and his pack of staghounds. But, forced to get off, he made his history out of standing, and now he settles in my mind somewhat like the tractor seats awaiting their farmers that are fixed in front of the slot machines at Caesar's Palace in Las Vegas. Ploughing your own furrow brings a harvest of indignities. Settling is to be ill at ease.

Custer stopped here. Many of his cavalrymen shot their own horses in order to hide behind them. And for a while Custer's body disappeared into this ground, his scarecrow straw hair combed with prairie soil; his dead mouth plugged with it. Everything is said to go very quiet after a battle. The meadowlarks that sit today on the death markers and bend their oriole bluegrass through the hot air would have stopped singing for an hour in the madness of the fight. Watching them, I wondered, as Edward Thomas did of moles in the trenches, if any were killed in the crossfire. As soon as the guns fell silent the birds would have started up again. In late June there is work to be done and the prairie sparkles with its workers' music. Custer would have been buried to lark song.

Though he hunted as he crossed the plains, bringing down wolves and bagging a bear, and was a keen amateur taxidermist (able to do a full elk), Custer was also a nature lover of sorts. He kept a pelican and a porcupine (which shared his marital bed on occasions). He allowed a field mouse to live in the inkwell on his desk and let it run up his sleeve and scurry through his grassy hair. He made over the cavalry's hospital tent for his travelling menagerie (a hawk, two owls, toads, rattlesnakes and a petrified tree trunk, a prairie bog oak). And there is a story that he once 'altered the regimental line of march to avoid disturbing a meadowlark's nest'. Sitting Bull, chief among Custer's enemies at the Little Bighorn, also had poignant dealings with the ecosystem. Before the battle he 'sang a thunder song, smoked, and prayed for knowledge of things to come'. He filled buckskin pouches with tobacco and willow bark and fastened these offerings to sticks, which he planted in the ground of the valley of the Little Bighorn. Later the same night he dreamed of soldiers falling on an Indian village like so many thousand grasshoppers. And after the fight, and not long before he died, a Sioux-speaking meadowlark appeared to him in a dream and told him that his own people would kill him. The bird's words came true in 1890 at Standing Rock when he was shot by two Indian Agency policemen.

* * *

Without the last 150 years breathing all over it, the prairie might have endured. But the worm cannot forgive the plough. 'Busting the sod' or 'breaking out' the land does as it describes. Turn over the grasses and topsoil of the prairie and it is no longer prairie. Rescue is hard. Grasslands are soil manufactories. But they need grass to do it. There was often more than ten feet of topsoil beneath the prairie surface. Most of any grass is underground; roots spread for miles allowing it to live in drought conditions and to survive fire. One square-yard sod of big bluestem, the once dominant native grass of tallgrass prairie, contained twenty-five miles of roots. To sever the roots is to destroy the surface of the earth. When the first horses pulled ploughs through the prairie, the sound of grass roots cracking and snapping on the blades was so loud it was described as being like 'a fusillade of pistols'.

Almost the entire prairie has now gone, the grass and its soil and everything following. Less than five per cent of the original tallgrass prairie (the eastern prairie type) remains. A few unploughed acres rise above the surrounding land, like the islands of wet undrained fens in Cambridgeshire that are higher than the farmland around them. Less than half of the original mixed and shortgrass prairies remain. One of the ironies that the straw-headed Custer bequeathed to the world is that the best surviving shortgrass prairie in southern Montana is at the Little Bighorn battlefield. Though the fight was over the grass, and though the battle dead have been buried and reburied beneath it, the 700 acres have never been ploughed. Nor has grazing been permitted on the Custer battlefield since 1891 or on the adjacent Reno-Benteen site since 1954. On ungrazed high plains, 250 plant species have been found at a single location; on ranches where the ground is unploughed but nonetheless grazed, the count drops to forty or so species. In a valley of old grass ploughed to wheat or alfalfa the crop replaces an ecosystem with a monoculture.

Below the battlefield across the shallow doodling river, Crow farmers were cutting wheat. The Little Bighorn is now at the heart of the Crow Reservation. Swallows cast a net in the air above the field to take its flies. The chaff from the combine blew up towards me through the trees of the little wood where Major Marcus Reno got into trouble in the Custer fight in 1876 and was forced into the timber. Reno's scout, Bloody Knife, was hit in the head by a bullet, and his brains wet Reno's face. The shrapnel of splinters killed forty men there.

Specks of straw stuck to my sweating forehead. There was a sign in front of me: *The removal of objects from the battlefield or adjacent Indian lands is illegal.* Later, when I rinsed my face in the visitor centre, three stowaway grasshopper legs swirled into the sink along with the chaff. The fold of their joints was the same angle as the crook in the grass stems that they had lived among and the same as the bend in the leg of the meadowlarks that had sung over them.

Some of Reno's men got out of the wood but didn't make it back up the hill. Those who did were besieged for two days; theirs was the longest of battles at the Little Bighorn. On the hilltop they dug 'rifle trenches' as best they could with forks, spoons and coffee cups to get as close to the ground and as far out of harm's way as possible. Soldiers used the molehills of a prairie dog town, little hummocks of turned earth, for breastworks. Some were buried in their own trenches afterwards. Lieutenant Edward S. Godfrey remembered fighting from the little scuffed up and scraped places: 'The excitement and heat made our thirst almost maddening. The men were forbidden to use tobacco. They put pebbles in their mouths to excite the glands, some ate grass roots, but did not find relief; some tried to eat hard bread, but after chewing it awhile would blow it out of their mouths like so much flour.' Several were so exhausted in their trenches they fell asleep holding their guns.

Grass stems scribble at the death markers on the battlefield. The low hills are planted with white marble stones, scattered in places, clustered elsewhere. The stones take you to specific minutes in June 1876. Those showing the outcome of the fight between Captain Myles Keogh and Crazy Horse struck me especially. In a scrape of grass in a shallow basin below a ridge, they look like a disturbed clutch of eggs – with some death markers practically touching, others tossed aside. This man died alone, these close enough to have held hands. Beyond the markers are open acres with nothing, escapes that never were. There are darker red granite memorials for Indian deaths too, though fewer of them are known (and fewer died: between forty and a hundred). These have been erected only in the last decade or so. Each, the white stone for the white man or red for the red, marks a last breath. Cornered in an open field and clobbered, cut down with axe or arrow or bullet, people fell to the ground. Here he died; right here, where now, as then, the grasshopper goes and the meadowlark sings. I am used to trudging to fixed stony monuments and reading the text – the words and the stone being all there is left – but these scattered markers shook me awake; a tombstone is after the fact, these stones mark the crossing places. Or so we think.

The markers were erected in 1890. Photographs from before show a chaos of human and horse bones across the abattoir of the battlefield. Some bodies were moved and many were mutilated after death. Ravens and eagles, coyotes and wolves, burying beetles and worms, all would have done their work as well. In 1866 in another battle in Red Cloud's War, ten years before the Little Bighorn, Crazy Horse and nearly 2,000 other Lakota, Santee and Cheyenne warriors killed eighty-one men of William J. Fetterman's command near Fort Phil Kearny (one hundred miles south-east of the Little Bighorn). It has been estimated that the Indians fired 40,000 arrows in the fight. Private John Guthrie was deputed to gather up the dead: 'We walked on top of their internals and did not know it in the high grass. Picked them up, that is their internals, did not know the soldier they belonged to, so you see the cavalry man got an infantry man's gutts and an infantry man got a cavalry man's gutts . . .'

Chapter twenty-three of Genesis tells the story of Abraham seeking to bury his wife Sarah in the land of the Hittites, where he describes himself as a 'sojourning settler'. Custer and the other immigrant dead were not intending to become settlers right away on the battlefield at the Little Bighorn but they had to be buried. The Hittites grant Abraham a cave at the far end of a field (the word is *sadeh*, 'a flexible term for territory that stretches from field to steppe'). The desire to bury our dead meaningfully and live among them – to put down roots

– is one reason to stop moving and settle. Some corner of a foreign field is not enough; Abraham buys the cave to bury his dead wife.

On the Crimean steppe, Scythian horse-riding nomads dug huge earthworks and raised conical burial kurgans, like lighthouses in the sea of grass, defying the rolling flow of the land itself. Inside they stowed their dead kings but also their dead king's horses and lots of gold. It was time to stop moving.

White America had similar ideas. The tension between the desire to push on, the sense that better things lie over the next hill, and the urge to make camp – to open the ground and live on it – run through the interleaved history of Americans and American grass. Landless but enclosed people left one continent for another and there sought fences. Out of Europe came bodies and minds that had registered what hedging meant, that understood the wish to be bordered, and that admired the pioneer but loved also to sit down. In Montana and elsewhere these incoming undertakers met a landscape that couldn't think like that, and inhabitants who had been shaped by living in the place: who had taken on its qualities, no more nor less than the immigrants who, even as they broke free of their European cages, had brought their fenced minds with them. We, the Europeans, wanted the grass the Indians had, and if we could convince ourselves that they didn't actually own it (since they weren't subduing the earth enough, as God commanded man to do in Genesis) it made taking it from them that much easier.

One summer in Montana I saw the Last Stand twice and I met six Custers. One, in buckskin, handed me his business card in a long caravan purring with its air conditioning at the back of a white farmer's field beyond Hardin. 'The people come out,' he said, 'they can actually handshake George Armstrong Custer, they can get an autograph; that goes a long way in saying they've touched a piece of history.' Another Custer, in cavalry uniform, handed me his card the next day. He'd just died and was husky as we spoke, 'I'm wore down,' he said. When not Custer he was Steve Alexander, a linesman running wires across the plains for an energy company. We were sitting on the temporary wooden bleachers erected on a Crow farm at the edge of the battlefield.

Restagings of the Last Stand happen all around but are not permitted on the sacred ground itself.' You believe that I look like Custer because I convince you that I am Custer, but if you take my picture and put it up against Custer there is probably not that much of a correlation, but this is as close as you'll ever be to the man, you will never find another person who will be able to portray him in this manner, who has put as much time into it. The ring I'm wearing is the West Point ring of June of 1861; I have cinnamon oil in my hair; I carry a tooth-brush in my pocket because Custer always carried a toothbrush in his pocket.' As we were talking, next to us, an Indian pony rider was being reprimanded for still wearing his socks. They were white. A brisk middle-aged woman was telling him to take them off the next time he rode. He asked her if he could keep his glasses on. She thought for a moment and said, 'Uh huh, that's OK; but make sure when you fall off next time that you stay down; don't go getting up too quick.'

Custer was thirty-six when he was killed. He was shot twice, beneath the heart and in the left temple. One account has him not scalped (his hair, despite all stories, was short on his last campaign) but sitting up and stripped naked except for his white socks with his thigh gashed so he couldn't ride horses again in the afterlife. Another says two Cheyenne women found his body and pushed the point of their sewing awls into each of his ears. 'This was done to improve his hearing.' A third report describes arrows driven into his groin (just because). He stopped, the last straw, in the sandy soil of the battlefield for a year. Then he (or the 'double handful' of bones that remained of him) was dug up and taken to what was thought holier ground, 1,000 miles east at West Point in New York State. But by then the resident alien had turned the green hills about and marked the earth forever.

'When the last stand was made, the Long Hair stood like a sheaf of corn with all the ears fallen around him,' said Sitting Bull. At the Little Bighorn the 7th Cavalry Custer battalion lost 210 men, and in the fighting further north along the ridge the Reno-Benteen battalion lost fifty-three. Indians, coming from their village and splashing across the river, looked like bees hurrying from a hive, Kill Eagle, a Blackfoot, said. The battle, according to another Indian, looked like 'thousands of dogs might look if all of them were mixing in a fight'. But the heart of it lasted, a third Indian warrior remembered, 'no longer than a hungry man needed to eat his dinner'. 'It was as easy as killing sheep,' Rain, a Sioux, said.

Though Custer and the 7th Cavalry were trounced, the Indians didn't linger at the scene of their victory. They gathered their dead and left the valley as soon as they could. Their possession of the place was as fleeting as it ever was. Late in the afternoon of the battle day, its little hour of blood already passed, the great joined camp of Indians at the riverside gathered their few things and began to leave. Reno's surviving men watched them through binoculars. First they set fire to the prairie around their tepees, so that flames swirled from its sweet grass, and smoke clouded the campsite. And through the smoke, 7,000 people and their horses and dogs moved west up the grassed ridges of the valley towards the distant Big Horn Mountains. The crowd stretched for five miles over the prairie. Charles Windolph, a member of H Company, recalled: 'It was like some Biblical exodus; the Israelites moving into Egypt; a mighty tribe on the march.'

I stood in the valley of the Little Bighorn and looked at it also from its eastern rim where the surviving cavalrymen would have watched the departing Indians. Having been there makes it strange to know that just a few years later some of those same Indians walked again a few yards from where I sit now in the evening of a wet English day. Extraordinarily quickly after the real event, Sioux fighters and even Sitting Bull himself were recruited to appear in various stagings of the battle promoted by and usually starring Buffalo Bill. Sitting Bull charged between one and two dollars for his signature as he travelled the world. On tour he wore goggles fashioned from green wire and found stairs difficult, never having known them previously. Presented with a telephone, he would offer his best (and only) English: 'Hello' and 'You bet!' One of Buffalo Bill's Wild West Show tours in 1891 visited Bristol. When not in the fens I live there and write in a room that looks out on to the Gloucester Road. This was the road taken by the cavalcade of performers from the railway station at Temple Meads to their performing grounds at Horfield. They walked from the train, field names everywhere, to get to their battlefield show, drumming up business as they went. I have often looked up from my table and out across the street to imagine the sound of Indian feet and Indian hooves, and the eighteen buffalo they also had with them, all passing my window.

Once the Indians had gone, the earth at the Little Bighorn became one great lodging for the white men. The first soldiers who came upon the battlefield after the fight mistook the naked bodies of Custer and his troop for skinned buffalo carcasses. The sun had already blackened the dead, the stench was nauseating. The smell of dead men persisted for the whole summer, it was said. The Indians had dismembered some bodies, many were stripped and many, like Custer, had been mutilated after death. Across the battlefield the fallen were 'disembowelled, with stakes driven through their chests, with their heads crushed in, and many of them with their arms and legs chopped off'. Most received only a shallow grave, a scoop of soil taken from beneath the body poured back on top of it. Officers were buried more deeply than ordinary men: 'to keep the wolves from digging them up'. The earth isn't hard to scuff. By late June the short prairie grasses are drying in Montana, their first green already silvering under the sun, the soil is fine and easily shaken from the roots. The summer of 1876 was unseasonably wet but most of the rain fell after the battle. Indians did not bury their dead, so the Custer graves were the very first turnings of the prairie turf.

Those who survived the battle but were wounded were evacuated at the same time as its dead were buried. The injured were carried on litters and stretchers made, in some cases, by tearing apart Sioux burial scaffolds that had been built adjacent to the battlefield. For fifteen miles they were taken through the grasslands to a steamer, the *Far West*, which waited at the confluence of the Bighorn and Little Bighorn Rivers. There the bleeding were laid on deck on a bed of freshly cut grass.

A year later in 1877, the bones and other scraps and remnants of almost all the officers and the civilians were removed from the battlefield. They were buried back east, nearer, as it seemed, the centre of things. Custer's remains were never returned to where he died.

In 1879 a military expedition was sent to the battlefield to tend to its graves and to collect still more bones. It was long claimed that the only official survivor of the Custer battle on the United States government side was a 'claybank' coloured horse called Comanche that had been ridden by Captain Keogh. The horse was shot seven times in the battle including through both of its back legs and a hoof but it survived. One bullet went through Keogh's knee and on into Comanche's flank. Many horses (and even a yellow bulldog) actually survived the battle, but many also died, often shot by their own riders. In 1879 the shambles of horse bones and human bones that was scattered across the hillsides was gathered into a heap and topped with a pyramid of logs. This – the Cordwood Monument – was the first memorial built on the ridge that became known as Last Stand Hill. One horse skeleton was identified as Custer's. Its hooves were removed and fashioned into four inkwells. Comanche lived to be twenty-nine and was stuffed when he died.

In 1881 all the remaining shallow graves on the battlefield were opened and dug over, and their contents placed in a new mass grave around the base of the new granite memorial that replaced the bone and log affair. Lieutenant Charles Roe of the 2nd Cavalry reported on his work: 'A trench was dug, into which were gathered all remains of those who fell in that fight . . . and deeply buried at the foot of the monument.' Thirty-nine horses, 'all sorrels of C Company', were buried at this time just beyond the humans in another pit near the memorial. This mass grave was discovered in 1941 when pipes were being laid and ten horse skeletons were uncovered.

The biggest cluster of the 1890 white stone death markers is across a hundred-yard square of the grass slope just below the crest of Last Stand Hill and the memorial. These are the only close-fenced markers on the battlefield. Custer's stone is in the middle of a field of comrades who are sown around him in death like so many bags of flour. The well-known *Last Stand* oil painting of 1890 by Frederic Remington shows this as well: Custer in the middle of a corral of men curved against the Indians who are circling like wolves. But both stones and picture are in fact fictions, early restagings of the battle. It is thought Custer actually died slightly to one side of most of his men nearer the hilltop on what is now a square of mown lawn around the granite memorial. The commemoration of the event has obscured the event itself and Custer is forced to play his part in a simulacrum a little way off.

A larger military cemetery on the edge of the battlefield was founded in 1886. It is a great depot for the dead, housing 4,950 dead soldiers and others from conflicts the USA was involved in from the Indian Wars up until Vietnam. It seems strange to have gathered the dead and to bury them on top of others' last moments but the blood shed in 1876 sacralised the soil for many, making it a good place, super-special, super-sad, to stake a claim. Though the cemetery is considered 'closed' it is still waiting for a few relatives of some of the already dead who had booked family plots. They are permitted to arrive in their own time.

Below the plots and the battlefield I could see silvery cottonwood trees hugging the banks of the Little Bighorn River and, beyond them, Crow ponies that had been let on to the aftermath of a cropped field to graze. On the far side of the valley a long coal train appeared on the railway tracks. I walked one section of the graveyard and still the same train was drawing down the line. There were hundreds of wagons, each filled with the same shaped mound of black coal. The whole stretched for perhaps four miles and the wild klaxon of the train's locomotive ran back over the coal wagons like smoke and met its echo from the answering dry hills.

In the cemetery those who had been previously buried in the army forts of Montana, Wyoming and the Dakotas were reburied here when those places were abandoned. As a consequence civilians are buried next to soldiers, and soldiers next to children. Some died unnamed at birth and are marked bluntly with a dash, a surname, and the carved word *Child*. Vincent Charley, the Swiss farrier in D Company of the 7th Cavalry, is buried here; he was shot through the hips at the Little Bighorn and tried to crawl after his retreating comrades. His body was later found with a stick rammed down his throat. Corporal John Noonan is buried here. He didn't fight at the Little Bighorn. He shot himself in 1878 after his wife died. She was known as Mrs Nash and had survived several soldier husbands but on her death she was discovered to be a man. Corporal Noonan couldn't take the ridicule that followed. John Burkman, Custer's orderly, is buried here. He was devoted to his boss and would hear no ill word said of him. He'd wanted to ride with Custer on 25 June but his commander had sent him back to the pack train. Lonely and adrift in his later years he moved to Billings in Montana so he could at least be close to the scene of the end of his hero. He shot himself in 1925. Captain Fetterman, or what remained of him, is buried here. His 'internals' were among those of his command of eighty-one that proved so difficult to unjumble when their tangled corpses were found in 1866.

In 1893 the first battlefield superintendent arrived at the Little Bighorn site. He built a house ('one of the first permanent structures in eastern Montana') and looked after the graves. The Crow, who had recovered their lands around the battlefield by this time, called him the 'ghost herder'. They believed that as he lowered the flag in the cemetery in the evening the soldiers' spirits rose from the graves and when he raised the flag the next morning the spirits hurried back underground.

I returned to the spot on the Custer battlefield where Keogh and Crazy Horse fought and Comanche the horse took his hits. It was near closing time and I was the last person out on the road. Far to the west there was lightning and a grey mess of rain. The nearer air began to sizzle in expectation. In the evening sky above me, Venus pushed through like a first match struck and then the silver dust of the night came prickling overhead all the way along the battle ridge from Last Stand Hill. Away from the storm, unvexed clouds lay quiet around the sky, darkening it where they ran, marshalling yards for the night. A female northern harrier bucked along beside me, silent over the grass and the death markers. The meadowlarks began to wind down and just as I turned to leave, a nighthawk appeared right at the roadside, flapping fast and ghostly over the grass, part of the dark coming into the end of the day.

The next day I drove south, reading signs as I went: American telegrams, letters from the people – *Native Eggs, Crawfish, Reiki for Horses, Worms and Frogs, Sewing for Babies, Support our Troops.* On the Sioux reservation at Pine Ridge there were different messages. Nailed to a telephone pole was a narrow plank, written on it in white lettering, *Jesus Saves*. Some miles further, on a different road but in what seemed the same hand, in red paint this time, an arrow pointed right, as if for the next turning, *Hell →*.

If the Little Bighorn is the beginning, Wounded Knee is the end of the end. In the shiny tubes of hay in the fields around the Little Bighorn is the terminus for the life of grass on the plains. At Wounded Knee – and Pine Ridge where it lies – is the end-station of a people. The massacre of Lakota Sioux there (between 150 and 300 were killed, no one can agree exact numbers) by the revived 7th Cavalry in December 1890 seems cruelly continuing, with the living forced to exist in a permanent day of the dead.

The graveyard for the Indians in the Pine Ridge Reservation is a wretched place. I have been there twice – fifteen years apart – and nothing seemed to have happened in the interim. The dead neither got deader nor had the living moved on. It is a stopped place for a stopped people. At the foot of a low hill is a dusty car park ringed with empty trinket stalls. One advertised 'cold pop'. The sign that describes the massacre and the end of the Ghost Dance movement is the same as before, except 'Massacre' has been stapled over an earlier word, perhaps 'Battle'. A thin man, looking like a sick bear with a smashed-in mouth, walked out of the grass giving me permission to take photographs if I wanted to and offering to sell me a dream-catcher for ten dollars 'for gas'. Fifteen years before a younger version of the same man offered me the same hopeless tat. The cemetery is on top of a hill. The mass grave for the victims of the massacre is fenced with grey wire mesh. It looked like what it is – a filled-in ditch. The fence was broken in places and old posies of plastic flowers had blown and bleached through its wire. There were two more Sioux with dream-catchers for sale at the gate to the cemetery. The girl said she was an artist. Her teeth were in a terrible state.

I asked her about Ghost Dancing but couldn't make much sense of her answer. She knew it had some connection to her people but was keener to explain the sacred colours of the Sioux that she had used in her jewellery. In the late 1880s, when most Indians were already cooped on reservations, the Ghost Dance movement travelled through many tribes. Half invented and half adapted by a Paiute Indian called Wovoka, who had a vision during a solar eclipse, it varied in its religious and millenarian aspects but commonly offered escape routes from the end of the world: a native messiah was expected, white men would be removed from the plains and buried under a new layer of earth, the buffalo would be restored to the Indians, and the Indian dead would walk abroad once more – up from the ground. A people with nowhere to go had devised a fake passport. The Sioux sent a delegate to check out Wovoka. When he looked into Wovoka's hat, he 'saw the whole world'.

Ghost Dancing took its adherents through exhaustion into trance. They would shuffle and dance themselves silly until they fell down into the dust and into a seeing state. Many reported visiting distant stars and meeting long dead relatives. 'Sometimes they brought back white, greyish earth – a piece of the morning star – as proof.' Some Sioux thought that symbols of the dance painted on their shirts made them bulletproof. There are historians that believe this idea of protective holy clothing migrated into Ghost Dancing from the Mormon underwear known as the Temple Garment. Meanwhile, non-sacred all-in-one underwear, known as a Union Suit, was de rigueur for many settlers at this time (and has been used in many recent cowboy films as an icon of authenticity). It is striking to think of these various extra skins or body bags, trying to contain the swelling population of the Great Plains at the end of the nineteenth century. The Ghost Shirts make for an especially sad thread in the story. The Union Suit keeps you together, intact and preserved, as you occupy a new space and open its soil. The Temple Garment saves you from yourself, sealing the fleshly horrors of the body beyond your own reach. The Ghost Shirt tries to erect a barrier, a first and last fence for an Indian, between body and bullets. It didn't work. Supposed evidence of where you had been in your dreams, the shirt became a way-marker for where you were going. And a target.

Ghost Dancing frightened nearby white settlers, agitated the Indian police on the reservations, and provoked the United States cavalry. In a botched arrest in the Standing Rock Agency, north of Pine Ridge, Sitting

Bull was killed. Buffalo Bill, his sometime employer, had been sent to bring him in. Circus masters can become policemen, just as cowboy actors can turn president. Events got out of hand. Guns went off. The grey circus horse Buffalo Bill had given Sitting Bull sat down in the chaos and started performing his tricks, kneeling on his haunches and delicately raising one hoof after another, just as he did on tour when the pop-guns sounded. History restaged as farce was repeating itself as tragedy. After the killing some surviving Sioux moved south, joining Spotted Elk (also known as Big Foot) and others and all heading, at midwinter 1890, to Pine Ridge to seek shelter with Red Cloud. Intercepted by the 7th Cavalry, they were forced to camp at Wounded Knee and the next day they were ordered to surrender their weapons. Some accounts say this prompted a Ghost Dance and a medicine man called Yellow Bird said that the Ghost Shirts would stop the cavalry's bullets. Shooting began. 'We tried to run but they shot us like we were buffalo,' said Louise Weasel Bear. The wounded (Indians and troopers alike) were taken to a church at Pine Ridge and laid on pews covered in hay. A photograph shows the body of Spotted Elk lying stiff and frozen in the snow on the hillside, his eyes half closed, his long and delicate fingers locked into a grip of something in front of him no longer there or invisible. He is wearing an overcoat and heavy trousers and has a scarf wrapped around his head as if he had a toothache. I cannot see a Ghost Shirt.

I bought a dream-catcher from the girl at the cemetery gates. With the money in her hand she immediately walked away down the hill in a kind of purposeful drift off the track and through the grass. People walk in the reservation like nowhere else I have seen in the USA. People walk there as they do across Africa in order to get to places they need to go to. Other people sit on the ground, again like no one else in North America. Some lie on it. A few miles from the cemetery, south of Pine Ridge, across the state line in Nebraska, there is a liquor store. The street has no paved sidewalk and dirt runs up to the broken wooden buildings. Scabby dogs, slung with raw pink teats, ran recklessly across the street; barn swallows stitched their way along it. For hundreds of yards on either side of the store there were people in various stages of collapse. I was shocked again by how absolutely the scene replicated one that I remembered from fifteen years earlier. Were these the children of those I saw before? One figure – it was impossible to tell if it was a man or a woman – was lying on its back, feet together and arms splayed, like a crucifix nailed to the earth. Others crouched in huddles, leaning against trees or ruined storefronts. The faces I could see as I walked and then drove past looked orphaned; they seemed open but bewildered, as if they were surprised by their own demolition and were caught up in some dream and dazzled by daylight.

Unadopted is what many of the village signs say around the reservation. Buffalo Corral was one. Surrounding a house, once a mobile home, was a stockade of dead cars and old coin-operated laundry machines. Down a telescope it would look like the orbital rings of some failed white-goods planet. The Indian Wars had turned into junkyard opera. The outer crap was older, among it a Buick grassed up through its broken guts to its empty windows. Closer to, the house was circled with more recent rubbish, the washing machines like a string of pulled teeth, and the verandah, one time definition of rest, piled impossibly with stuff, semi-rotten, rained on and snow-softened, and faded to the universal weathered brown. Out front three children took their parts, riding bareback on ponies towards two pickups that had stopped by the road edge. A medicine show masque between the opera's acts. The flatbeds of the trucks were wrapped in neon-pink paper and hand-painted signs: *Mustangs don't do drugs; I had a daughter; now I have a prostitute because of Meth; Breast-feed your children; Get help.*

I drove on to Sidney, Nebraska. I went looking for dinner but found only a bar where a covers band was playing 'Don't Fear the Reaper'. The twenty-year-old vocalist leapt about to the crash of drums.

There are other Indians. I wanted to meet some who had taken a different path through the grass after it was fenced. Back in Montana and thanks to Tim McCleary, a white man who teaches Crow students at Little Big Horn College and speaks Crow and knows more Crow lore and history than most Indians, I met Bill Yellowtail of the Crow tribe in a Dairy Queen in Hardin. Bill is a cowboy Indian – a rancher, among other things. He opted for a caramel ice cream, Tim chose a more lurid event streaked with red and paved with a rainbow of hundreds and thousands. I'd eaten a buffalo burger for lunch so was off all solids and sucked instead at a bucket of lemonade. Our talk between mouthfuls and friendly laughter was however, as it might have been in Pine Ridge, of the end of a people.

Bill was heading away from the Crow Reservation the next day but ten minutes after our meeting he had invited me to travel with him that evening to his ranch home tucked into the first hills of the Big Horn Mountains at the head of Lodge Grass Creek, a tributary off the valley of the Little Bighorn River. He drove and we talked and then we sat at the house he is building on his family's land and talked some more. We slept and then he shepherded me up a small mountain on what he called a 'Japanese Quarter Horse'. A first-timer on a quad bike, all I had to do was follow the old-timer on his, but still I crashed the gears, my beast bucked and I unwisely allowed the steering to decide its own route, twice having to be rescued when I thought the angle I was climbing was untenable. Bill was smilingly patient throughout. My day with him was full of jokes. He laughs like Yogi Bear.

The view from the top was good. For a thirty-mile spread, dry deer-brown grass flowed below us in rippling warm plenitude. Far away across the green gash of the Little Bighorn the land rose again on a blue horizon to the lone hill of the Crow's Nest where Custer scouted ahead and misread the scene in June 1876. The entire country of a people was laid out there, every feature holding a story from the past and Bill, though he half-pretended not to, knew them all. Coming down was harder than going up. I became attentive to Bill's waistline. By concentrating on his jeans and hugging close to his bike I managed to stay on mine, follow him and stay alive as we controlled our fall down the mountainside. No forty-four-inch-waist Levi's could be more inspirational.

Bill is an unusual Indian. 'I choose to identify myself as a Crow though it would be altogether easier not to be an Indian.' His father was Crow and his mother Scots-Irish. He graduated from Dartmouth College. He was a Montana State Senator from 1985 to 1993. He has served on the board of the National Audubon Society. He was Angler of the Year in 1991 in *Fly Rod and Reel* magazine. He has a university job. He doesn't speak the language of his people. Most strange of all is that he is an Indian rancher and part of a settled Indian family who took up the farming all the Plains Indians were pressed to do by the US government at the end of the catastrophic nineteenth century.

In the Dairy Queen, Bill showed me his Crow identity card. Among its facts: his height, six foot four inches, and his 'blood degree', which has him as 13/32 Crow. If that second number is 25 or lower, you are not, officially at least, a Crow. Tim remembered Tom Morrison who was more Crow than many but wasn't allowed a Crow identity since he was also seventy-five per cent Irish. He had reddish hair, grey eyes and alabaster skin but was raised by a Crow grandmother and Crow uncles. His spoken Crow was celebrated for its archaisms and much sought by language collectors. The only English words he knew were *Hello* and *Jesus*.

Both of Bill's grandmothers arrived into Crow country at the same time around 1887. One was a Scottish-Irish homesteader coming from Missouri to settle on the Wyoming–Montana border along the Big Horn Mountains. The other was a Crow restored to her ancestral homelands – which the tribe had lived in since at least the fifteenth century – in the aftermath of the Little Bighorn battle (she could remember hearing the news of the death of Custer) and the subsequent clearing of the occupying 'mean-and-nasty-Sioux – all one word to a Crow'.

The grandmothers' sons become friends and partners in a cattle business and their respective children, a son (Crow) and a daughter (European), found one another. Their love was risky and unusual at a time when there was pitifully little assimilation or accommodation between the contending peoples of the plains. The Crow faced an abject future and white Americans commonly behaved like a vengeful army. The young couple had to marry in secret, 150 miles away from the reservation. But they came back to settle on Bill's father's allotted property (all Crow had been given parcels of land on the reservation when it was established). His mother, the white girl, was welcomed by the Crow, although his father, the Indian boy, was not made to feel so at home by the white settlers.

'My mongrel pedigree!' Bill groaned. Not only was his mother white, his family put the paleface on even more thickly by taking up the white man's calling to become ranchers, 'a minority within a minority'. There are not many Crow (12,000 'enrolled members' of the tribe at the moment) and there are very few ranching Crows. The idea of an Indian cowboy, though such creatures have existed for nearly 150 years, is still hard to take for many in the Crow nation. It is a foreign concept or, as it sounds, a contradiction in terms. Bill and others like him have been accused of 'becoming white'. Some of this reaction comes from various inherited or received ideas. White ranchers think they are supermen; cattle herders came first to the plains and were often rather grand or even aristocratic. Farmers came later and were usually poorer small-time operators. The Crow are differently prejudiced. Horse people scorn those who run cattle. Sheep are even worse; Bill knows them as 'prairie maggots'. Farmers are not even included in the debate. There might also be some economic jealousy at work – Bill and his family are well-off in Crow terms. But overall the Crow suspicions about ranching and farming speak of a continuing anxiety in the people themselves about their very legitimacy. The wounds suffered by the fenced nomads have not healed and, worse still, they are being kept painfully open by the sanctioned victimhood (the Indian as evolutionary drop-out) of the present.

This is particularly sad since the Crow are known for their historical efforts to become farmers and ranchers. Among Plains Indians they were early adopters of the settled life. At the end of the nineteenth century, with the buffalo gone, the wars played horribly out and the reservation supposedly secure, many Crow followed their leaders, like Plenty Coups, and wondered if they might make farmers of themselves as the United States government would have them. The Crow are supposed never to have killed a white man in anger and in the Indian Wars they scouted for them, including for Custer at the Little Bighorn. The Sioux were a greater enemy to the Crow than the white man. The rival Indians had driven them from their buffalo hunting grounds and the Crow were keen to get back to their grass. But even so, even as the white man's trusted red men, they ended up jilted then broken then ruined, just like the Sioux.

Perhaps the Crow felt encouraged to try farming simply because they saw defeat coming anyway, having already scouted for and supped with the devil and tasted his tinned meats. Various so-called agreements in the early 1880s tied the Plains Indians to the new reservations. The Crow term for the 1883 rule that stopped them moving translates as 'Living Within A Line Drawn On The Ground'. They became semi-sedentary, most still lived in tepees for a time and horses remained important, but houses were built and the government doled out rations and slaughtered cattle to replace the buffalo. At Crow Agency, the tiny capital of the reservation, a flour mill was set up. The US government hoped the Crow might grow wheat to feed themselves. In Crow the name for Crow Agency is 'The House Where *They* Grind'. The Indians took the ground flour but didn't take to growing wheat. At Pryor, on the western edge of the reservation, Plenty Coups tried to set an example to his people and started eating biscuits made from the free flour. He also planted vegetables and moved into a log homestead house. You can visit it today and see a sweat lodge in the garden like a gazebo and some of the items the chief – named for the many enemies he had touched with his coup stick – once offered for sale in his pitiful Crow version of a corner shop.

In 1887 the Dawes or General Allotment Act allocated each Indian a parcel of their reservation land. A year before, from the other end of the great grass swath around the northern hemisphere, Tolstoy had asked 'How Much Land Does a Man Need?' in his marvellous story-parable of greed and trickery. The Crow and other Indians were told that forty acres was their lot. Tolstoy's answer is a six-foot grave after his covetous peasant-farmer Pakhom drops dead trying to outwit some Bashkirs of their land. The Bashkir were the Plains Indians of the steppes, semi-nomadic cattle-herding, beekeeping people from the flat-lands around the Urals. They drank kumiss and played pipes. Pakhom is an ambitious accumulator from elsewhere. He wants to own the earth. He sells foals and 'half his bees' to buy land, stepping on to an escalator of acquisitiveness, selling and owning and selling again. He learns that the Bashkirs' 'beautiful grassy steppe' can be bought for a few trinkets, 'a chest of tea and vodka for anyone who wanted it'. The Bashkirs take his gifts and tell him he can have as much land as he can walk around in a day, so long as he carries a spade to dig a hole at every turning and lifts the turf to mark his circuit. Pakhom is excited and starts early 'across the virgin soil, flat as the palm of one's hand, black as poppy-seed, with different kinds of grass growing breast high in the hollows'. This Tolstoy knew directly for, in the richly complicating background to the story, he himself had bought land cheaply from the Bashkirs and for several summers went for kumiss cures and to read Herodotus on the Scythians, dragging his family to the blasted plain to sleep on heaps of feather grass strewn across the mud floor of the hut-house on his land. Pakhom hurries, walking hastily around his would-be field edge until, increasingly desperate as he tries to enclose a larger area than he can circumnavigate, he begins to panic and run. As he joins his circle, under the watchful eyes of the Bashkirs, he collapses and dies. His servant buries him with his own spade.

At the museum in Hardin is a hand-drawn three-quarter-inch to one-mile map of the allotted lands of the Crow Reservation made in 1907 by Carl Rankin at Crow Agency. Most of the indicated forty-acre allotments are along the fertile river valleys, the Little Bighorn and others; some of the rising arid plains between the rivers are still marked 'unsurveyed'. Below the map is a list of the allotted. There are hundreds of names, each having their boxy tombstone plot numbered on the grid above. I filled a page in my notebook: Medicine Porcupine, Kills On Her Own Ground, Small Head, Balls, Bird Child, Sits Down Far Away, Three Wolves, Spies Well On Camp, Old Horse, Big Elk, Strikes The Enemy, The Wet, Strong Leg, She Sees It, Hoop That Moves, Mrs Mary M. Humphrey, Bad Baby, Like A Beaver, Lies In Bed With A Man, Her Medicine Is Medicine, The Other Heart, Wolf Looks Up, Fire Weasel, Shot in the Hand, Puts On A Hat, Walks In The Water.

To turn the Indians into farmers, to plough and run cattle, 'boss-farmers' were appointed on the reservation. These were government employees, sometime Indians from elsewhere, appointed by the Indian agent in charge. Some of these men were better at their job than others; just as some Crow were more receptive to change than others. Horses could be taken to water but not necessarily made to drink. For some boss-farmers and agents, horses themselves were an issue. One superintendent at Crow Agency, Charles H. Asbury, thought European-style farming was the only way for the Crow and wanted to outlaw as many native practices as possible. His assimilating severities still pain Crow memories today. He wanted to ban the Tobacco Society, the Crow organisation that sacralised their belief that happiness could be guaranteed so long as treasured and holy tobacco seeds were gathered, looked after, planted and grown. Asbury also didn't like horses and insisted a Crow farmer would need only two. In three years the Crow horse herd shrank from 40,000 to 2,000. The people's money, transport and definition for the previous 200 years were slaughtered or sent east by rail to be canned.

Asbury's successor as agent was a relative of Bill's, Robbie Yellowtail, and a Crow. He brought the horses back and there are still hooves all across the Crow lands wherever there are Indians. In the broken-down town and villages, horses are tethered outside people's houses. Nowhere else in the United States apart from here and the Sioux reservation at Pine Ridge have I seen people riding in order to get somewhere. Somewhere, though, turns out to be nowhere. At Crow Agency I watched some Indians riding their ponies up the paved streets and to the edge of the fields beyond them. The riders might own those fields but they almost never will be the farmers of them. When they got to the field edge, where the grass begins, they turned their ponies around and rode them back down the road.

There were some successful Crow farmers and ranchers in the early years of the reservation but the life didn't take hold and many left the land that they had been allotted. Instead of becoming farmers the Indians themselves were to be farmed. Within a few years of granting Indians their own land, the federal government wanted Crow territory opened to non-Indians. From his wooden shop at Pryor, Plenty Coups resisted. The 1920 Crow Act half protected the reservation and half prepared it for its journey out of Crow hands. All of the reservation was allocated to the then-living Crow; even babies were given land in their name. But Indians were henceforth permitted to lease their land to non-Indians: they didn't have to become farmers after all, they could become landlords instead. White ranchers and farmers moved in and leased land cheaply and the process of leasing is still in place today, with many Crow being a strange enfeebled type of absent landowner.

I picked up Raymond de la Forge who was hitching with his ten-year-old son, Raymond Junior, just outside the Little Bighorn battlefield and drove them through the Crow lands to the Northern Cheyenne Reservation that joins it to the east. Raymond is a Crow carpenter and separated from Raymond Jnr's Cheyenne mother. By stopping to give them a ride I was assisting in complying with the terms of young Raymond's childcare order that has him shuttling back and forth between his parents. They got into the car with nothing but themselves. I have never seen an Indian carrying a bag. As we drove and Raymond Jnr finished his can of fizzy drink on the back seat, his dad gestured vaguely to either side of the road. He had an allotment to the left hereabouts on some grazing benchlands above a river and he had another in some juniper timber, he thought, that rose in the hills to the right towards the Big Horn Mountains. 'White men' leased both plots. Raymond had never been to either place and couldn't remember how much rent his land earned him or his family, though he knew it wasn't much. His carpentry paid his bills, but he had to do that in Colorado, and if it weren't for his son he wouldn't have been standing by the road in his old country.

Nowadays much more of the Crow Reservation is farmed or ranched by non-Crows than by Crows. Leasing has turned into ownership and agriculture has become industry. The prime river valley croplands that grow wheat, barley and sugar-beet (corn in some areas too) and the upland rangelands and wheat fields are either owned or leased by non-Crow farmers. As he drove me to his anomalous ranch (it has no name and no sign, 'nothing that would say – look at me') Bill pointed out the farms up the Little Bighorn valley, the small grassy places where some Indian families (the Real Birds, the Moccasins, the Not Afraids) reared rodeo horses or bucking bulls, and the irrigated and fenced fields and tight-run rangelands where a millionaire farmer from Salt Lake City or billionaire corporations from who knows where make their money. Great, wheeled irrigation arms were drawing green circles of alfalfa on the valley bottom and corn grew there because so much water and other care was lavished on it. We passed Bill's mother's childhood home. Bill's grandfather had to keep a fire going outside that house all night when his cows were calving to keep the wolves from helping themselves. The white wooden house is still there; it is now owned by the Salt Lake City man.

The wolves have gone, but in keeping with his contrary-rancher-counter-Crow way Bill would happily see them back and running across his dirt road and over his cranky fences. The Yellowtail ranch is a far cry from the valley farms. The Salt Lake alfalfa is cut four times a year. Bill can 'hay' his un-irrigated crop just once. Ranching is hard on the scale Bill and his brother and sister do it. The ranch went bust in the 1980s and they can no longer afford to own land as well as cattle, so their species-rich and never-ploughed high prairie grass is let to a cow-man who trucks his herd of Herefords in and then trucks them out and away some months later to a feed-lot elsewhere where they fatten further on corn.

Bill regrets not speaking his father's language but doesn't think of himself as forced to speak the words of his conquerors. His life simply went another way. Moreover, he thinks the Crow, as a people, are too happy to cast themselves as irreparably wounded by their history. 'There is no better victim than an Indian victim,' Bill said. 'Even the Jews feel sorry for us! I don't want to relate to that. My grandparents were hardy, hearty and independent, and walking proof that in the transition time victimhood and dependency were not a condition of being an Indian. But as well as apparently being genetically the saviours of the earth, now, genetically we are its greatest victims.'

As we had driven towards the mountains up the Little Bighorn valley, passing Crow Agency, the battlefield, and then the small Indian villages, I had asked Bill if he could explain the mess his people make. I wanted to be told that I had misread what I had seen at Pine Ridge and saw here, the rag-and-bone forecourts slipping past the car windows, the squalor and the broken-down fabric of the lives of those who live among the crap. But Bill couldn't offer any better news: 'We speak most passionately about how we are the genetic environmentalists, but our very living space defies that. But I am not sure, though, that many Crow can deal with the psychological dissonance involved in contemplating that. It's pretty devastating.'

It is. What I saw of the reservation seemed not like a home for the Crow but more like a *field-hospital* where a people have been installed after a battle. The wounded are still too sick to move. Some manage to get on their ponies but don't travel far. Some wave their arms at passing cars and get out as best they can. Some travel no further than a few hundred yards. Dying, as they might say, within a line that is drawn on the ground. In Crow Agency one car passed us without a bonnet, its barrelling engine wobbling like an exposed heart. The roadsides in Montana, as in South Dakota at Pine Ridge, are skewered with white crosses marking fatal crash sites. Meadowlarks perch on them to sing. Larks and markers. They thicken noticeably around Indian places.

The Crow are poor and under-educated. There is seventy per cent unemployment on the reservation. The sorts of things the people can afford to buy don't last. But they who had nothing cannot let go of the nothing they now have. In the old nomadic times family refuse would be dropped outside each tepee but the rubbish was biodegradable and the Crow would move every three days. They were known for being a very clean people. They had to be; their enemies would smell them otherwise. Nowadays everybody smells clean but everybody stays put.

Crow life on the reservation is village life, but the villages are not villages, as many would think them. The idea of a village as being not only adjacent to but also intimately connected to the surrounding land seems not to exist in contemporary Crow country. No Crow village, not even Crow Agency, has a road that doesn't end in a field, but these apparent openings to rurality belie the truth. Crow life is as deracinated, as *ungrassed*, as any city life. Although they live no more than one hundred yards from the grass it is as if it isn't there. Nature deficit disorder, if it exists, is rampant in the Crow lands and never more acute for occurring in the midst of what has been commemorated as the birthplace of sustainable living, the home of those able to be at home even as they moved seasonally in a wholesome wheel across the land, like its buffalo and its weather and its birds; the birds whose name the people took, the *Apsáalooke*, the children-of-the-long-beaked-bird.

Bill dropped me off at my car and continued on his way to his university life in Bozeman. I drove back down some of the Crow roads. They were quiet without his talk and his laughter. A hot wind came heavily through the open windows. It smelled baked. I watched the birds that flew up around the car. There was a magic forty-five miles between the Crow villages of Pryor and St Xavier. Midway there, the road runs alone or rather on its own and for itself. Every ten miles or so there is a ranch gate, the name of the place given often by no more than a brand mark burned into a post, but no houses or farmsteads are visible and along the top of a series of broad-backed ridges through these rolling rangelands the road snakes like a flexing spine.

The grass stretched on, the wind now moving mazily across it, fetching and carrying light just as it does over the surface of the sea. Watching the swaying and seething, the fish flash and the weedy green turns, I saw how an aerial acre of wind crossed the plain, how the grass lived the weather. The same gust came up through the car window and raked my hair into dusty furrows. I slowed to keep pace with a male northern harrier as it flew parallel to me, hunting at between ten and fifteen miles per hour with its downcast owl-face interrogating the grass. I adopted its methods and its speed, a prairie lick.

It took me three hours to dawdle along the road, stopping every few hundred yards to look at the fields, pulling over to walk out into them, waving at the cattle five miles away on a ridge, trying to talk some prairie dogs into a meeting. In places the metallic ripple of a cattle-grid took away the fences. Then the grass, running from either side of me, made an even bigger scene, as close to the once high prairie as I might get.

Birds the same colour as the earth and its outgrowth came to the ground to be part of it. How does the earth itself paint the life above in its own shades? Over the cattle-grid I'd been delivered into the lark-lands of America. The grey smudge of a Sprague's pipit; horned larks with sand-brown backs, perfect matches for the soil beneath them, and yellow and black ear-tufts, prickling up like sharp thistle-heads; lark sparrows, streaked and drawn like a bottle of grass; and lark buntings, the females a thicker wetter grass than the lark sparrows, the males darker than anything for miles, with bright white panels on their black wings. Between the lark buntings and lark sparrows were western meadowlarks. Every higher stem or tussock stretching into the blue haze appeared to have one sitting on it, each like a hank of the grass with one yellow flower head pinned to their breast like a medal of spring. They panted like farmyard chickens in the sun but their songs, a liquid in-and-out breath with a following tumble of cooling water, came through the dust and the heat like a drink.

Fences strung to the roadside once more and under the same blue sky the grass changed to wheat, dry still but more intense in its ripeness, golden with its held grain. Two colours only, Ian Frazier says, would be needed to paint the plains: gold and blue. There was wire at the road but beyond it on both sides ran the largest cropped fields I have ever seen. One kept going next to me for five miles. The combines were busy, each raising its own weather of field-dust and wheat chaff, some clouds caught the light and travelled bright as a headdress, others were thick and baffled the sun like an animal skin. I thought of the fields being taken in, all of them through the metal grasshopper 'header' of the machine, their grain grown and harvested and lifted from them without once being touched by anything human. That night, in a restaurant in Hardin, I watched an exhausted team of custom harvesters (the travelling gangs who take their combines from Texas to Canada following the cutting seasons) lifting slices of a shared pizza and, even as they did, falling asleep one by one at their table, until four of the five slept while the remaining young man pushed the sleepers' beer and soda glasses away from them and rescued their drooping pizza from their drowsy hands.

Half a block away from the sleeping harvesters, I met the granddaughter of Thomas D. Campbell, the epic wheat farmer of Montana, outside the old German hotel. She had spotted me looking at a historic marker nailed to the wall and introduced herself. In the first half of the twentieth century, Campbell, farmer of the world's largest wheat farm, harvested in the Crow Reservation on leased land or land he had bought from the Indians. His family had first grown wheat in South Dakota in 1876, the year of the Custer battle. He was born in 1882 in a settler's sod house in North Dakota. By 1926 he had 95,000 acres of wheat in Montana. His tractors changed the place even more than Custer succeeded in doing; breaking the sod, and turning prairie ground for the first time in its history, and then ploughing its native grasses back into it, quite possibly for them never to return. The various prairie blades were hopeless before the plough blades. The winning was dangerously easy.

Campbell was a genius of mechanisation and of the industrialisation of agriculture. His fields were brashly vast, a single furrow in one of them is said to have run for five miles. Such earthworks, such scarification, might rival any marks our species has made on the face of the planet. But the bigger the cut, the deeper the wound. In drought years in the 1930s, soil that had broken from the opened plains blew away, some dust clouds made it to the east coast, news from the interior, like the Plains Indians visiting the president. Some fell through an open window on to a desk in Washington, DC, even as those around the desk were discussing erosion and drought and bad farming, and some of the dust went further east again, three hundred miles out above the Atlantic where it fell as dry prairie rain on the ocean's saltwater fields.

A few years later Campbell had his hand in another rainstorm. He was an inventor as well as industrial ploughman. In the Second World War he was credited with part-developing the napalm firebomb used in the Pacific theatre: seeds of sticky invasive pain that were scattered on people and their places from above. Odysseus acting strange in order not to go to war and sowing his home fields with salt might have devised such madness, such madnesses.

In the three hours on the Crow road only one car passed me but as it did it killed a cliff swallow. I was an accessory. The birds nested along the road in drainage culverts that ran beneath its surface every mile or so. When the road was straight I could see the next colony of the birds half a mile ahead, an *air field* of swallows flying and feeding, close above their breeding tunnel. Barn swallows joined them, though they must have been further from home. As my car drew towards the other oncoming vehicle, an old clapped-out coupe with an even older Indian at the wheel, we pushed the air between us. This must have agitated its insects for it excited the swallows. For a few seconds the near sky around our cars was crowded with the birds, blue-black and rust-red, and they flew low to the road. One went too low and then too close to the approaching car and was drawn under its front. I saw the bird pulled up towards the engine and fall back to the road instantaneously dead even before the car had passed over it. I stopped and walked back and picked it up. In my hands it was still warm. Its eyes began to dry and then slowly shut as I was holding it. Its smoky-grey belly had been split open and its intestines had burst. The colour of its insides was midway between the warm buff of its rump and the brick-red of its throat. It cooled even as I held it and I laid it back down on the road-side while the birds it had left behind twittered and busied themselves over my head and on out across the grass.

At Pryor I stood in the shade of Plenty Coups's log-house-cum-shop and looked towards the stream. I spotted a male yellowthroat, a warbler, sherbet-yellow all over apart from a perfect bank-robber black mask wrapped round its face. It flew busily through the brush after a bird twice or maybe three times its size, a cowbird chick, lumpen, dusty brown and demanding. Cowbirds are called cowbirds because they associate with cattle; they live in fields at the hooves of herds, feeding on insects disturbed by the animals and are tolerated beneath the cattle's feet because they eat irksome biting flies and other nuisances. They are able to move with moving animals across country and through the season because they are also brood parasites; they live like cuckoos or honeyguides, dumping their eggs in other birds' nests. The yellowthroat had been tricked into believing it must adopt the imposter and was raising the cowbird as its own. The cowbird has found a way to wipe its foster parent's mind. The chick begged and the yellowthroat hurried to fill the cowbird's open beak. The yellowthroat's own chicks were nowhere to be seen, were perhaps dead or, at best, back in their nest, feeble, underfed and out-competed by the giant incomer. The big brown baby was taking up all of the yellowthroat's day.

In an old mess-house from one of the Campbell farm complexes on the Crow lands, now installed in the outdoor museum at Hardin, there are photographs of the same building or one very similar. A print shows visiting Soviet agronomists in the 1930s sitting along a bench at a table eating their lunch. These men ('two hundred sod busters') came halfway round the world to be taught by Campbell or to learn by example how to make their collective farms grow during the desperate decade of famine and terror in the USSR. Campbell himself travelled several times to the Soviet Union, knew Lenin and then Stalin, advised on the first Five Year Plan in 1929, and continued until the 1950s to tutor the world's other great wheat grower in how to 'start from scratch on unplowed endless steppe'. After the 1950s he stopped going east, and the Soviets didn't come west any more. Spaces, meanwhile, were cleared deep into the soils of the Montana wheat fields and grasslands in order to plant intercontinental ballistic missiles that were to be aimed at the heads of the children of those who had walked the same fields twenty years before, learning how to turn the soil of the east-west plains into bread. For cannot pruning hooks be beaten into spears and ploughshares into swords?

Fred E. Miller, the one-eyed and highly sympathetic photographer of the Crows between 1898 and 1912, took several pictures of Curley, Custer's Crow scout. Curley had escaped the battlefield, he said, by galloping away with a blanket over his head. Miller's last portrait is a masterpiece. Curley stands in soft abundant summer grass that stretches to a pale horizon. Behind him is a row of trees, young plums perhaps, in the beginnings of an orchard. In the long exposure their foliage has shimmered into a blur and bright stars of light speckle the leaves like fruit. Behind the trees is the side of a wooden barn or house. The horsemen of the plains have become farmers; its scouts have turned fruit pickers. An invisible tree beyond the frame throws some shadow over the foreground grass and on to Curley's lower half. He stands looking straight at the camera, his eyes squeezed in the bright light. He appears older than in any of the other portraits I've seen although I think the picture was taken around 1898 and he still had twenty-five years of life ahead of him. His face has lost its young man contours and his chest has got heavier and dropped on to the beginnings of a belly. His hair, a quiffed pompadour, gives him a touch of an old rocker. A striped blanket that he wears like a loose skirt obscures his legs. In his left hand he holds a pale version of a reservation hat. At his right side stands his daughter Dora who was also called Bird Another Year. She was born in 1893 when Curley was already forty. She looks about five here. Like her dad she has two pigtails framing her round cheeks. She is wearing a long dress with a dark shirt that is sewn with elk's teeth down its sleeves and all across the breast. The teeth are white and roughly circular like ancient coins, each about half an inch in diameter. At least 150 spread across her shirt. They make a pattern like the lark bunting's wings that I saw near Pryor. She looks apprehensive as she peers from under her fringe at the camera but Curley's right hand is gently resting on her shoulder, bringing her to him, holding her still.

The young fruit trees, the new farmyard and the old Indian man in front of them holding his daughter clad in elk teeth are all markers of the same violent rupture, the grass-fight and the plough-down, that dragged the bodies of the 7th Cavalry through the soil of the battlefield in the years after 1876, that tried to make the Crow settled farmers of that soil, and then eventually in 1923 planted Curley's own body in the same earth that had eaten the white men's flesh and fed the plum trees. The white man's guide died not wanting to be known for what he'd done in 1876 but was buried all the same in the soil of the battlefield beneath a white tombstone in the military cemetery, one of a line among many lines of pulled teeth grimacing across the grass. The Crows otherwise didn't bury their dead in the ground. They feared the entrapment of the earth and placed their loved ones in a coffin or wrapped them in material and then took them out on to the prairie, to places the dead had loved, to a hillside or the banks of the Little Bighorn, and there they raised them for sky burial, six or more feet off the ground, on stilted biers or scaffolds they called *ghosts*. Birds – vultures and ravens mostly – would eat the bodies. Fred Miller took six mesmerising photographs of these rickety launch pads, and his pictures of the Crow ghosts surpass even his portraits of the living.

SUMMER FEN

The moment the music stops, the maypole-year collapses about itself, stepping out of its green finery, trampling its own juices into the soil. The festival is done, the tent abandoned in the swamp where the field once was.

At midsummer, rain fell from dawn until after dusk, and then again on the morning after the longest day. I stood at the back door and looked out. The general synopsis: marine. The whole busted flush of the sodden country to be rafted out into the Western Approaches and given there a drubbing. Whales expected inland, ships on the horizon. 'Summer,' Coleridge said once to Charles Lamb, 'has set in with its usual Severity.'

I went out in a raincoat and shorts. Cloud-wool clagged about my head. In the garden slugs worked as beavers, felling one tomato plant after another. Rank veg basted my legs and peppered them with seeds. I found a snail in my pocket.

Further out at sea, the sky had clamped itself to the fen, and pressed it low under its pedal of cloud. Fresh squalls came building, bellying, and bursting above me every five minutes. A downpour hurried off a field of beet leaves sounding them like umbrellas. A tight-packed wheat field made a machine hiss. When the rain was heavy the lode was tin-tacked; when it eased, the water puckered with frog lips. It burped once as a sunken parcel of disturbed dead reeds was hurried to the surface by the furious knocking at the door. I could smell beer as I passed barley, borscht from a bare peat field, and Vichyssoise between leeks and potatoes.

A blackbird sang a hooded version of its song from the brambles out into the seasonless rainlight. Young goldfinches and meadow pipits got wet in the kelpy grass, their pale pink skin showing through their waterlogged feathers, making them look cold and wormy, like pickled birds in a jar. Cows lay about the fen like walruses, dirty and thick-skinned. An old wet carpet smell came off their backs. One stood up to deliver a copious piss, then lay down in the lake it had made. It rained on and the water began to creep to the top of the banks, and the grass at Burwell Fen flashed.

One of Thomas Browne's shorter works is described by Samuel Johnson in his life of Browne as 'a letter "on the fishes eaten by our Saviour with his disciples, after his resurrection from the dead;" which contains no determinate resolution of the question, what they were, for indeed it cannot be determined. All the information that diligence or learning could supply, consists in an enumeration of the fishes produced in the waters of Judea.' This isn't a fen matter but it contains a fen truth. The last-fish-supper is not the answer. The fens and their facts slip and slide, sink and swim. Nor was this the end of Browne's fish thoughts. In 1662 the antiquarian William Dugdale wrote a rather tedious survey of fen projects from the Romans onwards, a *History of Imbanking and Drayning*. His book is mostly book-based – Dugdale was a reader and a compiler not a digger or a paddler through the earth – but he did send Browne a bone from a great and apparently marine fossil fish that had been found at Conington Down in the far south-west of the fens near Cambridge. With the bone came questions. How did the twenty-foot fish get into the fens? Were they once covered with sea? Dugdale knew there were marine silts in the fens as well as freshwater peat and that both lay often on clayey soil, and it was in this soil that he thinks the fish foundered. How could it get beneath the sea-soil? He asks Browne: 'when, or on what occasion, it was that the sea flowed over all this . . .'

From Norwich, Browne wrote back to Dugdale several times. He knew many things and had many ideas about things he didn't know. He reared ostriches. He coined the word *antediluvian* (as well as *electricity*, *precarious* and *hallucination*). He noted the first inland gannet in Norfolk, reporting a bird storm-wrecked and 'kild by a greyhound neere swaffam'. He knew otters were caught in marshy places and could be trained to serve for 'turnspits', being harnessed in such a way so that kebabs of meat rotated as they cooked. He knew the world of the drenched and drowned, the quaggy and the mired, fen and carr, the rescued and the doomed. He kept a stuffed pelican and a bittern in his house. He called mankind 'that great and true Amphibium'. He was superbly that himself.

Browne indentified Dugdale's petrified fishbone as a vertebra, 'solid, according to the spine of fishes' though 'too big for the largest dolphins, porpoises, or swordfishes, and too little for a true or grown whale'. He also knew that there are three layers of earth in fenland: 'ancient & proper soyle', 'siltie soile' and 'fenny soile'; but he would not commit himself to an explanation. In October 1660, he responded to Dugdale saying, 'in points of such obscuritie, probable possibilities must suffice for truth'. A floodful of fruitful doubts, the negative capability once again of the place and of the times, rises in Browne and he delivers a most exquisite evasion of certainty touching on elephants' bones and giants, the great Deluge and Flood, inexplicable seashells on Alpine peaks, and the recent use of whalebones for buildings. He is further troubled by the confusion that may be caused in the future by a maverick citizen of Norfolk who instructed that he should be buried wrapped up in the horned hide of an ox: 'How this may hereafter confound the discoverers, and what conjectures may arise thereof, it is not easy to conjecture. Sir, your servant to my power, Tho. Browne.'

On the western fens along the Nene Washes the corncrake has come back. Captive-bred birds were acclimatised in outdoor cages to the grass, its worm- and snail-foods, and to the sky-map overhead. Released into the summer, they knew they must fly south for the winter to the great tawny spread of grass through southern Africa. The following spring, because they had left the fields at the Washes, they wanted to return to where they started and some did. Those homed males called their hoarse double rasp, *crex crex*, and brought down totally wild birds, untouched by man, that were flying north over the fens. Generations of corncrakes might have been doing this – flying the same skies on spring migration – for a hundred years, without hearing anything of themselves calling them down from below. The new-partnered birds bred, the man-planted and the crake-captured together, and the wider fortunes of the species may yet revive.

Common cranes, an ancient fen bird, are back in their old haunts as well. They have bred on the Washes too. I saw one walking through the grey of a ploughed field just south of Burwell Fen one early summer day. The same colour as the soil, it also looked appropriately big in the wide spaces, a pylon bird, and it made me feel how I'd missed its scale and the fitting purchase it offered on the place. Its great beak out-did the rooks' bone-bill and looked like an ancient fen tool; its bum-end was muddied and dishevelled from sitting in fen earth; its stilted legs and wide-pattened feet were accustomed to stepping through wet. Cranes' feet not human webbed feet are true fen feet, the *pied de grue*, or the fen pedigree. Then it took off, with neither the mute swan's lumpen judder into flight, nor the 'big boan'd' bustard's stampede (see the twenty-fifth song of Michael Drayton's 'Poly-Olbion'), but with a triple-jumper's hop, skip and leap – the fen being long enough for its slow-motion hurdling into the air. Airborne, it was magnificent and, apt for fen skies, showed no shrinkage. A grey heron will fold itself away in a flying shrug; the crane, with everything fully extended, neck ahead and legs behind, seemed to frighten the sky into keeping it aloft. Peat from its feet fell back to the earth like exhaust fumes. The air-beating vans of its wings whacked at the grey tent of itself and kept it going in its slow transporter-plane climb. Migrating cranes were once believed to carry corncrakes on their backs. I could imagine it. My fen hero joined the stack of airforce heavies and headed east towards Lakenheath and out of sight.

In the list of lost fen things – the smell of 10,000 working horses, skateable fields, peat smoke, the punt-gun's sonic boom, mole gibbets, swallowtail butterflies – the sound of corncrakes must be the noisiest absence. It is one of the most missing birds in Britain. Since 1900 its population collapse has been more dramatic than any other bird species in our islands. During the last quarter of the nineteenth century the bird bred in every county of Britain and Ireland. Many people leaving their work in the fields on a May evening would have walked home to the sound of corncrakes. On the fens they were especially common:

the wet grass was ideal habitat. In the county in the 1880s 'nearly every small grass meadow had its pair'. Everyone sleeping between Cambridge and Lincoln – or trying to – would then have known the corncrake's call. Once started, the males will commonly sing their cracked come-hithers throughout the night.

Three times in my life I have been kept awake by corncrakes. On Coll, the island in the Inner Hebrides, which is now one of the last strongholds of the birds in Britain, I heard males calling through a chatter of adjacent sedge warblers, the whickering of snipe above, and the moaning of seals just offshore. On the Hortobágy of Hungary, about as far from a seal as you can get in Europe, I tried to sleep out one short summer night until the syncopated irritations of mosquito music and corncrake call seemed to get inside my head as well as all around it, and I had to seek insulated shelter in the spidery waiting room of a village railway station. And, aged ten on my first holiday in northern Scotland, I saw what I subsequently discovered was a rare thing. My parents rented a cottage at Oldshoremore in Sutherland. A walled potato patch ran around its backyard and from our first evening until our last we attended a corncrake concert. The light dipped but never fully went, the potato leaves grew heavier and darker through the night, and the raucous singers (or was it just a single running soloist?) kept up their song. It was so hidden in the gloom that on the first night we didn't know who or what the performers were – a vast frog, some sort of clunking machine, synchronised grasshoppers? – until the crofter asked us the next morning if the corncrakes had kept us up.

They sang on. Knowing what they were didn't help us sleep. The singing, which is not singing at all, is loud. The male takes his voice for a walk; one minute it came from one corner of the potatoes and the next from another. Even sung from the same place, the bird twisted his head and shouted like a strobing lighthouse, throwing his voice through all points of the compass. Nor was it continuous and eventually soporific like a soundbed of grasshoppers: it started; threw itself; moved; started again; stopped; started.......; started...; started.....; started..............; started. We listened every night having no choice, and I remember lying in bed, beneath an open window, and the birds' craking seeming to blow the thin curtains above me. We didn't see them until our final morning when, on a pile of cut potato stems at the back of the patch, first one and then another appeared, each like a little inconsequential chicken, brown and streaked all over. Both stomped a bit on their potato mound. The male then walked off the heap and as it did threw back its head and opened its pink beak as if to drink in the damp Sutherland sky and instead croaked its crake-trumpet and out and up came its name, *Crex crex*.

A sighting like this is rare. The birds are not often seen in the open. At the time, simply putting feathers around the call was exciting enough. And, indeed, since then I have only seen corncrakes for fleeting moments. They no longer breed in western Sutherland. The potato patch is still there; I went a couple of years ago to have a look and a listen, but it was silent. Even as a ten-year-old neophyte birdman I knew something was up with the species. The birds were deep into their decline in the 1970s. A kind of out of date thing anyway, they were undone above all by the mechanisation of haymaking. Machines cut the heads off incubating birds and cut their downy black chicks in two. My potato pair were unusual; most corncrakes do everything that they do in the breeding season in fields of grass. And although haymaking was late in Sutherland, and the grass was still cut, raked, and stooked by hand – the key essentials for the survival of nesting corncrakes – the fields there couldn't hold on to their birds.

Their life in these plots and yards has followed ours in them. The bird is tied to us. The Clearances of the human population from the Highlands were responsible also for the removal of the corncrake from there. When people were taken from the land and their hay fields, and arable crops in mountain straths were converted to sheepwalks, the corncrakes also disappeared, having nowhere to hide or to run to. Further south and closer to the fens, Marvell's 'tawny mowers' in his poem 'Upon Appleton House' accidentally carve corncrakes when massacring, as he says, the grass. Their scythes come up bloody from the sliced chicks and the 'orphan parents' call in dismay with what Marvell hears as a 'death-trumpet' or a 'sourdine in their throat'. Sourdine (from the Italian *sordino*) means a mute on a trumpet that produces a hoarse effect. It is a perfect summoning of the corncrake's call, as a last post or rusty taps, and proves Marvell must have been very familiar with the sound.

But there is something else about corncrakes that exacerbates their otherworldliness. It is not their fault, and I have no science to prove it, but it is something I cannot help feeling. They don't appear to be fully resolved on life. 'A sort of living doubt', John Clare called the corncrake and its music in 'The Landrail', his poem from the fen edge on the bird. Though it calls like a little god of the fields it is nowhere to be seen. They are full-time hideaways. At no point in their lives do they elect to break from cover. I have heard corncrakes for perhaps one hundred hours of my life, but I have seen them for no more than one hundred seconds. And I get this sense that before we messed with them and their places, they were already removing themselves, as if something hadn't quite worked for them as a species.

The skulking bird is also a reluctant flier, yet somewhere along its lifeline it has become a migrant, addicted equally to concealing vegetation thousands of miles apart, pretty much at opposite ends of the grassed world. Not long after my family and I watched the corncrakes at Oldshoremore, the parent birds would have done a midnight flit and lifted into the sky, their yellow-brown chicken feet trailing beneath them, their babies back in the potatoes. Somehow they would have steered south, flying now when for months they had only walked, crossing the sea now when for months they had crept at soil level under leaves of grass and potato stems. And somehow, even less fathomable, the young birds, knowing that they must, would later climb alone into the same following sky.

When I read about this aged ten it conjured an absolutely terrifying world. That same holiday, for similar reasons, I lost my briefly held head for heights. On Handa Island, I discovered that cliffs were out of bounds to me. In a swirl of vertigo, the seabirds I was intent on loving were lifted from me and taken into the air, as young guillemots still not able to fly leapt from their breeding ledges hundreds of feet to the sea below. For the corncrakes, all I could imagine was exhausted young birds falling unseen into the sea at night with the tiniest of splashes as they hit the water and it opened its wet embrace around them and took them down.

In David Thomson's magnificent account of seal legends in Scotland and Ireland, *The People of the Sea*, he asks an old crofter on South Uist what spells the seals are under, such that at times they become people and people become them. The crofter replies: 'it is given to them that their sea-longing shall be land-longing and their land-longing shall be sea-longing'. When I read this, decades after the potato patch, I thought straight away of those corncrakes. I still know of no better way of explaining and describing the driving migratory imperative that lifted the streaky groundsmen from the earth and took them over the water.

I haven't seen the corncrakes on the fens. Nor even heard them. It rained so much in the spring of the year when I had set my heart on a night of rasping that the room of the Washes flooded, and even if the creeping land bird hadn't abandoned the sudden sea-place it had certainly shut up. I did, though, at the other end of the same year, and at the other side of the corncrakes' life, watch one in early morning light along a farm track near Lazaro's honeyguides in southern Zambia: a wintering corncrake high-stepping from the long wet grass on to the red-rutted way and, stretching its wings like a brown cape, shaking the dew of the night from its body, telling me in its silent purposeful walk out of sight that, while I might be, it was anything but doubtful.

At the Temple of Heaven in Beijing on a cold autumn morning I once saw dozens of elderly men in grey suits carrying square bamboo cages. Crouching on the floor of each was a single sandy-brown, chunky-headed and black-collared Mongolian lark. The larks and their keepers walked between squadrons of tai chi dancers and bright fluttering kites tethered on sticks. The cages swung in the men's hands until they gathered on a square of open grass to the side of the circular Hall of Prayer for Good Harvests. The men put their cages on the park benches and greeted their friends, their breath smoking into the cold air. The larks, seeing others of their own, began to sing. Like all lark song, it was some sweet, burbling twitter mixed with drier notes. The specific sand and dust of their home-ground made music. It rolled on, between the cages, sky song kept down to earth, while the men, after their hellos, fell increasingly silent as their birds took over.

Skylarks were a bird I looked for even before I became a birdwatcher. Near my home when I was a boy, the wooded North Downs of Surrey opened to grassy hilltops. One of the first things I remember doing on my own, aged about seven, was cycling to a place we knew as Viewpoint and hunting for skylarks as they sang above me until, by listening, I found their singing dot in the sky, the colourless scribble of an impossible gnat. Best of all was to do this when lying down, when grass stems leaned over your face and the damp of the soil crept through your shirt. I would turn my head, the grass brushed loud in my ear and I could hear that the sprinkle of song fell more to one side of me than the other. I looked in that direction, again the song was offset, and again I turned towards it. Clouds stretched my eyes. The sky toppling over me brought the sensation of falling upwards towards the birds. I think of this every time I pass gasometers that have deflated, leaving a circular gantry and metal steps curling around the sunken gas-tank's nothing, holding the shape of what was there, the stairs climbing into the open air. Being on the top stair might be like falling towards the skylarks. With my hand at my forehead I shielded my eyes, a gesture that always seems old to me, like an explorer's in a new land or a sailor's at sea. But my ears had found it: up there in another realm, little more than a drift of air, spilling music around it without stopping as if it were breathing the sky in and out.

One reason we love birds is that they move in some ways as we do. They walk with two feet on the ground. Watch starlings crossing a lawn and you might be seeing people in a park. Then they fly and flying seems superbly different to walking, unencumbered and free. But, like walking, it is also essentially a continually averted falling. Our bodies – starlings' and mine – must work to keep us from the ground. Birds that don't appear to struggle to stay up or that have passages of flight where they are able to stop in the sky seem special because they have broken beyond gravity's pull. The lark above me on the fen now was all effort but didn't show it; its wings appeared to tremble with music not exertion. It rose as if the fountain of song it was spilling was pushing it from underneath. Having found its level in the sky it settled there and made its way through open country.

As the day warmed, a second and then a third lark rose with a rippling electrical call, breaking from the field to sing, to give themselves airs, each in earshot of each, a raised descanting chorus that moved over the grass like the searchlight beams that stream from the sun through gaps in the cloud. Both larks and light are aimed at the earthed world: the sun comes down on to the field, the larks sing their occupancy of the grass beneath them, but both are also glimpses of a life lived upwards, where we cannot go.

Wordsworth would have known The Backs when he was a student at Cambridge. He could have shot snipe as others did over the land now occupied by Downing Terrace, then known as The Marsh. But he wrote of the countryside, from where the garden fens were sequestered, only in passing ('level fields / Far from those lovely sights and sounds sublime'), or as a blank space for the screening of generic thoughts ('I looked for universal things; perused / The common countenance of earth and sky'). Perhaps the fens were too flat and too boring, too farmed and fielded already. Or were they too wet and too messy? *Fen* remained a dirty word for him, which was why he enjoined the shade of Milton to tidy the place up. But if he had explored them, he might have done for the molecatchers and eel men what he did for the solitary reaper and the leech gatherer. As it is, instead of romantic heroes buzzing with feeling and natural truth, the fens have come down to us as a sideshow of freaks. Old, unhappy, far-off things made jolly.

Missing their Wordsworth the fens got butterfly collectors, character-hunters and outward-bound chaps like the student members of the self-styled Republic of Upware in the mid nineteenth century, among them Samuel Butler, later author of *Erewhon*. They sought out the fens as a nowhere place, a quaint holiday site of specialness, of primitive energies and untutored wisdoms. They loved to fish and hunt and sail and skate and to learn field-craft and plunder tales from the canny rustics. Tennyson came out by boat to see the sunken sights of the *drown* of 1861 and wrote a poem about beer. Invoking Virgil's *Georgics*, others wrote doggerel: 'The wide, wide fens are drear and cold / And drear and cold the weather / But the skies are light and the fens are bright / When warm hearts meet together.' They recorded what they shot as well: '8th March 1852 Fell in with a flock of rare linnets *Linaria montium* [they mean twite] and shot about 50. Lunched, adjourned to the Fen and killed four [short-eared] owls *Strix brachyotus*.'

James Wentworth Day thought the republic 'hilarious'. His *History of the Fens* appeared in 1954; it was written in six weeks, he says, and joined his twenty-six other titles. He was perhaps the most incorrigible of the many writers (almost *all* writers before 1960) who milked and mined the fens for the characters those students would have loved to patronise. Much 'country writing' across Britain was imprisoned by this two-dimensional dehumanising of its own people; in the fens, with very few exceptions, it seems to have been endemic.

Dates and details were kept vague, but it always helped if you could sketch in at least the illusion of a direct encounter. Fowlers in Wentworth Day's book were 'near savages' who lived on Adventurers' Fen in peat hovels with horn-paned windows and lay about eating water rats on couches of sheepskin. Tom Harrison was one of them, the 'last' (of course) of the punt-gunners: 'a hermit of the fens, a man of the primitive wild . . . in his veins ran the wild blood of Hereward's Saxons'. Our author had a particular thing for the Saxons: Hilaire Belloc, fen prospector likewise, made a fetish of the Normans – there is no truth here. On Adventurers' Fen, Harrison netted lapwings, noosed redshanks, darted jack pike and, knowing 'the workings of the eel in the mud', stabbed them with a glaive ('pure Saxon'). He was part paid for his catch with laudanum for his ague.

A fitting rig of your own was required to even begin to match such a fenman. Wentworth Day had dug deep into the peat to collect 'the mandible of a small pterodactyl dredged from the bed of the Cam at Upware . . . together with the heel bone of what Sir Arthur Keith, the distinguished anthropologist, definitively identified as a "tree-climbing woman".' He also announced 600 years of fenland ancestry and his ownership of 'a few hundred acres of Adventurers' Fen' (he bought this, 'my fen' he says, in 1935). Perhaps he didn't feel the need to dress up.

In any case the entomologist Lord Walsingham, who went butterfly collecting at Wicken in the early 1900s (those extinct swallowtails . . .), had probably upstaged the whole century and the entire fen playground with his mole-fur jacket, snakeskin waistcoat and a cap made out of a hedgehog.

Along with the witch-doctor togs and the high old heels, the fens themselves were cast as a character: the misty embodiment of archaic nationhood. 'I bought the fen to preserve it,' Wentworth Day says, 'to save for all time the essential Englishness of it.' Quite what that would be is never disclosed but the Saxons are involved, providing, 'an indefinable background'. In addition, Wentworth Day recruited a home guard to defend his patch. His roster of friends and staff, though, are even more lost in time than the tree-woman or the auroch, also dug up from Burwell Fen, with a Neolithic polished-stone axe embedded in the great blackened forehead of its buffalo-like skull. Watch the parade as the film runs, once again, backwards: 'Lord Lloyd, dark, incisive, and gay, the greatest Proconsul of his age; Ralph Okeover Curzon, who would get up at two o'clock in the morning and cheerfully motor sixty miles to be in his butt before dawn; the present Duke of Manchester, an old friend of many Fenland forays; "Chubb" Leach, the Newmarket trainer, a boyhood friend for whom no day is too cold, no water too deep; Sir Jocelyn Lucas, that engaging man-of-all-work, Member of Parliament, Master of Hounds, gallant soldier . . . and overlording it all was Ernest Parr, my keeper, quiet, sunburned, tough as old iron, with the water-wisdom of an otter, the eye of a hawk . . .'

But it was all for nothing. In the war, farm-improvers or 'little Hitlers', raucous with 'bureaucratic self-praise' and severe in their 'extravagant, ruthless, soulless form of "efficiency"', drained his fen thereby 'destroying not only the beauty of the English countryside [but] killing the spirit, the soul, and the independence of the countryman'.

When we hear the word *countryman* we might reach for our eel-glaive but, in any case, the fen was long drained and growing leeks and potatoes by the time Wentworth Day wrote his dead letter to old England. The three books on Adventurers' Fen appeared within twelve years of one another. All are rather quiet about the nearby writers. Alan Bloom mentions neither Ennion nor Wentworth Day. Ennion, first on the scene, doesn't call any other writer by their name. Wentworth Day, with his *opera buffa* Adventurers' Fen and his 600-year stare, talks of 'Dr Ennion's . . . charming little book'.

At last the rain stopped. Under the dry zinc of the sun the days grew heavy with the smell of nettles and heated with ragwort crowns and rosebay spikes. Flies hummed the fields. The stubby ponies tethered in the lee of a hawthorn were hypnotised by the buzzing. Only their trembling flanks said they were alive. Sheep cooked in their fleeces. There were grey stockings of dried mud on the cows' legs. Nobody had anything to say. The larks had finished and the rooks and crows were silent and moved like black damper felts over the ground. The erotics of the year here were remaindered to the close scrambling drone of a bumblebee into a pale purple foxglove, the pansy-dark tongue-spots on the flower's lip quivering beneath the bee's boozy crawl like moulds in a dish. The fen had never seemed so inland, so quiet, so far from the sea. Somewhere offshore, through the days and nights, puffins swirled between the wings of gannets. Above the fen, an afternoon woodpigeon climbed a rotting stair, stumbled and slipped.

As a child, I liked to stand on summer days for minutes at a time inside the thin tent made by a bed sheet drying on a washing line. The cool shaded fresh interior and the warm burnished smell of the outside made the summer for me. The hot quilted week on the fen after the soaking gave me something of the same. Towards Upware, a second haying was underway. Walking the field twice, in the morning and then in the afternoon, I tasted its drying, from bleeding green stem-juice to the dusted grey biscuit of hay.

Ruined mallards sat around the fen pools: the boys, demobbed, looking like girls, the girls like they were wearing their brothers' old clothes. This annual catastrophe, a fag-end anti-masque, is politely called *eclipse* plumage by birdwatchers. Both sexes moult but the drakes have the most to lose. Their spring flash and quack must give way to unemployed loafing while their new feathers grow. An old pillow had been shaken out over the fen, the water was clogged and messy with shed plumage, medals of the blown season. The men, in their underwear, peered at their reflections.

There was an emerald-green fly on a dead shrew on the fen track, the finger of a glove with a jewelled ring worn on top. The fly flew and the shrew moved. From under its snout appeared its puppeteer, a corpse-burying beetle, fastidious sexton in orange and black scrubs, busy shaving the body beneath, or laying its eggs, or doing whatever it must. Shaking itself free of its prize it paused and cleaned its feelers with its front legs, the left feeler stroked by the front left leg, the right by the right. The tiny morsel's sugary rot rose above it in a little scented tower about a foot high and four inches wide. A day later I walked the same track. There was nothing to smell or see.

I had waited for the last frost before I planted my maize in the garden, but the first swifts above the house distracted me and I forgot to dig and the corn went in late.

The village next to ours is Swaffham Bulbeck. There, between 1820 and 1831, Leonard Blomefield kept, and eventually published, *A Naturalist's Calendar*. It is a list of species – of birds, flowers, trees, insects, agricultural crops, amphibians and one or two bats – and the 'Mean, Earliest and Latest' dates of their occurrence in and around the fen village.

Phenological documents like this are of immense value in charting not only lost species but also cycles and rhythms of animal populations and climate change. We know how bad things are because of the banal entries in gardeners' diaries that have recorded, over many years, the first annual mowing of back garden lawns. The dates have crept earlier and earlier.

Blomefield was born Leonard Jenyns, but later changed his name. Blomefield is perfect for his book. He lived near Bottisham Hall, on the edge of Swaffham Bulbeck, where he held the living. From 1818 to 1854 he was the vicar at St Marys. The beech trees, along the edge of the park of the hall, are a good place to see little owls (which Blomefield didn't know, as they were yet to be introduced and established in the country) and tawny owls (his mean date for 'hoots' was

2 February). His father had inherited the hall from Soame Jenyns, author of *A Free Inquiry into the Nature and Origin of Evil*, which much provoked Samuel Johnson for its mealy dealings with serious things. Leonard seems to have been a rather cautious and singular man. He was invited to travel on the *Beagle* as the ship's naturalist, but turned down the offer, suggesting Charles Darwin took the job instead. He knew Darwin from beetle-catching expeditions they had shared to the fens (Darwin's fen beetles, pinned and labelled in a box, are on show at the University Zoology Museum in Cambridge).

Blomefield's own interest in order and systematics started early. At Eton he reported arranging his belongings 'with great particularity' and was nicknamed '*Methodist*' – 'This I did not like but it was true all the same.' Also at school, terrified that he might never see the book again, he copied out nearly the whole of *The Natural History of Selborne*.

My copy of Blomefield's *A Naturalist's Calendar* is small and khaki, like an army manual, but the list within is the poem of a green man. The book's title page describes him not as the author of the *Calendar* but its *keeper*. The earliest a song thrush began singing in Swaffham Bulbeck was 1 January. The pipistrelle bat was 'last seen abroad' on 31 December. Blomefield has wonderful sightings from the late-summer fens to record: the appearance of both the ghost moth and the goat moth, the hatching of hen harriers, the shining of glow worms. Many of his noted creatures are no longer found on the fens, but the list doesn't read as an elegy. Blomefield knew so much, and had noted so much, that to be in the field with him must have been like walking out with a recording angel who could channel the song of the earth. If we could take down the world like this, in long- and shorthand, we might, it seems, save it and ourselves.

His mean date for the cessation of blackbird song is 16 July. Wheat is cut on a mean date of 30 July; mushrooms abound; the stridulous notes of the great-green *acrida* grasshopper are heard, and all else falls quiet. And then, on a mean date of 8 August, the last swifts are seen.

In October 1974 Georges Perec sat for three days in various cafes around a square in Paris, the Place Saint-Sulpice. He noted down what he saw – pigeons, people, traffic – as a birdwatcher might keep a tally from a hide. Subsequently, he wrote a short book on what he'd been doing for those days called *An Attempt at Exhausting a Place in Paris*. He had had in mind an investigation into 'what happens when nothing happens' or a study of what he called the *infraordinary*. His fifty pages list the activities and scenes that he witnessed one after the other. It is wilfully banal and humdrum stuff and the square is drained of drama. His commonest entries are for the buses that cross in front of him. They prompt the most continuous passage of writing in the book:

> why count the buses? probably because they are recognisable and regular: they cut up time, they punctuate the background noise; ultimately they're foreseeable.
>
> The rest seem random, improbable, anarchic; the buses pass by because they have to pass by, but nothing requires a car to back up, or a man to have a bag marked with a big 'M' of Monoprix, or a car to be blue or apple-green, or a customer to order a coffee instead of a beer.

Not that it's important but I remember what I was doing in October 1974. My field days were in jeopardy. My young teenage life was rather bleak. My parents were rough-riding an unhappy relationship while my sister, in love with horses and ponies, was lost to me. I was at a school twenty miles from where we lived. Instead of teaching me how best to count buses or other useful skills, the teachers seemed more interested in making sure that my hair didn't creep below my ears. Kept from weekend birdwatching by Saturday classes and oceans of homework, I took up trainspotting on my long rail journeys to and from school. It didn't work. I needed something to identify, to count, and to write down, but I needed whatever it was not to come predictably towards me trapped by its own metal rails. Not even Clapham Junction with its great snake-head of tracks was wild enough. I left the school and moved to another where they had a Field Club and I joined it at once.

Perec's book is fascinating mostly because it is a failure. The place cannot be exhausted. But the book's failure makes it happier than it would have been had it succeeded. Perec sits in his cafes trying to be objective and empirical but finds he is part of the scene. What he notes down is increasingly conditioned by what he has already noticed and by what he already knows. To begin with he sees more than he knows but rapidly he knows more than he sees. He discovers, as the Russians have it, that life isn't a walk across an open field. On first glance what might have looked like a *tabula rasa* is soon shown to have a history, as do those people who are traversing it, and so does he who is observing. His first sightings are as bald as can be, a time and motion project, but within minutes he is working on what has already become a phenological poem: now is different from then; that has changed; this is new. Everything thickens.

I think of Perec, a rare specimen of a now near-extinct species – the hardcore but playful literary avant-garde – starting out as a kind of regular birdwatcher trying to work his local patch but discovering, having gone into the field, as much about himself as about the movements of the gulls he watches, and, as he does so, discovering that the gulls are also infinitely more complicated than they seemed at first. These complications and his elucidations of them change him as well as shaking out the birds into Caspian and yellow-legged along with the herrings and lesser black-backeds. As he watches the gulls, the diary of his heart and his carefully written bird list become interleaved, and when he gets up to go he has just one notebook in his hand.

The more we know, the more there is to know, and the more it all joins up. The harder we look, the less straightforward seeing becomes. At the end of his life Linneaus, the greatest namer the natural world has known since Adam, no longer knew what he himself was called. Leonard Blomefield, anxious about putting things in their proper place and struggling to order Swaffham Bulbeck's bird song and flowering successions, might have found the Galápagos too much to take in. His decision not to go on the *Beagle* was probably the right one, but it has also left us with a theory that makes sense of everything (Darwin's) and a transcendental account of life in a few fen acres written as a list of names and numbers (his). After (what proved to be) the wild life of Saint-Sulpice, Georges Perec wrote a 600-page account of an imaginary Parisian apartment and made, in *Life: A User's Manual*, an ordering of the domestic world into his origin of species.

169

On 8 January 1964 Elizabeth Bishop wrote to her fellow poet Anne Stevenson about Charles Darwin, one of her favourite authors. Her thoughts in her letter have much to say about her own poetics yet also, accidentally but brilliantly, capture Perec and Blomefield too, and find the whole unlikely gang on the same bus: 'reading Darwin one admires the beautiful solid case being built up out of his endless heroic *observations*, almost unconscious or automatic – and then comes a sudden relaxation, a forgetful phrase, and one feels the strangeness of his undertaking, sees the lonely young man, his eyes fixed on facts and minute details, sinking or sliding giddily off into the unknown'.

Those gulls are being shaken out these days in the Cambridgeshire fens and on its gravel pits, rubbish tips and reservoirs. Species are being split and there are new and obscure featherings to learn. Caspian and yellow-legged gulls didn't exist by name when I was sorting out my birds, and this has made it hard for me to believe that I could pull them from the world around me into knowable life. I have never consciously seen either in Britain, but I have promised myself that I will one day work them out. And my maize? Late planted in the lack-lustre summer, it never grew higher than its first foot.

The big projects to fix the fens always ran alongside smaller and more local negotiations for living with them. The Romans tried to do what they did everywhere, rolling out their strict and straight brand. Their tidying of the place was unsurpassed for 1,500 years, but the fens were slippery and tricky even for Rome. Their causeways had to crook and curve and meanwhile, as their lost silverware dulled in the peat, the *custom of the fen* grew up – a looser, more pliant give and take, saturated usually, dissolved sometimes, knowing always. It was an ambience not a fact and denoted a lived environment, an accreted neighbourhood of shifting uses that had become patterned into habits. You could see it in the common sense of the commoners over their common wealth. Like a conversation preserved across centuries, it was a muttered and reinterpretable agreement between a people and their place. It blew in the wind and the words got carried away, but when it worked it was like the best of farming or like seeing how wild animals live. Life goes wrong and comes right and goes round again as another year brings another chance.

The wet demanded adaptations. And although the people didn't think of themselves as oddities until outsiders repeatedly cast them in that role, their strategies for survival were tailored to amphibian life. On census forms, fen natives were usually denoted as labourers or peat cutters; local differences alone separated them from other farm workers up or down the Roman roads. Only others dressed them as full-time stilt-walking fen *slodgers* or plover-trapping eel-stabbers. It is true they sometimes worked this way, but that wasn't all that they did. Some did catch waders with nets and some did use stilts to navigate flooded fields: in the fourteenth century a boy walking on pattens or stilts into a marsh, looking for ducks' eggs, was drowned; in 1610 Isaac Casaubon watched one stilted man and a single small boy drive 400 cattle to pasture. Summer grounds, also called *half-lands*, were often reached by boat. But on them, fen people grew hay and grazed cattle like anywhere.

Parts of the fens have been a near-industrial agricultural landscape for many centuries. Medieval fenland was remarkably organised. Fishing rights were arranged with such precision in some fens that the night was divided into eight separate bank-side sessions. Minute regulations also controlled peat cutting, intercommoning between villages, and the maintenance of ditches. In the presentments and inquisitions of medieval courts, the failure of individuals to play their part in the common upkeep is repeatedly noted. When the custom of the fen had been ignored and things had gone bad, the arraigning documents were jammed with Fen-Latin verbs: *obstruitur, inundantur, submergunter*. The detailing of what was neglected and went wrong intimates what was otherwise done well and went right. In order that water might flow for all, your channel had to be kept clean, your *clowes* (sluice or floodgate) cleared, your sewer sorted.

Through the seventeenth century, as the fens were mangled most severely and clobbered closer to submission by outsiders, the people who had lived on and from them became identified with the recalcitrant non-complying swamp. Obstreperous Lincolnshire fen people were said to 'live at large, and prey, like pikes, upon one another'. Straight lines were demanded, meanders and porosity were threatening signs of a backwards or dangerous character. Some fen dwellers rioted against drainage, threw down ditches, broke open sluices, and found common ground with parliament in the Civil War years. Cromwell's own fen tide went in and out: the fenman was first against drainage (his national reputation was made as a defender of fen commoners who opposed drainers), then, when in charge, turned in favour. The unknown writer of the *Anti-Projector* from around 1653 described how the fens provided a livelihood for 'many thousand cottagers', with those locals gathering 'reeds, fodder, thacks, turves, flags, hassocks, segg, fleggweed for fleggeren, collors, mattweede for churches, chambers, beddes and many other fenn commodytyes of greate use both in towne and countreye'. The alternative, the Anti-Projector declared, was 'Cole-seed and Rape', and what were they 'but Dutch commodities and but trash and trumpery'. A Dutch-engineered landscape prevailed, however: Vermuyden and the Adventurers had their way and the waters began to obey, for a time at least. A poem of 1685, attributed to Samuel Fortrey, toots the drainers' triumph from the height of the Restoration years of zealous surveying, embanking and pumping. The poem lumped the bogtrotters with the bog, and suggested the wild man would be tamed like the waters he had stilted across. The floods were new 'muzled', rivers 'govern'd', streams dammed with 'bridles' and, as a consequence, 'there shall a change of Men and Manners be' so that 'Souls of Sedge shall understand Discourse'.

As I read the old fen books I began keeping a list of flood dates – of *drowns* as they are called in the fens – until I realised I was writing down almost every year in some decades. Floods were part of ordinary fen life, part of the custom of the fen. Flooding water was once thought of as 'mother' to the fens. For this reason, some people resisted drainage just as the fens did themselves. Their livelihood looked better to them wet. Parts of the medieval fens were more valuable in their half-natural condition than they would have been drained to winter grounds. They were highly productive bogs. For centuries the meadow grasses of a seasonally flooded summer ground were worth more than an arable field. A heath, William Cobbett wrote, might be more valuable for the bees it feeds than for anything that might come of its enclosure. It was the same on the fens. Eels paid their way. So did the sedge.

An astonishing aerial photograph of the great flood of March 1947 east of the Ouse Washes shows three farms, Causeway, Doles and New Willow, as three trinket clusters of matchboxes and sugar cubes in a vast grey plain of sheeted water. That year the banks couldn't hold the flood, but the same year the farmers there grew bumper crops out of what had been drowned fields. In a flood in 1918, around the Little Ouse, Frank Harrison carried his eight pigs, one by one, upstairs to safety in the bedroom of his cottage. In 1613 when the sea flooded the silt-fen at Terrington, some took to the church for its protecting height and some to their haystacks. In 1861 a windmill took off, sailing across the flooded fens it had failed to drain. In another flood a sea boat was driven inland and came to rest on the roof of a fen house; three sailors saved themselves by clinging to the chimney. Elsewhere old boats were used to shore up banks and keep the water from making the land a sea. Attacking Hereward, when the Isle of Ely was still an island, the Normans built a pontoon bridge by inflating the skins of drowned cattle. Stone for fen churches came by boat and sometimes didn't make it. The huge blocks destined for Ramsey Abbey were tipped from their ferry by a storm. Each weighing a ton, they sank to the flooded fen floor and are now stuck on the long-drained fields of nearby Engine Farm like a henge dropped from the sky. In June 1693, around the town of March, 30,000 acres were underwater: 'where wee should be now plowing the fowles of the ayre are swimming'. Another photograph shows men trying to harvest standing up to their waists in water in a field. Each stook of wheat rises like a straw mountain peak from a sea.

There is no doubting the severities of the floods and the casualties they caused, and even a regular crisis is hard to prepare for, but the flooded fens were part of fen life for centuries, and people lived alongside the water with their own expert if sometimes sunken knowledge. Fen people once understood the fields, wet or drained, in ways we cannot fathom. The custom of the fen has all but disappeared. The closest we can get to it nowadays is the flooding Washes and their man-made creation each winter (or flood-time) of a wet broadway twenty miles long and half-a-mile wide that stops the nearby rivers from flooding the fens. Vermuyden planned the Washes so that 'the water, in time of extremity, may go in a large room to keep it from rising too high'. The image is telling. Looking at the banked waters, the housed wet, spilling over the fields into the Nene Washes near Whittlesey, or the Ouse Washes between the Old and New Bedford Rivers west of Ely, it is possible to see some late lingering reflection of how the wider fens looked and how they worked. No fen river, even as they are routed and managed today, can carry its winter load without further help. On the Washes a sanctioned flood is floated in front of us. Water is ushered into a room. The flood flattens the flat place still further. Field lines and fence posts grow like the raised stitching of the earth. Whooper swans scull over half-sunk gates. Gulls slide and dip over the drowned grass as over the sea. And then, two months later, cattle graze in the lush summer meadows that the Washes become after the winter water flows on. The grass there is thicker and greener than any I have ever seen elsewhere on the fens.

A story is told about a punishment reserved for those who most severely ignored or denied the custom of the fens. A penalty at the disposal of the medieval Court of Sewers for those who neglected or deliberately breached locally raised and vital banks was to have the offender buried alive. The culprit would become part of the defences he had ignored or wrecked. He was to be bound and planted into the gap he had created, peat doing for a concrete overcoat. Can we believe this happened? Like a lot of fen stories and their near-neighbours – the Dutch boy at the dyke and Canute at the waves, or the fens themselves as flow country with their endless brokering of the dry and the wet, of land and water – no one knows where this story begins or where it might end, or where, if anywhere, its truth lies among other fen burials and disinterments, the melting of solids, the fixings of the eel and the bog, the swimming of mole and mist.

The blackbird in the rain was the last I heard singing for the year. Through June, birdsong drains sweetly and slowly to the reductions of midsummer. In the bushes hidden blackbird fledglings take over, with their punctured-tyre *pseep* noises. One day all you hear is flies and you struggle to remember what has gone. In the village, I caught the last juice of blackcap from the sloes, the beak-snap of a spotted flycatcher on its sallies from the gravestones, and the tinnitus of goldcrests – the white noise of a hangover – from the cedar in the churchyard. Then – unheard and unnoticed at first – space opened in the hedges. From now on, if the sun is to come back before the winter, it will be in the legs of grasshoppers or the dry wheezing calls of young starlings. They flock as soon as they leave the nest and then crash about in gangs, flying the tattered matt flags of the season that they share with young rooks and crows. You can see this even in May. Long before the school summer holidays begin the winter is signed up. Only the woodpigeon tries again and again his cracked tuba. He sounds far away and out of date: a lullaby sung on an iron-lung. Through the summer his sorry song tightens the chest as old grass shrinks taut over the field and harvest chaff and thistledown come to stuff the air. The Earth, the whole planet, is slung out on its slingshot arc and on the fen you feel it, coasting without power, all traction spent.

Swifts make July bearable, almost rescuing the month, swinging through its otherwise hammock-slump on scything wings. But, by the third week, the village birds are done with its rooftops, the skittering and screaming is over, the beetling scuttles into the crannies and the bale-outs from the eaves no more. If they come over our house they are higher and quieter than before. In the first days of August most hunt out above the fields, rigging the wind and fattening on flies. Ant-flights one day steered them over the fen in a brilliant black frenzy. Black-headed gulls gathered for the insect bonanza as well, clomping about the sky, pulled and tugged after the aerial morsels; wooden spoons to the swifts' steel blades.

That same evening I lay on my back in the middle of the field and looked up. The winged ants had lifted in the still of the afternoon but now the wind had risen and with it the late light grew ruddy and loose. The gulls sloped off into it, turning gold as they went, but the swifts were still there flying above me in the way they always fly, describing their continual motion, their permanent entrance into the sky: endlessly, effortlessly, blackly uncoiling, always moving yet always there. Above me were birds that wouldn't make contact with anything that touched the Earth for at least ten months. One swift that summered in Oxford was known throughout its life. It lived to be eighteen and in those years had flown 2 million miles, the equivalent of four round trips to the moon.

James Ferguson, the eighteenth-century Scottish astronomer and instrument maker, began his life as a farm labourer. Aged ten, in 1720, he minded the sheep on a neighbour's farm in Banffshire. He was a precocious astronomer and already fascinated by the night sky that cloaked him on his way to and from his long days in the fields. In his autobiography he described how, with his flock folded, he would lay a blanket on the sheep-turf and would lie on his back and hold beads on strings over his head to measure star distances and patterns in the fields of space. These measurements he then transferred to paper star-maps that he had spread beside him on the grass. The reckoning of swifts' flight is no easier but just as alluring as Ferguson's celestial calibrations: how a handspan might make a light year; how a bird that lives in my neighbour's roof might fly to the moon and back.

Above me the swifts were quiet. So quiet they seemed to silence the air. They seem to darken their surroundings as well, their blackness spilling from them. They sleep on the wing. There are beautiful black and white photographs of radar screens blooming into life at night, capturing swifts leaving London in all directions to sleep in the sky. The night-screen is black, the birds appear greyish white. The image looks like winter breath parsleying on a pane of glass. The birds I saw lifting themselves into the sky beyond my eyes were probably preparing to sleep. In their sleep-flight they rock from one side to the other as if they were being swung in a cradle. It is thought this motion is prompted by a sleep pattern that dims and then alternates brain activity. First the left side of the swift sleeps and then its right. The sleeping half begins to fall through the air, the waking half corrects the fall. *Nocturnal harmonic oscillatory orientation* is the term given for the shuttle of the bird through the loom of the night. Flying above the Earth they move around the world as it moves around – beneath and above – them, their globe-curved heads like little planets, half-lit, half-dark, swaying above the swaying earth, the bending grass, and the curved reeds.

One year, out on the Wash, from a boat riding the mixing waters of the North Sea and half the rivers of eastern England, I watched two swifts slicing like flung peat between three gannets, cruciform flints, all piling south towards the fens. Neither gannet nor swift is a bird of the fields. Both are useless if set down on the earth. Once, on ploughland far from the sea, I saw a storm-wrecked gannet looking like an abandoned wedding dress. Once, in a field after a thunderstorm, I found a swift grounded – a dropped glove. Both birds are wrong for my story, but both, between them, are sentries keeping watch when airborne. Lie in your summer bed in Britain and know that gannets are flying around the island's every edge and swifts are flying above your head. The light walking on the sea. The dark swimming through the air.

Midnight on the fen, a half-hearted dark in the dog days of the year: all quiet and still but for the leaning air of summer which came over me like cow breath. Everything was here – the fen was flat but full – and yet the engine of the place seemed elsewhere. Whatever was once noisy and colourful and fresh in these same fields was worn out and run down. Labouring up through clouds a slice of moon cheese sweated into the muzzy sky. I looked as far across the murky plain as I could. There was little to see. The horizon was flat with a few trees hanging at its end like dark chandeliers. But the smell was strong – a low-tide vegetable ooze with a salted edge. The sea.

The sea is not here but it once was and perhaps will be once again. At the dead end of the road, where the tarmac stops and the grass begins, I slipped off my shoes and socks and waded out. Most of the fields there were lying under wheat, almost ready for harvest, their gold gone to grey and in the dark they looked like tiles of worn carpet. But I went on to paddle in a grass field, one of the few. Where cattle had stood, its earth was warm, wormy and black under my toes; further out the grass bit at my feet like insects and a few tired dribbles of dew brushed my shins. It smelt: green but old. Cabbage not lettuce. Rot not ripe.

The sky misted taking the feeble stars still further away. From invisible clouds it started to rain. The long-buried sea stirred in its basket of sleep. Just before the first drops, I felt the field breathe in and hold a deep quiet for a moment. Then I heard the rain as it hit the sleeping grass at my feet and the earth sighed. The grass stems bowed beneath each tiny wet punch. Away across the fields, in the almost dark, a hidden quail called twice like a damp electrical contact fizzing in the night: *wet-my-lips, wet-my-lips,* a fen prayer signalled over the waves of green.

As a crop grows, tight-packed and uniform, it closes a field, like bread rising in a loaf tin. Then the harvest cut comes that releases the ground and, with it, the itch of all its welcome irregularities. By the end of the dry week the fields next to the fen were transformed in this way and it was the same for every mile around. The corn-top of the world had been lowered by two feet, close-cropped and clear-felled. With the wheat taken, the soil, its earthenware, was to be seen once again. And the ruins, the leftovers, seemed more homely than what had grown before.

The farmers drove their cars into the half-done fields and left them there while they were combining, stopping every other hour, walking across the toast and marmalade stubble and straw. They sat with the radio on, smoking and texting in their cars, the last fade of the linen cloth carried at noon to the field, a jug of cider, thick-cut sandwiches, and a snooze in the shade.

The combine started up again like a taxiing jumbo. The field was shaken and heated and shouted at. The machines made their noisy, partnered dance around the square. All the years, all the people, the barefoot bending to the ground, the cutting, the raking, the stooking, the threshing, all is now put so quickly through those metal mouths into those playground-bright trundling bellies. I stood and watched the harvester make light of the harvest, and the field was done in an hour.

All night the combines drove on across the fens with dragon roars and bright lamps, as if this gold rush was an emergency, and the molten gush from the Earth's core must be tapped and capped at any price. In the floodlit dark between the roaring engines I heard lapwings bleating anxiously around the stubble fields, woken and inconsolable.

SWALLOW

Afterwards I threw away my rucksack and a pair of socks: I had put my bag down on the ground in some dusty places and grass seeds had got woven into the knit of my ankles. I should really have binned my jeans as well. My fingernails grew unbitten for a week. I put my contact lenses in with diligence, eyeballing them for flecks of alien grit. On the third day my throat ran with mucus before drying to chalk and I thought I'd been delivered to the end in double-quick time but, after a hot night of dire imaginings, a regular cold took hold and I shivered on and off through the rest of my stay.

Chernobyl is flat, as flat as the fens. Its horizons are local and edged with trees. Rarely does the view extend more than half a mile in any direction. The green at the rim of things curls up the sides of the sky. Nowhere can you stand on a hill and feel that, like the Little Prince, you are on the outer edge of the planet and towering over its curve. Everywhere you are held in the bottom of a shallow spreading basin. Somewhere there must be a gradient, something that tilts or rolls or drains, but you do not feel anything of that here. Somewhere, you remember, there is sea too, but here that would only be a rumour or, at best, a defrosted fish finger in the canteen of Chernobyl town.

Any and all wide views close down when you arrive at the checkpoint barrier across the road two hours by car north of Kiev. Before the Exclusion Zone that begins here, flat fields had been coursing next to the road for miles, tangled with old grasses or stubbly with wheat straw, each already finished for the year. At the fenced border of the Zone, a tall wild hedge of shaking aspens at right angles to the road squared off the last field and from there on to the plant, a further forty-five minutes away, only trees crowded to the roadside.

The red and white barrier had the English word *nice* printed on it several times. I don't know why. No one goes into the Zone who doesn't have business with it. And nice is not the word. We waited for our papers to be processed. A redstart sang half a phrase of song and then called from a pine next to the road on the Kiev side of the barrier. Its orange gape opened a cave in its black throat. As it sang, its silvered back and warm red tail trembled against the scabby bark of the branch. At the same moment, on the Zone side of the barrier, a black redstart called from the corrugated roof of the policemen's hut and shook its dustier back and rustier tail. The fountain sparkle of one bird passed into the metered buzzing of the other, their tails quivering like needles across the line. The policeman raised the barrier.

Hemmed by pine and birch we drove towards the heart of the Zone. Staring into the trees I caught glimpses of open space, flashes of yellower light through the green dark of the woods. There were villages half-hidden, and industrial sites, and then a town. A lead-grey pipe crossed above the road like a gateway and we passed under it.

We drove on to somewhere flat somewhere else in the trees. We did this for five days. Away from the town we saw no one for there was no one to see. At fifteen or so places we stopped and collected plants, bugs and grasshoppers. We wanted variations and aberrations. Radiation levels were metered and noted. Leonid was at the wheel of his old saloon; our minder, Igor, issued directions from the passenger seat and helped with paperwork at the two or three other barriers we met. On the back seat with me was Anders Pape Møller, a Danish scientist based in Paris, and Tim Mousseau, a biology professor from South Carolina. There wasn't much talk. They were both on their second study trip to Chernobyl this year alone. Between their weeks in the Exclusion Zone they had had a summer holiday to Fukishima in Japan on a first visit to assess whether they might be able to start gathering biological data in the shadow of the devastated power station.

Above the redstarts at the first checkpoint there were barn swallows calling as they cut around the government buildings, and for the rest of our stay there were loose gangs of the birds over our heads almost everywhere in the Zone. Often they were the only birds that we saw or heard for an hour or more. Their lovely chittering flights, warm, sociable and unhindered, seemed to come from another time and place, the best of a summer farm thrown up into the autumn air above a forest. There are no longer wires between the telephone poles at the roadsides of Chernobyl, and the poles themselves have often rotted and fallen like trees in a swamp, snapped at their knees. The swallows must make their gatherings on the top twigs of limes or birches or on the loose tiles of the collective farm buildings and houses in the abandoned villages. As you approach, the birds shake from these places like dead leaves or brick dust.

Later in the week the weather closed. The swallows stayed on and flew lower. Even dulled and reduced, the air where they lived came increasingly to seem like a place you wanted to be. A place where you might revise your life upwards, lift your head and see beyond the trees and beyond the Zone to a freer and more open space less poisoned than the place we have been given. By their flights and calls through this air the swallows advertised it as habitable. But the swallows of Chernobyl are sick. The air might be their zone but the insects they take from that air pull the birds heavily down to earth.

We know this thanks to Anders. Most springs since 1991 he has come to study swallows here; for twenty years before that, and continuing to this day, he has also followed swallows breeding on Danish farms. His father was a dairy farmer and Anders has known swallows domestically since he was a child. His scientific research is among the longest continuing study of a bird by a single scientist ever. 'Someone', he said, 'did' common gulls for almost as long and there was a 'Finnish count' who worked on pied flycatchers for forty-three years, 'but he had a chauffeur and a servant to carry his stepladder'. Anders has ringed 50,000 birds himself – every one passing through his hands and many of them swallows. And those birds at Chernobyl join the swallows he knows from Jutland and elsewhere. Cradling so many in his palm to fix rings on their legs and take measurements and samples has allowed him to look deeply into the birds, understanding them as a species, but also and inevitably registering their individual characters. 'I have known hundreds of swallows personally,' he said, with half a joke, as ever, playing over his face, 'and it is not my fault.'

His voice is dry and quiet. You have to lean in to hear him and he leans away as you come close. In the car he sits still; in the field he walks with steady steps and a straight back. His hands are small and tremendously calm. When they are not working he holds them, I noticed, in a way that suggests an old painting, a still life, as if they are not solely or fully his. He is mordantly funny but doesn't laugh out loud very often, nor does he even grin, but something like a smile is always hovering at the tight corners of his mouth. As a scientist he is extraordinarily productive. A monograph on the swallow by another ornithologist flits between Anders's studies, with half the book indebted to things he has seen and thought about and its bibliography thick with the thin man's name and his references. He is fiercely clever – the only scientist I have met who I imagine lives fully in the stark light of what his behavioural ecology teaches him, its iron severities and truths, its granulated accounts of love and desire. Being a Danish dairyman's son contributed to this, he said, and Anders also told me that he was a teenage reader of Kierkegaard and, at the same time, debated vehemently with his local priest. In rural Denmark in the 1960s you were, he said, included in a list of believers in your parish unless you demonstrated that you weren't one. He duly did. Forty years on I found myself momentarily pitying the priest. It is still easy to feel stupid in Anders's company. I did that but I also liked him very much. Another possible reaction to his cleverness is to turn against him. Some biologists have done this. There was a spat a few years ago with serious consequences that ended with him being accused of manipulating his data. His ringing permit was revoked in Denmark. He was to be kept from his swallows. An academic tribunal subsequently cleared him of all the charges but watching him walk through the abandoned farms under the shadow of the reactor in the Exclusion

Zone, it is hard not to think that Chernobyl and its hot and testing seriousness is answering all of this, and that there is proving to be done in the remains of its fire. However, that is not the end of things. Anders's work with Tim Mousseau in Ukraine goes far beyond the personalities of the two men and whatever local motivations I might guess at. After repeated journeys in and out of the sick place and the painstaking accumulation there of evidence and understanding, they are now writing what amounts to a book of the end of things, nothing less than a Revelation and an Apocalypse.

This summer, between the poisoned places, Anders returned to Denmark and its swallows with gadgets that human runners wear on their wrists to record their heart rate. Previously, with birds in his hand he had noticed that when another swallow flew over calling or singing he could feel the held bird's heart racing against his fingers. Some hearts pumped harder than others. This year he sat in his car in assorted Danish cattle-yards clutching swallows he had netted and holding the runners' gadget against their chests while the car cassette machine played various swallow contact calls and alarm notes and songs. The length and complexity of the electric bubbling at the end of the male swallow's song indicate his testosterone levels. Listening birds, especially males, reacted strongly to the beefiest messages. But no two birds were the same; each swallow was either more agitated than the next or less. These variations offer glimpses of what nowadays are being called bird personalities. An individual might be defined by the way its blood is pumped. By your pulse we shall know you. Indeed, if you go ringing great tits, you can feel a whole society travelling through your hands in a single morning. Some come easily out of the net and lie meek in your palm, others attack like dwarf woodpeckers drilling at your fingers and drawing blood. Every bird is different. In Anders's hands some swallows flinched more than others when they heard alarm notes. These variations may well indicate how successful these individuals are likely to be as parents or long-distance migrants or as birds struggling to live in inhospitable places. Every bird being different, the more swallows you know the closer you get to the truth. There can never be enough data but each bird handled narrows the gap even by the tiniest amount, a feather's width. This is what brings Anders and Tim back to Chernobyl when so many have left. As well as its book of the dead they are working on the map of its life.

In Chernobyl the swallow variations are vertiginous to contemplate. Every living thing is more or less ill, that is true of all life everywhere, but in the great sick room of the Zone this given comes to mean something far darker. The long dying that is life is horribly truncated there. Gerontologists talk of *twisted growth* in elderly humans as a way of understanding how we age into death. In Chernobyl you do not grow old with twisted growth, you are born with it.

To my eyes there seemed to be plenty of swallows in the Zone, but the map-makers know how to see beyond this seeming. Everything is to do with counting and the more that can be counted the better. By your pulse, but also by your neighbour's pulse, we shall know how things are. Good or bad. At Chernobyl another pulse, the throb of invisible radioactive particles, complicates the picture, marking it brightly and terrifyingly if you know how to look. The radiation released when the nuclear reactor at the power plant exploded in April 1986 ruined the woods and fields, villages and farms, fishponds and towns. I could see that. There is nobody there and trees grow up through the village bus stops, libraries and schools. But the ruin goes on, thriving as it ruins, and there is much to be learned from how those events are putting a kind of continuing stop on life. There is, it turns out, a gradient in this flat place, Chernobyl is a sink: it takes life in but gives next to no life out.

Radiation has triggered variations that no swallow personality can possibly cope with. It is eating them alive. Anders has been ringing birds since he was fifteen but before he started working at Chernobyl he had never seen a visible tumour on any bird. Of the 3,000 swallows he has handled to date in the Zone, at least fifteen had external growths blackly bursting from their bodies like cankered fruits. The red throats of other swallows were blotched with partial albinism, and others had asymmetric outermost tail feathers. Anders has also held birds whose toes pointed in the wrong direction, whose beaks wouldn't close, whose eyes were deformed by cloudy lenses. Cataracts increase in a human population exposed to higher than normal levels of radiation. A near-blind bird is a soon-dead bird.

Overall, fifteen to twenty per cent of the swallows in the Zone show aberrations or mutations. Every fifth or sixth swallow that flew over me was blighted in some way. One in ten of all birds of all species are afflicted in the Zone. From the ground I couldn't see the thinning red on the throats of the damaged swallows, nor the tail streamers that curl, but they were there. Aberrant birds seem able to breed (sperm has been collected from males and brood patches have been seen on females), but no one has yet watched the young of these birds or counted how many leave the nest. But it is known that their survival rate is low. Adult swallows show a bewitching loyalty to places familiar to them. We love them for this. Pulled by a rough half-moon of spit and mud, they try to come back to the same nest in the same barn that they previously bred in. Half the adult swallows elsewhere in Ukraine return at least once to breed (the exact number is 0.49). In Chernobyl only one in five makes it back the summer after it hatches (0.28 to be precise). If they don't return to where they started in all likelihood they are dead.

Getting back is not enough. There is neither escape, nor home-coming. The clocks of those swallows that do return are running down. In radiation-contaminated areas swallows are breeding two weeks later than birds in cleaner fields. This is bad. Though springs are warmer, encouraging birds to nest earlier, mutations are holding back breeding. Early birds get everything. Returning breeders, birds that have survived the winter, are much more likely to have hatched early themselves. Leaving late because you hatched late is almost certainly a death sentence. Anders glanced at the swallows above us. 'It is not good to be a slow starter if you have to fly to southern Africa on wings this big.' He spread his thumb and forefinger apart into the outline of a five-inch swallow curve. 'The old is dying,' Antonio Gramsci wrote of a different place and another time, 'and the new cannot be born; in this interregnum a great variety of morbid symptoms appear.'

*   *   *

186

'Don't chew the grass or put anything else in your mouth, and wipe your feet whenever you leave the field.' Anders offered no further safety advice. He and Tim both laughed when I asked if they had any extra health checks after their visits. My five days in the Zone, they said, would radiate me no more than a single X-ray at the dentist. But in the Red Forest on our second day, they encouraged me to put on a thin white bodysuit over my jeans and shirt so that, when I stooped to the ground, the creases of my denim knees wouldn't fill with radioactive grains of sand.

I was kneeling in order to pin down my grasshopper victims in a butterfly net – my contribution to the week's work: forty grasshoppers from each site we visited in the Zone. After the first day of looking I began to be able to do the job: attend to what you would otherwise ignore; follow whatever filament of moving light flicks ahead of you as you walk; watch for where it stops moving and, at that place, something slight will have been added to a stem of grass or will have scratched a new mark on the ground; go there quickly and quietly and if possible without a shadow. For five days I peered down for hour after hour. Never have I looked so intimately at grass before, never scrutinised the places it pulls up from the earth, never felt so many dry feet on my fingertips.

There were bigger grasshoppers. I saw two the size of locusts, and others beautifully cryptic, their bodies dark chocolate brown with cream tramlines like the back of a great snipe. Some brighter ones too, paintbox green mantises with lashless professorial eyes, and others with cornflower-blue skin stretching from their legs into papery wings that helped them flee. But the grasshoppers I had been deputed to catch were half-an-inch long and the colour and texture of old grass; some had a little brighter green on their bellies, some a rye-red – those colours, you only really saw when you were holding them between your fingers.

Every day my hands smelled dimly of silage and my thumbs and fingers were stained brown from the tobacco-spit that bubbled at the grasshoppers' tight-lipped faces. The sodden chew was their last mouthful. I put them in a plastic bag. Every time I opened it to add a new recruit, those already captured leapt upwards, kicking off from the backs of others, or managing to get some grip where their spit had stuck on the slippery walls. Once one escaped, sailing free back to the field, but for all the others being caught was the beginning of the end. The bag sat on the table in the tent that Leonid and Igor erected for Tim and Anders at every stop. For a while, as the grasshoppers jumped within, it twitched; the clicks of their legs against the plastic like the ticks of the radiation meter next to them. Having finished his other tasks at each site – the dissection and photography of evening primrose flower heads (an American native, here an invasive weed) – Tim would take the hoppers from the bag one at a time. Their genes, like the primroses', were to be plumbed. In deft doctorly gestures he manoeuvred the animals between his fingers on to their backs and with the blades of a pair of surgical scissors snipped their bodies in three or four places. Their legs kicked a few more times, each kick with less certainty, drawing last hieroglyphs in the air, before they were posted into small glass tubes filled with liquid preservative. The three of us sat in the tent for a moment after the final delivery. Tim recalled doing his master's degree and how his dreams at the time became sinister distortions of his fieldwork that required him to pull the legs off more than 20,000 crickets. Anders admitted that he 'wasn't good with blood', and that the snip of Tim's scissors across the camping table took him back to the sound of his wife being cut to allow their first child to be born.

The grasshoppers were easy to catch on sunny days in the Zone in areas of lower radiation; they were hardest in the blasted clearings of the Red Forest, one of the hottest radiation spots. Highly contaminated ground here might have at best only one grasshopper every square metre; a similar area of clean grass might accommodate one hundred. The Red Forest is a mix of pines and birch (some originally planted, some wild growth) and clearings (some natural, some enforced). It is the nearest woodland to the west of the vast yards of reactors, chimneys, cooling towers, ponds and pylons at Chernobyl. All of these are now defunct and the trees are growing closer to the fences and wires.

In the aftermath of the explosion and nuclear fire that burned for ten days in 1986, the forest was the first dropping-off point for the radiation cloud. Its trees turned red. The wind blew towards the west and rain fell and both sowed radionuclides over the land. In particular, isotopes of three ductile silvery-white metals drifted where the air took them and sank where it left them: caesium (at Chernobyl, caesium-137), discovered in mineral water in 1860 and named for the sky-blue electromagnetic radiation that it emits; strontium (strontium-90), named by Humphry Davy in 1808 after the Scottish village Strontian where it was first discovered; and plutonium, the baby of the family, synthesized in 1940, though identified subsequently in nature, and named after the former (now dwarf) planet and the god of the underworld. Of the last of these, the isotope now found in the Exclusion Zone (plutonium-239) has a half-life of 24,100 years.

In the Red Forest, the birch trees are doing better than the pines. Birch seems to possess some superior ability to repair its own DNA. In the abandoned fields around the villages and collective farms a little further away from the reactor, it is the flimsy and short-lived but pushy birch that first steals a march across the grass. In the Red Forest I walked among birches half my age and three times my height, the wispy children of Chernobyl. The open acres of thin sandy soil scattered with a few of these rangy trees might have been in the Brecks of East Anglia, except that this was a clearing made by the explosion – the trees that grew here once were killed by radiation. Many of them still lay on the ground, preserved in death since 1986, their grey trunks wrapped in a fogged and brittle marquetry. Fall-out was so potent in these woods that for a time it destroyed microbial activity as well as most other living things. Rot was killed, decay arrested and the dead kept immutably dead. There were no friendly worms. Death, needing no colleagues, moved as an absolute master through these woods and fields, armed solely with itself, raining death beyond death down over the trees and grass, keeping everything dead. Dante, genius complicator of hell, would have understood; Achilles trapped in Hades too, a permanent king in the underworld wanting to be a ploughboy above and make things grow; and perhaps also the architects of the gulag, those men who devised death sentences given cruelly warped names like *twenty-five years without the right of correspondence.*

Even wrapped in my everything-proof suit I felt nervous in the Red Forest. It was ineffably strange: to be in a calm clearing that could kill you, where soil is dangerous, where the air might violate you, where standing under a blue sky is risky, where dust is lord of everything's future. I had walked only a few yards but had arrived on to an orphaned planet where nothing speaks to nothing. I started moving with flat feet, making deliberate low footfalls to try not to kick up the sandy earth. This made the grasshoppers hard to catch. The counter ticked hot at more than one hundred microsieverts per hour. Humans prefer their background radiation level at less than one. A little whirlwind got up from nowhere, as if looking for a Tarkovsky film, and brushed past me, picking up pine needles and then turning back with its cargo to stipple my white suit. My eyes smarted in the brilliance of the day. I began to imagine I could feel my own porosity, the soft membranes of my body, and the weather moving through me, the air coming inside and laying ash on my tongue.

Eight ravens came wheeling above me, each arriving separately but lingering, and calling hoarsely as I crouched to collect grasshoppers. A breeze riffled the birch leaves, already yellow and old. Older still, curled pages of bark scrolled from their trunks. Birches, wherever they are, look like they have got into the tree business rather too quickly. Here they leaned into some hopeless sickbed vigil at the edge of the pines. But the pines are beyond help, for in the Red Forest they have gone mad.

Eyes down for grasshoppers I nearly bumped into a standing stone of grey concrete, a twenty-foot-high stele marked 1941–1944 in fading black numerals. Fallen to the foot of this lost memorial was a tin crest, like a cheap fruit bowl, embossed with a wheat sheaf and knotted leaves and 'CCCP'. A pine tree scratched at the concrete and I could see weird sprouting balls of needles, dense and black like sea urchins, hanging from the ends of the tree's branches. Some malignity had driven extreme levels of needle over-production; another had concentrated these like angry iron filings leaving the rest of the branch twig-less and bald. At its dirty fingertips, the tree had grown its own wreaths.

Back at the car, Igor had laid on the bonnet a mushroom that he had picked in the woods. It had a cap three inches across, the colour of a brown envelope, and a chunky cheese stalk. On such a day in such a place it looked one-legged. Outside the Zone, the weekend before we started, Igor had been collecting mushrooms to eat. He pursues four species; one is dried, and three are bottled after being boiled with herbs and spices. They see him through the winter. On the way from Kiev to Chernobyl, men clutching black bin bags had been walking from the roadside into the woods. A lorry driver clambered back into his cab with mushrooms thickening both his hands to boxing fists. In many lay-bys and the forecourts of petrol stations, vendors squatted on the oily earth, next to blue and pink plastic buckets piled high with more mushrooms. Others, some as wide as eight inches in diameter, were laid head to the road on tea towels. All the mushrooms have high concentrations of radioactive isotopes, both in and out of the Zone, and the Ukrainians eat them throughout the year. This is not a good idea. Ingesting radiation is much the best way to absorb it. A single particle of plutonium can give you lung cancer: your own mushroom cloud.

In the autumn of 1986, four months after the disaster at Chernobyl, I moved to Budapest to study for a year. In the Nagycsarnok, the big covered market on the Pest bank of the Danube, a white-coated man with thick-rimmed glasses was often stationed behind a stall. You could show this mushroom doctor what you had collected in the Buda Hills and he would identify the species, separating the edible from the poisonous. He wrote authenticating chits so that the old men and women who got off the trams and trolley buses with baskets of mushrooms might sell them from the small tables at the back of the market. This little area was one of the best things I saw in the workers' state. The capitalist concession to the last peasants in the communist city. I liked the little altars of honey and herbs, of two eggs and ten mushrooms, and the ancients steadying themselves behind the tables. I bought jars of honey and its gloopy sunshine to light the winter, but I was always wary of the mushrooms, even with the doctor's notes. The first autumn after the explosion, and nearer to Chernobyl than I had ever been before, I wrote in my diary wondering about radiation and how it might be laid invisibly into everything that was banked so richly through the market: carp like old shoes lying in tanks of dirty water, glistening seams of pig fat, headcheese, huge bruised apples, collapsing curds, strings of hot paprika like dried tongues, barrels of chopped vinegary cabbage that made you wince as you passed, and buckets and baths of plums and grapes smoking in their own bloom.

I didn't know at the time, but the radiation had blown north and west of Budapest and the food I'd left behind in Britain was probably more at risk of contamination, but in any case my fears moved on and landed elsewhere. A mix of curiosity and trepidation had drawn me to Hungary. It was a European country but one that had made me a target through the cold war, that I had grown up in, and that had the where-withal to kill me. I half knew this was crazy but I also knew that I wanted something from the same angled light that had cast these distortions and refractions as it passed through the curtain (made of who knew what?) across Europe. I went east to see myself more sharply, but of course I carried my own bent light with me. A vagrant, even a vagabond, even a master's student, always comes from somewhere. The novelty and remoteness of Hungary then – I heard no English spoken except in my head for weeks at a time – revived and refocused two almost invisible madnesses that had clouded my childhood and teenage years. These were not my madness – they were the world's: the fear of poison and the fear of the bomb, bad stuff forged from the dust of life, brightness falling from the air turning everything dark.

At school when I had learned about the Earth, it was obvious that it was imperilled, and that we had poisoned it and, not content with that, were on the brink of destroying it. All my school projects were about extinctions and pollution. Aged ten I wrote about mercury in Antarctic penguins; I filled test tubes with pond water and sent them for analysis; I learned the word *epitaph* reading a book about dead elm trees. My favourite bird book of the time, J. A. Baker's *The Peregrine*, was a toxic account of a sick and self-hating man stalking wintering falcons in Essex ('a dying world, like Mars, but glowing still') during the decade the species came close to global oblivion. Agricultural insecticides, DDT and Dieldrin, were wracking the birds' bodies with poison, thinning their eggshells, and, in one of several gothic moments in the book, sending them falling to Earth on their backs, their yellow talons and legs clutching hopelessly at the sky.

This, I thought, was how the world would end. If the chemicals didn't crawl up the food chain to get us, then the nuclear blast surely would. I imagined the coming flash at the horizon and the burning wind. When I was thirteen a schoolmaster confiscated a hippy ring with a mandala design that I liked and the silver and black CND badge I'd tried to wear on my lapel. I never got them back. I watched *The Survivors*, a television serial about the aftermath of a catastrophic chemical weapons spillage, as if it was a manual for life, knowing, though, that I wasn't a winner and would have fallen at the first scything.

In the Zone, we drove back from the Red Forest to our hostel. There are two in Chernobyl town itself, one for Ukrainian visitors and one known as the Foreign Experts Hostel. It costs one hundred dollars a night to stay; the toilet paper has the colour and feel of woodchip wallpaper and comes in solid rolls, like a cut log of birch. The wind blew elsewhere in April 1986 and, although it is less than five miles from the plant, the town survives, the only living streets in the Zone. But it is a strange thing, oddly flat like a film set. As we drove I asked Tim and Anders if they remembered where they were when the reactor exploded. Tim, who was in Canada at the time, had no memory of the day; it barely featured in North American news bulletins. Anders knew exactly the place: 'a cabin made of moss and twigs,' beyond Uppsala in Sweden, 'hidden from the world' but under the same skies that bowled over Chernobyl. With a student, he was watching the extraordinary display of a male capercaillie, the giant woodland grouse of northern Europe, a boreal troll-turkey. Its name, coming out of Gaelic, means the horse of the woods. And it is. The male wears Jacobean doublet, ink black with pearl drops, and fanning his broad tail, shying at nothing, and puffing his wobbling throat he throws his head back and up and sings. Sings, like a drunk, what might be an account of fumbling at clothes, undoing a top button in extremis, and of pulling, meanwhile, a final cork. It is all told through neighs and whinnies, stamps and shivers. The ladies, hidden in blaeberries, look on discreetly, professionally unimpressed, sober in the dove greys of Morningside, and showing nothing of their secret decisions vis-à-vis sex. Anders saw all this and more as the nuclear fire was burning. He watched a beta male, a little less drunk, a little less camp-butch, make an unprecedented run at the boss-man and in a huge shoulder barge drive the alpha from his dance floor. The upstart pecked the toppled bird in the head until it was dead.

By the time I told my version of that day we were walking to the canteen in the town. The sun bounced on the western road at dusk. Mosquitoes became jewellery. Coming out of the sunset an old woman walked past us in a headscarf and home-knit jumper, steering herself with a wooden staff. She wished us *dobroho večora*. She was, I realised, the first elderly person we'd seen in the Zone. We saw no other. There are no old people in Chernobyl, or children. There are no house sparrows either, only tree sparrows. No rats. Outside our hostel, two not-right cats waited every day; one with a livid green scab across the back of its neck, the other with the face of a mother in a siege. At the edge of the town where the tarmac turned to dirt, a delinquent pack of five or six feral dogs hung around most of the time. The default canine regression in the Zone is greyhound-like, long, lean and pale: ur-dogs on the wolf-path.

Two gardens are maintained in Chernobyl town. One is watched over by the angel Gabriel, the other by Lenin. Gabriel sounding his trumpet is newer, a metal skeleton made out of stiff black cabling, the sort of rods that reinforce concrete. Behind him and his silent black horn is an avenue of crosses, more than a hundred, receding for a third of a mile across wet grass. Written on each is the name of a village that had to be abandoned after 1986. Out of sight of Gabriel, Lenin stands pewter grey amid a floral clock. In his mausoleum in Red Square in Moscow his preserved head and hands with their strangely childish fingers (who knows what goes on beneath his suit?) would recognise his Chernobyl self – the gardener of men and electrifier of the Soviet Union. His local incarnation is a little less waxy but clearly a variant bottling of the same fruit. In honour of some Japanese dignitaries who had been comparing disaster notes with the Chernobyl management, someone had buffed up the bald man.

Although the plant is dead, it still needs looking after. Rainwater is getting in; a new tomb must be built on top of the old one, a fresh concrete overcoat, and the buried reburied. The town is where the graveyard shift sleeps. Immediately after the explosion in 1986 they were allowed to approach Reactor Number 4 for only forty seconds before they had to retreat and be relieved. Many died and are dying as a result, nonetheless. Liquidators, they were called. Men and women now work four days at a time on the sarcophagus that cloaks Number 4 or elsewhere on the shut plant and then leave the Zone for four days before coming back. The town and the works are militarised; everyone wears a camouflage jacket and trousers. Some twisted idioms from the old days survive. People are in uniform but no one walks done up like a soldier any more. The workers' buses are Soviet-era with round bonnets and a hatch that must be opened at their rear to ventilate their engines. But they have dainty curtains at the windows and their old stencilled military numbers have been painted over in Ukrainian toyshop blue. A middle-aged woman with lacquered hair, pearl-drop earrings and patent black shoes that peeped from her camouflaged turn-ups, cycled slowly around us on a squeaky bike, her plastic briefcase tied on the rack at the back. Between two apartment blocks, a man, in the same fancy dress, attacked the last growth of summer grass with a sickle. He raked his hay beneath the escaped metal pipes, some naked, some clad in insulating bandages, that take (in common Ukrainian practice) steam or hot water cartoonishly on stilts over roads and from building to building but seem loath to enter any of them. On the way to our dinner of *varenyky* – parcels of something like old ears and the same colour as Lenin – we were sent through a scanner turnstile, which forced us to stand like applauding robots held mid-clap in a silent film, whilst some invisible account was made of our innards. We did this every day but I don't think the machine was ever plugged in.

The day the radio news in Britain announced the Chernobyl disaster

– three or four days after the event – I saw my first swallows of that year and also my first swift. The swallows were late and the swift a little early but I hadn't been doing much birdwatching that spring. Birds had become my business and I had an appointment at the British Museum's bird collection at Tring in Hertfordshire. My job was with the dead; my task to write a report on the status and distribution of the 106 species of endemic birds of Madagascar then known. These birds have evolved over millions of years of isolation and are some of the most extraordinary in the world, but the short book I wrote about them is one of the most monochromatic and lifeless imaginable. I am no map-maker and nothing I wrote could revivify the birds. The problem was that the nearest I got to Madagascar or its endemics was walking the narrow and dark corridors of the museum, pulling open cabinets and drawers, spending forty seconds here and there in one sarcophagus after another. Lying there, mostly on their backs, were hundreds of gutted specimens, what scientists call skins, many with a stick driven up through their insides and a dab of cotton wool in their eye places: vangas, ground-rollers, mesites and couas, the bizarre and magically complete avifauna found only on Madagascar but which I knew only as stiff and sorted, eyeless and grounded, and wrapped into themselves like all dead birds, whether under a hedge or in a fridge, on a beach or in a drawer. I took tray after tray to a work-table to decipher the details written on the labels tied to the leg of each bird. These labels are passports, information for the next world, like the cards tied round the necks of evacuee children, or coins placed under the tongues of the dead. They are small, no longer than an inch and a half, and usually written by the person who had collected the bird. To collect a bird means to kill it. That ought to be interesting, the written words ought to allow you to reinflate the moment and the hollow skin that came from it. I stared at the birds as I turned them in my hands, blue couas, sicklebill vangas and scaly ground-rollers; they were beautiful but strange, airy, fading smudges, somehow further away from me at an arm's length than they ever were before or have been since. A whispered lost language in an alien script. There was nothing to assemble beyond the colourless string, the greying card, and the inky lines recording dates and weights, measurements and localities. Laid out in rows in the trays like sorted bodies after a disaster, the dead awaiting repatriation, I had no way of helping them home. In death and tethered to their facts they were, to me at least, invisible. No news from nowhere.

Driving back I switched on the radio, spreading the words of the day into the car with talk of nuclear fire and airborne contaminants detected in Sweden and heading west. I couldn't picture Chernobyl, wasn't sure where it was, but that, I saw, was the point. The sky was the same colour as it had been the day before but now was utterly changed. We didn't know it but we were joined to it all. Perhaps the wind *did* blow from the Urals. Swallows fresh out of the blue from Africa and southern Europe cut and bucked around us, as they must have been doing above the roads and villages of the Kiev region too. Nadezhda Nikolaevna Timoshenko (her surname, my mother's nickname for me, coincidentally) lived in Borshchyovka village a few miles from Chernobyl. Her memories of 26 April 1986 begin: 'It was a very warm and sunny day, very quiet and still. Some birds could be heard singing in the sky. It was just an ordinary spring day . . .'

Anders and Tim had a coloured map of the Zone and kept a copy in the car. On my lap it spread from pale green to dark red. The colours record degrees of contamination. It was exquisite to look at. Didn't Francis Bacon keep a handbook of diseases of the mouth because the plates were so beautiful? On the map, scarlet areas plume west from the reactor in a narrow tongue of intense flame. Further west, the colours pale to orange and yellow but then in several places the red resumes as isolated lesions or bruises. Cheek by jowl with green areas, where the background radiation level is unexceptional, are hot spots that thicken on the map red, dark and dangerous.

Birds in the Zone are doing their own mapping, or rather it is being done to them. Anders has counted returning warblers in Chernobyl springs and found contaminated areas quiet in April, while blackcaps and willow warblers thronged elsewhere. Perhaps they can detect the ticking of the isotopes and thereby know the contaminated areas to be already occupied. More likely there is simply nothing there for them.

I took a tape machine with me into the Zone, but it was so quiet in September I stopped trying to record. Straining to hear anything, I pushed the input level so high that all I got were buzzes and clicks, the noise the machine itself makes when it has gone haywire. Beyond that was just the sick Earth's feedback: the hiss of a dry place, the needle-thin calls of a few tits and chaffinches moving on, the mist of mosquitoes, nothing else.

Nature even when driven out with a pitchfork is said to return. We have lived in the world believing this. At Chernobyl it isn't coming back. On 5 October 1893 Tolstoy wrote in his diary: 'They say that one swallow doesn't make a summer; but, because one swallow doesn't make a summer, would that swallow which already senses summer not fly in, but wait? In that case every bud and blade of grass will have to wait, and there will be no summer.'

We drove thirty miles west of Chernobyl to Vesniane village, still locked deep in the Zone. Like everywhere else away from the town, it is totally deserted. As we left our hostel we saw three official cars on the road, then no one else all day. We put on boots and stepped carefully but we could have walked naked and loud and not frightened anyone, except perhaps a moose. Anders stumbled on a dead one in a pond on his visit here in the spring. Only three sounds marked the day, other than the tick of the radiation meter: a grey-headed woodpecker attacked a rotten telephone pole and, finding nothing, laughed his high, resigned laugh; a jay screeched mid-air, the flying Mr Punch; and once a chiffchaff let slip its thin autumn music, two near-whispered rounds of its spring tune, a song before parting.

The village lies in the middle red bruise of three on the map, between the abandoned collective farms of Novyi Myr and Lubianka. Such names! By the old milking parlour Anders's meter showed 200 to 300 times the level of normal background radiation. The same number of people – between 200 and 300 – was evacuated from the village. Overall 130,000 people were taken from the Zone. At first, seventy-four settlements were evacuated. Later, further west, an additional clearance was undertaken: forty-eight villages were abandoned, a further thirty-seven partially evacuated.

A milk churn lay on its side at the doorway to the parlour. Inside, each plastered brick stall where the cows ate and were milked was rubbed and scuffed differently, signed by their late occupants. Further in, about twenty birch trees grew up thickly from the floor through the broken roof. In the village, trees are moving across the old fields, blurring their edges to dusk, but nowhere do they grow so excitedly as up through and out of its barns and houses. Perhaps browsing moose and others are reluctant to enter old buildings to eat; perhaps the barns are floored with old manure that provides some vestigial nutrition for saplings. Beyond these explanations the walled woods rise in front of you like flags of the Zone, the heraldry of its dark green law, drawing attention to what was there before while showing the way life will increasingly grow here – clearings closed, castles hemmed from within, timber walls, the death of grass. Soviet power turned churches into granaries and stables; here a village has become a nursery for a forest. This is a country that *wants* to be trees.

The grasshoppers were not difficult in Vesniane. The sun shone and they were easy to net in the scrapes of sand ploughed out of the old meadows by the rootling tusks of wild boar. The insects like this opened ground for laying their eggs. Along the village street, birch and lime trees crowded and pressed close to the buildings. Some cottages had all but disappeared or turned tree-house: now beamed with branches and roofed with leaves, their deal-planked rooms indistinguishable from the stockade of trunks that pushed at them, green papering the walls. The village school had limes filling its playground; in its assembly hall was a row of infant chairs, yoked together and facing into the rank heart of the building, home of hungry mosquitoes. Across the street, through the trees, was the library. It had been ransacked at some point since it was abandoned and someone had filled its porch with rotting books to mulch like dying woodland flowers. Through twenty-five dry summers and twenty-five iced winters anything humanly bright had been switched off or driven away. The same or other looters had put outside every ruined house any even remotely salvageable scrap-metal object for a later collection that never happened. In its slow rot the iron-age was chasing down the nuclear: on one verge the metal handle from a manual water pump lay next to three candle holders, nearby was a child's bike, strands of wire, a pram, a bedstead, lampshades, a madness of pipes, some birdcages, a heap of mousetraps, a motorbike sidecar, and more buckets and pans than I could count. It was as if some magnet had been pulled through the village, dragging everything we had made to the roadside so that the junk might bid farewell to the departing people. Let the scanner pass over our treasure at the crossroads of Vesniane, where we cannot live any longer in the world that we have fashioned. Here is our Scythian gold, our Roman silver, our cave paintings, our ghost shirts and dream-catchers, here all of it dreck and trash and the colour of old blood, our pigment gift to the world's palette, our rust.

Grasshopper quota bagged, I turned my attention to shoes and fruit. At the village bus stop, once tiled in blue, a birch grew where villagers would have stood. On the roadside was a single green plastic slipper, nearby three separate and different soles walked through leaf mould; at the crossroads a child's shoe, furred now with a petite sock of electric moss; further into the trees a leather boot like a dead calf. One hundred and thirty thousand Cinderellas waiting for a last bus, sabotaged.

Between the shoes there were apples: overlapping constellations of grounded things. Every cottage had fruit trees and more grew along field edges and at the roadside. In September there was an abundance of fruit, half was still on the trees, half had dropped. The fallen lay where they fell, bright and undisturbed, red, yellow, green: demonstrations of the physics of cluster, roll and drop, the way things fall down and fall apart. I walked closer and red admirals that had been feeding on the fallen sweetness lifted over the fruit like small flying carpets. Spun around other trees there were pears and plums as well as apples: atomic models, planets, dwarves, moons, small and large, red, yellow and green. Some were perfect, others crabbed, some going the way of all flesh, others hurrying there, every fruit forbidden, galled and inedible, bad seeds at the heart of every one. The *pink* of a chaffinch hit a tiny metal hammer on the sky and I heard an apple fall into a soft receiving sleeve of grass. The sound summoned all the others I wouldn't hear and a thought of how, 1,000 years from now, the A14 and the other main roads and motorways of England and the once villages of Chernobyl, sick places both but lined as they are with accidental apple trees, might be identified as linear orchards, good things, threads of fruit through forests.

On a low branch of a green apple tree was a male black grouse, a poor man's capercaillie: black and brilliant and a dancer too, just smaller and slightly more sober at his lek than the horse of the woods. In Britain a dawn start and hard walking up hill is usually required to see one – here they could be found at the bus stop. I stepped too close and flushed him; his beautiful lyre-shaped tail combed the still air and hummed through the blue as he flew up to a top branch on a tall lime further along the road. A grey female I hadn't spotted on the ground, where perhaps she had been on the cider, followed him, whirring up and away.

There are wild things in the Zone like these black grouse. Moose, and wolves too. But Anders and Tim insist that there are very few. Everything they have studied bears them out. In all his travels and transects Anders has glimpsed a wolf only once. And those animals that are living here have a hard time of it. A white-tailed eagle clambered heavily into the air as we were leaving the village and whinnied to a mate and both, huge and tremendous, did their flying stable-door impersonations, calling like Pegasus through the sky. But the male may well be sterile, the female warming dead eggs summer after summer until she dies. In five days of walking through what some have wanted to call a resurgent wilderness I didn't see a single mammal. I hardly saw a bee.

The moon was alone in the sky when we finished. Half of it, only.

Chernobyl's flatness is the flatness that comes from the middle of a place; there is also a flatness that comes out of the sea. To confuse matters, the Crimean steppe, the wild grass at the southern shore of Ukraine, is flatness – a mattress – of the middle place that comes out of the sea. But because the sea here is nested within seas – the Azov to the north of the Crimea nested in the Black, the Black in the

Mediterranean – and the ocean very far away, the prevailing conditions are still interior. If the wind blows it is from the land. The air is salted from within not without.

Calandra larks are abundant on the Crimean steppe in early June. I counted 400 in one mile along the split asphalt of an old military road just inland from the Black Sea near Kerch. There were another 400 singing in the sky above. They are big and heavy-headed as grasshoppers and, similarly, look like country boys, hayseeds, chunky and grassy brown. But their song is magnificent and on the steppe it is as common as light; it carries from the fields into the towns and through each village, and it doesn't stop from dawn to dusk. In June it starts at three-thirty in the morning and ends at eleven at night and in each singing bird is an account of everything worth saying in the lark-lands. One woke me in my tent on the Baherova steppe before the sun had begun its climb, another shepherded me off the plain long after the first stars were out. The calandra is generous, good things from other singers are included in its song, and riffs on those good things too – new volleys, asides and embellishments, found tunes and footnotes to those tunes, and made up things like shopping lists and gossip, hymns and snores. Always fast and always full-mouthed, it is a jabber but done entirely without stress. As a swallow sings as if it had a beakful of flies in the way of its music, so the lark sings with dust and grass seeds rattling in its syrinx: a dry song but running with the memory of water like a streambed in summer. Lark song is steppe weather. It comes up through you from the birds singing hidden in the grass at your feet and rises to the birds hidden high in the sky until you catch them as they shudder down through yards of hot thick air on their stiffened wings, black beneath, slow-flapping and stroking slowly like a rower gathering water or a reaper cutting grass. I ate a sandwich of neon-pink salami and drank a bottle of warm beer and the same lark was singing the same extended song from my first mouthful to my last slurp.

In Marfivka village on the steppe was a shop, and for sale along with my salami and beer was a two-foot-wide brick of pig fat (no lean, just fat), dusty bottles of Ukrainian cola, and several pink mattresses. On the road continuing through the steppe and beneath the hot shouting sky, a bare-chested man in wellington boots, nylon football shorts and a cloth cap was standing between his horse and his child, a boy of about eight. Straining its neck, the horse had managed to eat the hay in the cart it was meant to be pulling. The man hit his horse between the eyes with his fisted hand and then he turned and slapped the child on its cheek. His son he hit with greater force. In the same village, just beyond a football pitch chalked into the crumbling road, a young man in hard-core cyborg nightclub kit – black plastic t-shirt, tight black cycling shorts, ant-eye sunglasses – was walking to his hay, a long-handled scythe slung over his shoulder. Civilisation and its discotheques.

I arrived hot and dusty from the steppe in Koktebel looking for a bed. The hotel was shut. 'Remont,' the owner said, interrupting her mobile phone call on its front steps, waving me away. This condition is endemic in Crimea. Everything was being *renewed* but nothing was finished. In Kerch a brigade of elderly women in washing-up gloves scrubbed at the rusting railings, Ukrainian blue as everywhere, at the foot of their block of flats. Others swept dust with worn-out brooms into spiral patterns around chestnut trees. The water was off in Theodosia but I found a room. Just after dusk I went to the seashore there. A nightjar flapped like a stray letter, something Cyrillic, along the railway line on the front. I met a man from Armenia who had brought a green python to the sea to make money from tourists or sailors who might thrill to have a snake draped round them like a scarf. In the photograph I took, both his almond eyes and his snake's caught spits of street lamp reflection. Man and snake spend their winters in a warm apartment in Yerevan, sharing a bedroom or, if the heating fails, a bed. Next to the snake-man two prostitutes leaned on the seawall, their hands on their bony hips. In the bay beyond them and the railway track, visible through the crook of their elbows, common dolphins slipped like slivers of soap through the skin of the oily night sea. Once I'd let them follow the black scythe of the fins through my binoculars the women told me their rates: a hundred dollars to lie down, sixty dollars for anything standing up.

The next day: early into the grass. Black-headed buntings were already awake and singing on wires, black-headed wagtails leapt around the feet of some sheep, and a group of calandra larks landed ahead of me on a narrow road. In their arrival, they showed me another nightjar sitting on the verge under the full sun, its eyes dark tar bubbles below heavy lids, its head, back and tail overlapping layers of browns, obsessively worked like a madman's painting, stuffy in its complexity in the wide spaces of simpler grass. It flew awkwardly, craving dark and moths and wanting movement only when the cowled buntings and wagtails slept on the steppe. As it went swallows appeared around it, drawn to mob the freak, chittering, as they would around a cuckoo.

Every thirty miles across the plain are military listening devices pointing towards Turkey, widespread skeletons of crucified wire, like an X-ray plate of a giant bird with outstretched wings. You cannot tell if they are listening any longer. Sheep, with their heads down, goats, with their heads up, crowded around the legs of the big birds. In the empty shed of a vast and ruined collective farm was one muddy cow; its milkmaid, an old lady in boots and pinafore, sat on a recycled car seat to milk her charge by hand. As I passed I could see the chalky squirt into the tin bucket wedged between her shit-caked boots.

The Baherova plain began to shake in the heat of the day. Rose-coloured starlings, like squares of Turkish delight, lifted from the grass and fizzed towards the swimming horizon. Beneath them three displaying male great bustards were turning themselves inside out in their lather, switching themselves on by their undressing, three rival beacons bright enough even in the oven-heat and whump of sun to impress a lady or lure a traveller across the steppe. The calandra larks sang on. I became fascinated by how little they strayed from their quarter of air, their acre of grass: it was as if they sang *of* the field below them and *to* it as well, always working over the same place, and reworking. *Remont*.

The steppe is open but not flat. The bowl of Baherova, a circle of low hills cupping a four-mile-wide crater of grass, makes a beautiful amphitheatre. It runs north, joins more grass, and dips into the Sea of Azov; through binoculars I could see, as if in a mirage, brown cows cooling their legs miles away in the shallow seawater. The grass of the steppe here is continuous though not uniform: I counted eight species in four yards while thistles, herbs and purple vetches swapped places in between. In the warm wind some grass shakes, some trembles, some wobbles. The two-and-a-half-foot-high feather grass, *Stipa capillata*, is the most striking, its seed heads form hoary white plumes, eight old-fashioned-looking strands per stem. I picked a bunch to dry. Later in my car they seeded in the heat and exploded across the back seat with a crackle. Studded through the grass were burnet moths and blue butterflies I couldn't identify. Countless empty snail shells crunched beneath my every step. Rooks dug at the soil and one, rubbing against some thyme, launched a little low-slung scented cloud that climbed the hill towards me.

Walking through the feather grass on the far side of the bowl were two demoiselle cranes: new to me, specialists of the place and wonderfully made, it seemed, from the steppe. They are big, leggy and grey, with a rumpled pillow at their rear but exquisite and delicate to the fore, with silver white plumes that flow in a perfect curve from above their eyes around their faces to the top of their necks. These feathers are uncanny replicas of the steppe feather grass, and the wind blowing through Baherova lifted and blew the feathers and the feather grass in the same way, the various plumes waving in the various light. Below their pale curves, the cranes have long black stoles on their breasts like a velvet scarf reaching between their legs. The two birds walked as if attendant each on each, as if they knew without following each other's steps exactly where they were, relative to one another. Were they married? They looked it. A king and a queen surprised in their finery, wearing it for themselves, and out for a walk through their fields, which, being theirs, had come to look like them.

I slept badly that night in a tent on the steppe, put to sleep by the last lark song and woken by the first. In the few dark hours between the rising dry towers of lark music, mosquitoes passed close to my ears like cars. I hadn't realised it when camping but as I left the next morning I discovered that I had put my tent up in the grass on the edge of a ruined military base and airfield. West of where I'd been birdwatching

I followed a dirt track through the steppe leading on to an old metalled road that climbed from the basin to the flat tops. All at once my narrow route became a runway and I was driving down wide concrete lanes, bumping every hundred yards or so over the little green ribs of grass that had grown between the blocks of poured concrete. There was no fence, no signs, no people, and the steppe leapt over the criss-crossing concrete ways and carried on. There were larks as before. I headed towards some half-ruined and derelict buildings – old rusting hangars and a brick tower – that were grouped at the edge of the place and, close by, I saw the first people I'd seen for a day: some men in overalls standing around an old patched-up plane and pouring a liquid into canisters that were strapped rather provisionally to its wings. I guessed they were getting ready for some crop dusting. They didn't look up as I bumped past in my little car down the runway. It was like a scene from the beginning of time. Or the end: old machines with men in dirty clothes bending over them to keep alive something that should be dead.

Later I spoke to a Ukrainian friend about the airfield. Larisa is a kind of human metal-detector and has spent years passing her various sensitised monitors over the ruins of all sorts of Soviet and post-Soviet military darkness and other buried secrets across Crimea. At Balaklava, as we sat in a dockside cafe eating lunch, she showed me the marine caves carved out of the sandy rock across the inlet that had been the hidden berths for Soviet nuclear submarines. And Baherova base, she said, was not only a military airfield but was also one of the projected southern landing sites for the Buran, the Soviet rival to the United States' Space Shuttle – a nuclear weapon delivery device dressed up as something less nasty. The unmanned Buran flew once only, completing two orbits of the Earth and landing successfully at Baikonur in the desert steppe of Kazakhstan. The end of the cold war and the collapse of the Soviet Union aborted the development programmes of both the shuttle and the Energia, its rocket launcher. It never came to Baherova. What did, Larisa told me, was something nastier still. Nuclear waste from forty years of weapons testing at Semipalatinsk (the Soviet Union's principal test site), also on the Kazakh steppe, was removed by truck and by plane and, the rumours at least suggest, the airfield at Baherova, a closed and highly secure military establishment at the time, was one of the burial grounds. There might be dead machines entombed beneath the concrete runways now, ticking away with only their own poisonous clocks for company.

There was one last collecting site in the Zone at Chernobyl. It was to be the most astonishing of all. On the way into Prypiat, the town where the reactor's workforce had lived, we had to show our papers at another barrier. As the sleepy policeman ran his fingers down our names, a black woodpecker flew over us, coming from where we wanted to go. A carpenter-bird of big trees and deep forest, it leapt through the sky like a tool, a black hammer bouncing off the air it had tempered beneath. It landed behind us, clasping its sooty iron to the trunk of a tall pine.

After my year in Budapest I became a devotee of the frayed and failing communist empire and of the birdlife that went with it. I held on tight to my passport but relished travelling through the rubbish and the ruins. Though it was on its last legs the Eastern bloc felt unfinished and that made its people, even as they suffered, alive. I liked that. And I liked the low-watt interiors and the contrast with outdoor brightness and the birds that didn't care either way. But none of my scrapyard-pastoral adventures prepared me for the abandoned town of Prypiat where now only the black woodpecker is at home. We spent half a day there and, between the policeman on the way in and the policeman on the way out, we saw no one else. Fifty thousand people have vanished. Built to serve the plant at Chernobyl in 1970, it lived for just sixteen years. After the explosion in 1986 its population were put on buses and driven away over two days. 'Please make sure you have turned off the lights,' said the evacuation note that was issued to each household.

The town had been fully planned and purpose built: a space-age city for the happy atom plant. From the air its outline shows like a petal on a radiation sign, an inverted triangle on a stalk of road that runs from the reactors at Chernobyl. All the town buildings were boxily modern with flat roofs and austere facades. Ten-storey apartment blocks cut canyons away from the central square with lower civic structures between them. There were 160 residential buildings, a city hall, a palace of sport and culture, a hotel, a hospital, fifteen primary and five secondary schools, twenty-seven restaurants, thirty-five playgrounds and a funfair.

All the buildings are still there but now Prypiat is a forest. In a place we thought we'd made our own there are thousands upon thousands of trees. A green tide is lapping at the town. Wild trees returning to ground they were previously cleared from have met planted trees in the streets that have grown up and escaped from their concrete cordons. Everything else has stopped and is falling down and since the trees are still tenaciously alive and heading up they have taken charge. The effect is like rain inside your head. You cannot see out of yourself. A few of the roads through the town are still passable but trees narrow all of them. The asphalt surface is split as if rotten, and welters around strapping trunks. Every two- and three-storey building has been overgrown and is deep into its long dying in tree shade. Leaf ghosts camouflage grey concrete panels, where last year's emulsified foliage has printed itself on to the walls. This year's leaves are adjacent and ready. In other places the concrete is veined with green deltas of moss and water runs up the walls. The buildings seep. All the street lamps are now below the level of the green ceiling of the tree-canopy. They look tired. Rusted red stars hang from many of them like something between a bat and a discarded Christmas decoration. The upper parts of the eight- or ten-storey blocks remain above the forest but branches and leaves brush up against their lower floors like imploring children. And many of the blocks now have trees growing from their roofs or from a balcony or out of a broken window. Where, you wonder, do their roots reach? Is this what it feels like to have a bird nesting in your hair or a worm living in your head? A consoling birch cuddles a twenty-foot-high metal CCCP wreath-crest on top of one of the tallest buildings, the tree younger, smaller, more fragile than the concrete it grows from, but here for the duration.

Birnam Wood come to Dunsinane; Piranesi's crepitating Roman ruins; Mayan temples lost in the jungle; monkeys overrunning other gods in India; Max Ernst's vegetable-slime paintings; the ever-renewing Golden Bough; Ozymandias's instructions to the deaf desert; the revenge of Gaia – it all crowds in as thick as the pressing trees but nothing can truly assist with the profoundly unsettling task Prypiat puts before you. To stand in the forest that was once a town is to look *after* us. Down the wooded streets of Prypiat's arrested past you are bowled into the aftermath of man, into a future that has already arrived. I have been nowhere else that has felt as dead as here, been nowhere that made me feel as posthumous. And the strangest thing is that in this house of the dead, the dead have gone missing. To make fuller sense of it you would have to be an archaeologist of cities not yet built, or an interpreter of languages as yet unborn. Except, Prypiat is now and actually exists. Or was and did. And as bewildering as this is, this poisoned rewilding, it is all also bleakly appropriate to this concrete corner of the old empire.

'Actually existing socialism' was a sad coinage from the 1970s that described the way-station to happiness where the communist train had stopped, the best the Eastern bloc could then manage. It was meant to suggest that the radiant future was still on the timetable and that, despite difficulties – the grey cruelties of life and all the grief – what the east had was at least not what the west had. That, of course, was abundantly clear to everyone. The spurious ideological tag just rubbed the collective nose deeper into the rust. Soviet citizens were already well versed in double-speak and skilled at the clunky backwards living that was required of them. They knew the disappointment of the inevitable shortcomings of the imminent future, long before it arrived. 'Life has improved, comrades. Life has become more joyous,' Stalin famously said at the first all-union conference of Stakhanovites in 1935, having just presided over the terror-famine in Ukraine and on the verge of unleashing his great purge. 'The great shepherd' was one of Stalin's favourite epithets; grass and grasshoppers, the famished of Ukraine were forced to eat, until, when there was nothing left, they started on themselves. The louder Stalin's fanfare, the more cracked the trumpet sounded, though few dared declare it. The Finland Station was a terminus. Lenin, pickled, could last forever but no one could bring him back to life. His arm might be raised to the horizon and beyond or perhaps, as the joke used to say, he was just trying to hail a taxi. A taxi, because he'd missed the future which, long announced, turned out to have already arrived – though not at a railway station, but at a bus stop, and one where a tree grew where people might once have stood.

Lifeless neon letters marched across the pelmet of the 'Palace of Cultural Energy' at the dead heart of Prypiat. In the entrance hall there were flaking murals of science (lab-coated workers, test tubes and other laboratory kit) and agriculture (a basket of fruit and a hand severed by rot from the arm of a stout Soviet Ceres reaching to pick a red apple). I walked into a room, treading only on broken glass. Lying around an armchair pulled into its centre was a map of the best of us: cigarette butts, one sock and some scattered books about fish – the outline of a life. Someone had got up and left this room. Since it is forbidden to take anything from the Zone, I decided to leave something instead. I'd been using a postcard as a bookmark, a 1970s photograph of Wicken Fen (the windmill and reed beds, Adventurers' Fen beyond), and wrote on the back 'Field One for Field Four' and propped it on the brown armchair. Leaning against the walls of the next-door room were 1980s May Day procession portraits, ten-foot square and hand-painted, of Gorbachev and Eduard Shevardnadze and two others in uniform whom I didn't know, all blithe, optimistic, almost handsome. Their flat faces suited the place. In Prypiat everything human is thinned to screens that creak and judder through the solid and continuing trees, the apartment blocks like canvases flown in from grey skies, their broken windows like dark painted squares. Once in the foreground we are now barely part of the scenery.

One floor above the former leaders, two twenty-foot birches had grown through the parquet of a sports hall. Their green leaves throbbed in the interior light. They looked like trees brought inside to make a point. A Chekhov production could make use of them, the unsellable orchard inside us all, but that would be too easy, too glib. The trunks, the branches, the leaves have nothing to say. The Prypiat forest doesn't teach, it simply grows. It is not sublimely indifferent, not even plainly indifferent; it is just different. The real point is there is no point. There is no need for one. Overgrowth is not intrinsically menacing, it has nothing to do with us, even if we are what is overgrown. Other bosses, other regimes, pertain: yellow plums roll into life, rosehips bud like weapons. In an agricultural machine yard the huge grasshopper head of a rusted combine was tethered by three limes growing through its intricate mouth. In the vehicle workshop there were three inspection pits, a chair in the bottom of one. I climbed down and sat on it, five feet below the surface. The tiled trench seemed to close around me. I looked up and all I could see was silent green leaves.

We came out of the Exclusion Zone the next morning (though *out*, as Anders and Tim would remind me, is only relative). The sun hadn't shone for our last three days and the winter seemed keen to get on. We passed the old cooling ponds around the edge of the reactors and stopped to feed stale bread rolls to the ten-foot-long catfish that had got big on hot water. They came to the surface of the dark pond and opened their mouths, their pale jaws widening into drowned moons. Mementos of the nuclear days. As we watched I heard the creak of flying swans and six whoopers flew over, new in from the north, the colour of old snow, pulling the freeze with them. The swans alarmed a blackcap in a yellowing vine at the edge of the pond and it called a harsh cold *chack*, its concession to winter and perhaps the last thing it said before moving south. A handover of the seasons was underway for some. The politburo of cormorants, old men in old suits, stood unmoving on a gravel island.

As we crossed out of the Zone heavy rain came on. I asked Anders who his heroes were as a young naturalist. He laughed immediately at my question; he was struggling, he said, to even remember the Danish word. The clear-eyed scientific rigour of his youth shone from his face, but matters were further complicated because, he said, the Danish for *hero* is the same word as that for a species of freshwater fish found in the centre of Jutland.

The rain eased and the world was made good in front of us. We were released into it. There were bees and horses. Chickens dabbed at the roadside verges. Two dirty cows seen across an open field looked beautiful.

A cowherd with a furled umbrella under his arm moved towards them. Smallholdings were good too. A cord of cut wood was stacked between two apple trees. Old men in hats and women in headscarves walked to and from their gardens and fields; one man was carrying a white chicken under his arm, another a tin bucket bumping with muddy potatoes. Small boys rode by on grown-up bikes. In a puddle on the road, a drowned baby grass snake floated like a single cut stem of grass. Painted cottages sat warmly in the sun-bright. Orange nasturtiums fell over the wooden door of an outside privy. In gardens there were watermelons the size of boulders streaked lengthways, green and yellow, like cut fields. Concrete walls zigzagging Ukrainian blue and yellow ran along the village street. Between two plum trees a washing line was hung with pink knickers the size of small flags. Six pairs. I almost cried to see them. All the spotted flycatchers of Europe seemed to be snipping between the fruit trees and the cottage eaves in a non-stop tidying of the air. A table cut into the base of the trunk of a fat apple tree gathered windfalls from above like a ready-meal. There were hayricks and storks' nests and they looked the same. An orchard purred with bees as the sun came out. A one-legged man in a beret drove a motorbike with a sidecar down the middle of the road. A jay flew over a scarecrow. I collected my grasshoppers (the village was a control site for Anders and Tim) and picked a stem of grass; a dot of sap beaded at the break and I sucked it. Pulling wooden carts shaped like open coffins, the horses looked like they still lived in this place. After the rain they steamed. Anders asked: 'Perhaps you don't remember the smell of wet horse?'

Leaving Ukraine, you may proceed through the Green Channel at Kiev Airport if, as the sign says: 'You haven't got: Weapons, Explosives, Poisonous, Narcotic, Psychotropic, Drastic Substances and Medicine. Or Radioactive Materials. Or Flora and Fauna Objects, their parts and products obtained of them.'

I got back to England and in my waiting post was a letter from the council telling me to cut my hedge: 'I am aware that branches/foliage from trees/bushes growing within your premises are causing a partial obstruction of Happy Lane.'

Months later by chance I asked a friend what Lubianka means in Russian. Something, he said, like the place made of bark, or a basket made of bark, or a hut lined with bark, a cork-panelled room if you like, or a quiet place to sleep, or a place surrounded by trees where, whatever you said, or shouted, or wept couldn't be heard.

Autumn Fen

There are turf farms on the fens. Turf in the current sense of the word. The old diggings or turbaries where peat (also called turf) was cut for fuel are gone. Now the fen grass and its cradling fen earth are cut and shipped out in other ways. The level fields and the rich peat are good for growing lawns. Emerald-green squares alternate on the fen with arable acres and grasslands, and these brilliant smooth plots are the most disconcerting of all the fen fields.

One of the common effects of the fens is a roomy feel. You often catch them seeming spacious but hardly ever fully open. Despite appearing edgeless and held in their shallow basin by nothing more than the horizon, their fields have an interior air. The lawns of the turf fields give off this atmosphere more than anywhere else. They are like something incubated or cultured in a greenhouse without glass. The grass suggests walls that ought to be there but aren't. The lawns are so smart you expect a civic building, a crematorium, the stonework of an old university, or something comparably solid and grave to rise from them. Without a human edge their stage is very empty. Apart from a few rabbits and wagtails and the odd crow nothing ever stands on them. They are so level and smooth and the sown grass, when it comes, is so uniform and then so neatly managed, that looking at it you sense a missing dimension.

It is just *surface*. And that surface is cut by a giant lawnmower and then shaved by a machine that rolls up the lawn with a thin backing of peat into uniform widths to be stacked on a pallet and wrapped in clear plastic. Lorries drive on to the open-cast fields when the turf has been sliced from them and load it up and take it away down the lanes. The fens are unrolled like prayer-mats wherever they are required. A

214

kind of thin topiary is effected on these farms: the needy and parodic human transformation of nature, its diminution or its prostitution, into what Marvell, in his poem 'The Mower against Gardens', called a 'green seraglio', whereby fields of grass are cut to resemble a lawn which is grown to resemble a field of grass.

On a blustery early autumn day on the fen I once saw swallows settling on a turf field. At first they came with an air of exploratory trepidation and then, as more and more of them joined in, their dangling over the field took on a playful insouciance that looked like bird fun. They flew to the grass, as they do over water, angling their bodies horizontally above it and sliding lower and lower to its surface. And because that surface was so smooth and so flat – even smoother and flatter than water – they slowed their wings and gently stepped down on to it. Then they sat around on the short turf on their short legs as if they were doing it simply because they could. I have never seen that before. But it suited the lawn. It was a temporary fiction: a playground or a holiday. And the birds knew it.

Sometime around 1815 Coleridge wrote in his notebook: 'If a man could pass thro' Paradise in a dream, & have a flower presented to him as a pledge that his Soul had really been there, & found that flower in his hand when he awoke – Aye? and what then?' The fen, too, throws up flowers from paradise once in a while.

Chalk and flint break through the eastern fen edge like an exposed skeleton. The fens themselves are boneless. But for the remains they cradle, they are fleshy, soft and giving. So stoneless indeed that, as has happened, you might sink into them: 'I have known a riding horse to be bogged and have to be shot to save it from cold and starvation.' So stoneless that the song thrushes that live in the rare fen hedges find it hard to make an anvil for breaking open the snails they love to eat, and I have seen them use the bottom rung of a metal gate for the purpose, leaving it sticky with snail guts. You cannot build on the open fen – houses lean and roads ripple on the moving surface of the soil. Only on an island could Ely cathedral be built. Only on an island would you bury your dead.

It wasn't always like this. The fen has had a wooded past as well as a marine one. When Alan Bloom and his men were attempting to deal, as he thought necessary, with Burwell Fen, opening drains, ploughing up reeds, filling the turf pits and generally scrabbling around in the earth, they found assorted relics: a trepanned human skull alongside beaver skulls, deer antlers and the jawbones of wild boar. Others found wolf remains and a 'Roman slave-chain' with a 'lock for the attachment of the log of wood'. More commonly, Bloom bumped into a buried sleeping wood itself. Lying on the blue gault clay below the surface peat of the fen was a preserved thick lattice of fallen trees, a layer of wattle through the daub. The first day they opened up the soil on Burwell Fen they hit a trunk. Parts of the fen went on to yield up to thirty trees per acre, a corner, Bloom says, of 'what was once a mighty oak forest'.

Bog oaks have long been found across the southern peat fens. They still turn up. Shrinking peat and deep working ploughs pull them to the surface and they continue to make the local news when they appear. The wooden treasure, keels of oak, lying beneath a wet treeless place have excited and exercised almost every fen writer and it is a given that fen books will pitch in to the debate around the origins of the vegetable antiquities. Often there are photographs of men standing in bare muddy fields staring into a trench with a blackened trunk lying there like a great dead thing. These oaks were splinters in the fen flesh. Clearing water not trees was thought to have fixed this place. That the wet of the fens wasn't their first story was baffling, troubling even, and the discovered woods, like the fields in drag, were attacked with a furious zeal as if there was something devilishly wrong about them.

Bloom solicits the opinions of his fieldworkers: 'one man said he was sure they floated there, washed down from the uplands in some great flood. Another said that the Romans cut them down. But the belief that they raised themselves to near the surface naturally was quite prevalent.' Bloom himself doesn't credit the fen version of Birnam Wood come to Dunsinane, the oaks' spontaneous birthing and upward climb, but the trees trigger a mixed reaction in him: they are amazing 'primeval monsters', the leftovers of a bigger world, some with trunks up to 108 feet long and four feet thick; but they are also a terrible nuisance, 'great ugly things' that offend a farming man and which must be blasted out of the ground with gelignite.

Some of the wood was hard, some soapy soft; as it dried on the fen top it often shivered to bits. Thomas Browne, writing in 1658, guessed that the 'Moore-logs' that he knew well in Norfolk were the 'undated ruines of windes, flouds or earthquakes' and older than the cypress of the ark of Noah, which was believed otherwise to be the oldest of all wood. Alan Bloom ages the trunks on Burwell Fen at 7,000 years. Eric Ennion, in his book, thinks the oaks half that. James Wentworth Day, magus of Wicken, declares their age to be 'unguessable' but guesses anyway at ten times Bloom's estimate; they are, he says, 'not less than 70,000 years old'. Charles Lucas, like Ennion and Ennion's father a doctor in Burwell (in the latter part of the nineteenth century) and also a keen local antiquarian, would prefer to have the oaks falling in a crisis at the Crucifixion, as if to deny Christ's murderers their raw material, but his literal mind won't quite allow this: 'the Fen cataclysm was certainly not then, because that was in the Spring, and the Fen trouble was not till the autumn – probably about September, as the trees were in full leaf and fruit was abundant'.

Neither the beavers of Burwell nor Roman executioners felled the trees. The oaks were horizontal long before either. And they are not only oaks: alder, birch, yew and pines have also been found. All of them pre-date the fens and, indeed, it was the fens that killed them. Most bog oaks are thought to be between 3,500 and 4,000 years old, though some older trees aged up to 6,000 years have surfaced. They grew in drier times across dozens of miles of ground that is fen now, but wasn't then. Wicken Fen thickening with carr woodland as it dries out is the bog oak story in reverse. Between 5,000 and 4,300 years ago with rising sea levels came a great flood, more properly known as an extensive marine transgression, which inundated the northern part of the fen area from the Wash southwards. The sea dropped marine silt and the fenland basin became flooded with fresh water as its drainage systems stalled. With a new gradient to climb to reach the sea, the rivers draining from the south were hindered in their progress. Wetlands spread over the waterlogged ground. The trees that are now under Burwell Fen drowned and fell into the emerging and accumulating freshwater peat, which kept them buried and preserved. In some places the trees are scattered erratically, elsewhere stands lie with their crowns all pointing to the north-east, and appear to have fallen together, perhaps in a wild storm harrowing out of the west.

Another photograph in one of the fen books shows a single bog oak lying lengthways in its trench in the foreground, while behind it at the horizon, across miles of flat grey fen, is the ghostly outline of Ely Cathedral like another fallen trunk or a beached whale: huge hopeless things under the withering sky. Seeing these tree-bodies cradled on the plain summons the moment of their collapse: a single tree falling on its own into the peat, one splash across twenty miles of new fen and then nothing but the wet ground closing over the trunk. John Clare knew that sound, two or three fallen trees away, across the fens in Northamptonshire. He has a word for it all to himself in the dictionary, a word for those downed fen trees. *Gulch* as a verb can mean to fall or plunge heavily upon, and the only citation (though spelled differently) in the OED is from Clare's 'The Village Minstrel' of 1821: 'Ne'er an axe was heard to sound, / Or a tree's fall gulsh'd the ground'.

Bloom's heaving out or blowing up of bog oaks, long after their gulch, takes its place in the great and general gutting of the fens – the removal of what is in them to make them what they are. The trees are also part of something like a conversation that has gone on along-side the digging and the draining between what is buried and what is known. Rinsing the water from the fens and drying their soil hasn't really worked in the way that Bloom and the Adventurers and others would have had it, but the attention downwards has meant that a lot of hidden things have come to light and have been spotted, prodded and poked. The eastern edge of the fens, where Burwell and other villages run along the base of a chalk ridge, is dotted with Roman settlements. In 1942, the same year that Alan Bloom was tripping over bog oaks on Burwell Fen, the Mildenhall late-Roman treasure hoard was ploughed up. A little to the north, about nine miles from Burwell, just over the county border in Suffolk, twenty-seven pieces of silver were found on a run of land at the point where it crept out of the wet. The jewel of the hoard, a great dish nearly two foot across, was made in the fourth century a long way away (the nearest likely workshop was in Trier in present-day Germany) but its half-amphibious half-pastoral relief decoration is apt for its final resting place in the earth of a field on the fen edge.

The dish, like the fen basin itself, tells stories of the meeting of the wet and the dry, the exuberant and the sober, the planned and the unpredictable. The central figure is the mask of a marine god, Neptune or Oceanus. He is a green man salted to sea with large staring eyes, a beard of toothed seaweed and four dolphins plunging through his long wild hair as through surf. Around him are two concentric friezes of anarchic bliss. The inner ring is a revel of nereids or sea nymphs and assorted seahorses, crab-men and eely things in the thick of a marine transgression or orgy. The outer, broader, ring depicts the triumph of Bacchus over Hercules 'in a vivid manner' as the British Museum catalogue says: 'Bacchus stands naked, his long hair crowned with a diadem and his foot resting on the back of a panther.' As well as the drunken and meandering Hercules there are satyrs, dancing maenads and a priapic and shaggy Pan whose skipping hooves and parted furry thighs are terrifyingly well done. The find of the great dish close to and in the same year as Bloom's bog oaks is a coincidence, of course, but the possibility that other worlds – wet or green – might exist around or beyond the world we have made plays across both sets of reliefs: the carved silver figures and the corrugated surface of the fen.

There is a further and related strangeness about the fallen trees that worries at the fenmen, and it is because of this, I think, that the oaks are lodged so often in their books. Raising them out of the earth breaks up the order of things. The fallen wood undermines our sense of how farming works and what the soil is for and, for a moment at least, it shakes our understanding of the world, suggests that the spring might sometimes fail, and catches at the permanent awkwardness of farming, the way it wants to be in step but is always tripping over, the way the surface is always determined by its undertow. Earth is made of dead things and is a place to put dead things but life springs from it. We know that. Without rot there can be no green. And green in time will feed rot. Dung heaps smoke with the life of their deaths. The peat of the fens is made from dead and rotted fen, mostly reeds and sedge. The earth is served. New reeds and sedge grow out of dead reeds and sedge. Mole-sticks grow into willow trees and scythe handles are kept fresh under water and wet grass.

Yet on Burwell Fen the peat has chosen – the trunks in the trenches show it – to keep some things unrotted, to preserve the fallen trees and even – magically it seems – some green leaves, but only so long as the tree and its leaves are kept underground. At the surface, the very place we make green things grow, the treasure – a bloom out of paradise – cannot be kept. Its gold becomes dross. It seems wrong that by bringing stuff up into our air we kill it, but the buried truth of this shivers us awake. And deep down we have known it forever, known that the growing season is only part of the year, that death rhymes with life, that Persephone comes up out of a crack in the earth but must return there, that winter is a rehearsal for oblivion, that we grow old as we think on these things, and that it is a shock each time we discover them to be true.

What lies beneath and what will it tell us? Near Whittlesey swaths of mown grass were found beneath five feet of peat. Did a sudden summer flood come and cause the mowers to leave in a hurry? Why didn't they return? At Upware a blacksmith's forge was found beneath ten feet of peat, with tools, and some metalwork ready for use and some half-finished. Where were the horses and where were the men? On Burwell Fen James Wentworth Day reports, 'they found the dead, dried and pickled body of a fenman of a thousand years ago, standing bolt upright in the remains of a dug-out canoe. His long black hair hung down the leather skin of his face and neck. His right hand was poised and crooked as though to throw a spear, whilst on his legs were still the leather buskins and cross garterings. He could not survive the outer air and crumbled too soon into desiccation and dust.'

Green suits couldn't make the Manea commune grow. Only so long as Burwell man and the fen oak leaves are buried, will he be ready to fight, and they stay green. The upper green world, our green world, turns out to be inhospitable to other green worlds. Grass grows up green but other life brought to the surface dies. On Burwell Fen Alan Bloom dug up a namesake: 'we found leaves that were still almost green at the instant a tree was rolled out, leaves of some other shrub like large privet, but within minutes of exposure to sun and air they faded and crumbled away'.

Watching a 4,000-year-old green leaf die on a would-be green field is to sit once again in the little cinema on the fens where blind Milton's creation film flickers forwards or backwards (it is hard to say which) on an old white sheet hung between two hawthorns, the earth moving with death pulling free from it, while a bittern bumps somewhere in rusty reeds in the background, and countless moths are drawn to the stream of projected light.

At the end of each afternoon for an autumn week, I went on to the fen at Wicken to watch snipe on a pool. A watery flash on an old field of Alan Bloom's one-time farm had dried out enough to reveal a tongue of soft peaty mud. The snipe liked the mud. The feeding was good and the birds, which otherwise favour the cover of grass and sedge, had moved out into the open. I'd last seen them here in June when the displaying birds tossed themselves into the sky as feathered rockets, dancing and drumming like midsummer hippies at a solstice festival, but these autumn birds were different. Around six o'clock most days sunlight streamed clean and low from the west and brilliantly lit the pool and its birds. By the end of the week more than a hundred snipe were on show. There were scarcer species as well, ruff and black-tailed godwits and green sandpipers, and I confess that I was hoping for something rarer still but, through the week of watching, the snipe came to be more than enough. I spent eight solid hours looking only at them, the birds filling my vision, big in the telescope. Not that I could now accurately reproduce what I saw or properly describe the bar code of browns across their backs and wings, the tussock of dried wetland grasses, rushes and sedges, which they have taken for their plumage. Part of the genius of snipe crypsis is that, although when you see them you are in no doubt that they are snipe, the birds declaring their *snipehood* immediately and obviously (round head, beady eyes, long bill, all else streaky), the moment you look away, you cannot rebuild them as anything other than a clump of fen grass.

In the pool the snipe were at home. On an inventor's blueprint their bill would seem unrealistically ludicrous, like a bird with a trunk. Looking at them, working the ooze, that thought never crossed my mind. They fed by dipping and tip-tapping into the mud either directly or through the water. Most tip-tapped once every five seconds and, roughly once every three tip-taps they got something. They would then pull their bill halfway from the mud or the water and draw up whatever they had caught in little nibbling actions. This is the 'suction' that Byron said woodcocks used. If they had waded out into the pool, the snipes' dipping sometimes went up to their eyes. I watched them tighten their faces as they winced a little. Now and again they dipped deeper still and their heads submerged entirely, but they were less keen on this and after any plunge like that they would shake their heads clean and dry, and stop feeding for a bit. Some, straying deeper still, had to swim back for a foot or so towards shallower water, and looked as they went like hastily opened coracles made out of straw.

Whatever they were doing each bird would occasionally cock its head to one side and look up at the sky with one eye. When they weren't feeding, they preened, twisting and stretching themselves around the tip of their bill, never getting within five inches of their face. Parties of the birds put the wind up themselves sometimes and hurried off the pool, their *crisp* calls as they took flight sounding like an elastoplast being ripped from the skin of the fen. Though they fed close to one another on the ground, there was always some agitation in the air, and this infected them when they first landed again. Coming back to earth, they made curious matador-style movements for a few moments, fanning their tails and laying their beaks on to their breasts, as if half remembering their courtships. It was like seeing the end of a dance with the dancers inadvertently continuing their steps after the music has stopped.

There was something of a country-disco or a ceilidh about the whole scene. The snipe, like farmers, fresh from their fields and dressed in the colours of the acres around them, squeezed into smart-suit versions of the land they live and work in, the mud cleaned from their fingernails for one night of the year only.

The nature reserve at Wicken Fen has been preserved for more than a hundred years. But the fens being as they are, being the fens, means that *preservation* is not the right word and nor is *reserve*. Wicken might now be intended for nature but the fen is really a ruin, an abandoned open-air factory or series of out-of-town workshops with centuries of human use behind them and many different quasi-industrial lives. But because everything has been greened over, the old working fen is hard to see. The signs say it is the last of the undrained fens. And, whatever you know of the worked past of the place, its vegetated fullness today encourages you to think that the landscape must have been 'natural' in the old days even if the fen was busy: the floods kept coming, the crops were wild, there were many people on the fens but they were foraging rather than farming. We should guard against this thought. And much work has been done at Wicken itself to teach us why. The fens before the twentieth century were not really any more natural (or less) than they are now. Natural, indeed, is another of those bastard words.

Wicken was once a place where, to catch moths, white sheets were hung over bushes, and treacle smeared on corks that were nailed to posts. People came to the fen and worked the sheets for science; others did the same for cash. But the fen has also been a farm, woodpile, brickworks, turbary, charcoal kiln, fishery, and greenhouse. It was once what could be called a plant-hire centre. The harsh and durable leaves of great fen sedge, *Cladium mariscus*, a native present at Wicken for at least 5,000 or 6,000 years, made it a highly valuable crop for thatching. Before the prevalence of daily newspapers, dried sedge also made good kindling. It was carried off the fens on a shallow-boat-cum-giant-floating-haystack. It was landed at villages around the fen edge and carted to towns further afield. Testimony to sedge's importance as a crop is the host of local laws and regulations that governed quotas and harvesting dates, and ruled against the employment of sub-harvesters or hired gang-labour. Sedge cutting was lucrative and fiercely protected work. Like eels, sedge at times became fen currency: payments were made in *seggesilver*. Through the twentieth century, sedge cutting – and almost all the old functions along with the customs of the fen – came to an end. For a few years during the Second World War, some ghostly echoes of the busy and exploited countryside came back. Alan Bloom's farm in the fen nibbled at the edges of Wicken from the south-east side of Wicken Lode. Burwell Fen was drained once again – Eric Ennion's recovered wilderness dug out into 'productive' land. And on the reserve at Wicken itself, a new use was found for old trees. Charcoal made from alder buckthorns was a crucial ingredient in shell fuses and since the trees were invading the fen, they were dug for victory as well as to keep the fen fenny.

The rich flora that was found when the reserve was established at Wicken was associated with these long-running harvests of the fen. Wicken was thick with plant life *because* it had been worked. When sedge cutting was stopped and the fen 'preserved', vegetation succession led to the reduction of some species and the loss of others. This happened to the fen orchid, *Liparis loeselii*, with its delicate-fingered yellow-green flowers that entwine as if they are holding hands. It was discovered in Cambridgeshire in 1660 by John Ray, who found it 'in the watery places' of the fens, and knew it as the *Dwarf Orchies of Zealand*. It was last seen at Wicken in 1945 and is now extinct in the county. When peat cutting ended the orchid went with it, vanishing hand in hand with the turf pits.

In the middle of the twentieth century at Wicken, the botanist Harry Godwin and others realised that taking a sedge crop every three or five years, or cutting grass and rush litter annually from what was called the 'mowing marsh', 'did not arrest the main reaction of the primary succession'. In other words, unrotted vegetation accumulated, and from it peat continued to form even when the sedge was harvested. The ground rose higher above the water level and in places the fens were naturally drying out. Similarly, submerged vegetation was shallowing the water it was submerged in. Soon enough it wouldn't be sufficiently wet for water plants to grow. Trees and shrubs would have liked the way the fen was going, but because it was being cut for sedge their saplings were as well: trees couldn't become established so long as the fen was worked. When the fen was 'reserved' and no longer cut, the trees eagerly made their way. Active management has been needed ever since to stop Wicken Fen becoming Wicken Wood.

I was on the fen when summer turned to autumn. Each incoming season is made out of the ruins of the last. Summer's drying gives way to autumn's fall. A quiet and still day had come and passed. In the autumn the sun itself can look dead in the sky, as if its light has already been switched off somewhere, and all we get is the colour of the bulb. This was such a day. But then, in the late afternoon, a little local breeze cooked up close to the ground of the fen at Burwell. There is more thistle than grass in these acres in August, and I watched the dry lick of the warm air beginning to lift the thistledown. Every thistle-head had seeded and there were so many that the whole fen was draped in a long loose scarf of dirty snow. The tiny seeds on each head are dark and the plumes of down sandy pale and almost transparent. As the plant grows, both seed and plumes crowd tight together but the whole head loosens as its dries and sets and the seeds (the outermost ones first) are pushed up and out while the down froths around them. This was the day. Again the year rhymed with itself: the season now ended with thistledown in August that began with willow-down in May when the trees along the lode shook their swaddled seeds out across the fen in drifts, and I had watched a party of swallows rag-picking at the ready-made nest-lining.

On the first autumn day on the fen the wind sometimes took a whole thistle-head and sometimes just a hank of down. The loosest heads were the first to be prised from their prickly anchor but even these lift-offs involved countless local struggles, the breeze picking at the ties that held the down to its plant, the down committed to its flight but still not going willingly. Once these negotiations were over the cottony seed heads were lifted, raised, and then encouraged above the thistles and the rest of the field of grass, sorrel, loosestrife, wild carrots and docks.

As they blew, the strands snagged on one another, riding the air like soft chain-shot, wool-gathering as they went. Everything was floating towards the south-east in a silent, spreading, milky broadcast. I stepped off the bank and followed. Like snow pushed away from the earth, the down sometimes rose in the wind and climbed upwards. Other clots of spindrift thickened the spiders' webs on the fences to caricatures; or caught at the corner of the eyes of the bullocks on the field or stuck to their shitty tails; or bearded the stubble on my chin. Most of the down seemed to catch and stop on other thistle-heads within the big field, but some floated out of my sight far beyond the fen. A stray I followed with binoculars seemed to buck the breeze and move sideways over new lands where its novelty attracted a passing black-headed gull, prompting it to scoop its wings overhead and redirect its flight to try to catch at the morsel.

There was more. Thistle is goldfinch food and there were dozens of them, at least 200 all together, feeding in loose jingling flocks on the burst heads. Their expert beaks made repeated intimate delvings into the thistle hearts. The wool of the down smothered their red faces as if it were dabbing at a wound, until the birds surfaced and superbly husked the tiny seed they had picked. But the breeze and the blow distracted them and made them flighty. Group after group lifted as one from among the thistles, each pulled by the bird ahead of them and pulling those behind. Their departures and their landings released still more down and fanned the drift yet further. The golden bars along their wings caught the light like the slub of silk, and twinkling their toy piano music they moved off through the floating down like itinerant weavers flying their precious thread through the homespun, until the whole fen became a field of the cloth of gold.

Draining and pumping have finally achieved what they have been trying to do for 2,000 years: the fens at Wicken and nearby at Burwell no longer flood. But the place remains unsurrendered. Lowering water levels across the wider area have reinforced the effects of vegetation succession and of the soil being raised by accumulating peat above the water table. The fens are drying out. But where part-rotted stuff builds up the land, the wastage of the drying peat takes it away. So long as peat is waterlogged it remains intact, but if it dries, then oxygen is able to worm into its top layers and exposes them to bacterial and fungal attack (the rot truncated resumes) and to direct chemical oxidation. The wasting soil that remains changes, too. Because of its desiccation, the surface peat at Wicken had acidified to the point where more than sixty species of 'acidicolous mosses and liverworts and ferns', all new to the fen, had been reported by the time Harry Godwin wrote his book in 1978.

To my shame, I don't really know what a liverwort is. I've looked at the pictures and fingered the guides – detailing the 300 British species of these overlooked and under-sung neighbours to the mosses – and I realise I have probably trodden on some but I am not a botanist and still less a bryologist. I like the sound, though, of those who not only know but love their liverworts. One of the extraordinary facts about Burwell and Wicken is how many people have raised, on its few squares of fen ground, their liverwort flags and others equally lovely, equally obscure. These hundred fen acres have prompted an astonishing harvest of close-focused scientific discoveries and exploratory inventories, of *slodging* or *glaiving* with a hand-lens or a notebook. So much so, that we must open a new chapter for the liverworters, the mosquito men and the followers of the harvestmen, and many like them in the great soggy encyclopaedia of the place, drying now on the washing line slung between the pylons marching across the fens. We must add their names to the pages of prospectors and projectors, the old-guard fenland drainers, the new-fangled rewetters, the bird lovers and mole haters, and all the soft-spotters, curio-gatherers and pseudo-historians in between.

This epic surveying is best captured in a book that I cannot afford to buy and could hardly read anyway, but which, because it exists, makes me happy. It proves, I think, that attention to detail is a species of love. *The Natural History of Wicken Fen* edited by Professor J. Stanley Gardiner in six parts and running to 652 pages was fully made hereabouts. Published in 1932 by Bowes and Bowes in Cambridge and printed in the city, it is a vast sponge that has taken up the greatest draught possible of peaty water and with that everything that floats in the fens. It raises a model of the place even though it is made of flat type on a flat page (perfect for the flat lands), and draws a bright map of it even though it is made of words and figures without colours or contours (perfect for the zero-line fen). In the library it barely stirs in its sleep within the leaden chest of its covers. But this book-sponge, which is also an ark and which is also a brain, could be set back down over the place and would fit it perfectly, so fully has the looking at absorbed the looked at. Here come the plants, and the Lepidoptera, Orthoptera, Paraneuroptera and Neuroptera, Hirudinea, Hemiptera-Heteroptera, spiders and harvestmen, Phytoplankton, Ichneumonidae, Mollusca, Coleoptera, Oligochaeta, Thysanura, fossil vertebrates, Collembola, Diplopoda and Chilopoda, sawflies, Copepoda, the Cambridgeshire Planarians, Cladocera, Trichoptera, Bryophyta, mosquitoes, Psocoptera, Ephemeroptera, Ostracoda, and the Entomostraca, and then, mopping it all up once again, on pages 637 to 643, the freshwater sponges of the Cam basin.

Last but not quite, for on page 644 of *The Natural History of Wicken Fen* begin the 'Omissions and Additions'. And here is the most articulate scientific incarnation imaginable of the fen trope of the open ending, the wet fade, or the dissolve. Life forms have been missed. We forgot the fungus flora! And the Diptera! And, as the professor explains, it is not entirely our fault: 'I have long tried to find a student who would be interested in the free-living nematodes of this country.' I know the feeling. You get can get laughed at if you have a pair of binoculars, let alone a butterfly net or a pooter. But, even incomplete, I love the *Natural History* for its extravagant harvest and heave-to of all the tiny things, each threshed for their truth and laid into the great floating barn of the book. Actually, I love it for being incomplete as well, for ultimately not being able to cage or net, drain or preserve the teem that passed in front of J. Omer Cooper, the Rev. C. E. Tottenham, P. W. Richards, Robert B. Benson, D. J. Lewis, G. J. Kerrich, A. G. Lowndes, G. P. Bidder, R. Moylan Gambles, and so many more. And I love it also for illuminating, if only for moments when you open their dry pages, some of the bright filaments that made up the lives of those initials and doctorates, all of them now spun into the dark along with their samples and gone down, like them, with their nets.

I did see a rarity. Not long after she had moved to the fens and we were exploring the local area together, Claire and I bumped into a vagrant, a collared pratincole, that should have been on the other side of Europe but which we flushed from the muddy scrape at Tubney Fen on our first visit there. It was exciting enough, the bird is beautiful like a large sandy swallow with an equally buoyant flight and a rather piratical hawking manner, and when the news got out people hurried from across the county to see our prize. It was the fourth ever seen in Cambridgeshire. The first record in the county was reported not far from our bird. Leonard Blomefield, great diary keeper of the turning year, sent notice of one shot on Wilbraham Fen on 21 June 1835. Like that one, lost and shot, gone into the dark, the bird we saw revealed little of itself. It had appeared from nowhere and it flew on the same afternoon when our backs were turned and without us seeing it leave. The bird had gone wrong in its journeys and perhaps was trying to correct its ways. Or was it less purposeful than that and forced to fly without direction, unable to rest, though exhausted and disoriented? Or was it sick, its compass skewed, its head screaming with bad noise? Or perhaps, more simply, the Tubney mud didn't suit. We would never know if it found its home again.

The same day, just before we spotted the pratincole, we heard a wood sandpiper whistling once and then the triplets of greenshank calls. From the overcast August sky six birds spilled down, one sandpiper and five greenshanks, tumbling towards the small pool of water on the fen. There were lambs in the field next door, newly separated from their mothers and crying miserably, and the birds' calls made them sound even more bereft and feeble. To see any migrant bird alter its flight course, to know that below it – as it flies – it has seen a place it either knows or wants to know, prickles at our sense of the Earth and the seasons. The waders lingered even less than the pratincole, the wood sandpiper merely dipped towards the mud and never landed, but the inland day on the roomed fen was released by those birds moving through it, plumbing south, tugged by the flash of silvery wet beneath them. The bar-tailed godwits I had watched coming down to feed in the spring half a mile from here arrived from the south and went on to the north; the wood sandpiper and the greenshanks came from the north and headed south. It was as simple and as good as that. The world moves, and watching those moving birds you feel it doing so.

The Fenland Research Committee, and five strips of fen known as the Godwin Plots at Wicken, followed up and extended the work of *The Natural History of Wicken Fen* by, in effect, bringing all its authors and all its life forms together into one ecosystem. The story of the fens was fully worked out from their heart. They grew it themselves. Geology doesn't come close enough to the surface of the fens: too much has happened too recently for the rocks below to pertain. The fens are too young, too plastic, too earthy and too wet. To be explained, the rubbery place needed ecology, with its understanding of the bend and give of life, of co-evolution and of the tangled mingling of things, the way dryness gives way to wet, and wet in turn makes dry.

In 1921 Cambridge University's new-formed Botany School Ecology Club got on their bikes and cycled north from Cambridge to the fens. The riders were led by Arthur Tansley, sometime clerk in the Ministry of Munitions and future student of Sigmund Freud, as well as crusading new phytologist or plant scientist. Among his *domestiques* was Harry Godwin, who later joked he was 'pitchforked' by Tansley into becoming secretary of the British Ecological Society. But at Wicken, Godwin got interested. With Tansley, in 1923, he marked out five scientists' fields, five fen plots, and began an investigation asking questions about plant succession that is still evolving today and which counts as among the world's longest-running scientific experiments. The first plot was never to be cut. The second was to be cut every four years. The third every three. The fourth every two. The fifth every year. This management, with its echoes of Biblical crop-rotation and Joseph's harvest dreams, has, over many years, produced different vegetation patterns and different degrees of succession. The plots further underline how Wicken Fen is not a natural relic of undisturbed vegetation, but the combination of wild growth and anthropogenic change, or a kind of green archaeology.

The Fenland Research Committee, which started in 1932, the year *The Natural History of Wicken Fen* was published, worked on a kind of succession of the mind. Stratigraphy was at its heart – the meaning of each layer of the fen and the different ways those archived strata might be prised apart and interpreted, and then re-laid with cumulative effect. To learn to read the ground, people had to know about pollen and the sea and ice and rivers and rot. Archaeologists were needed, biologists and geologists, professionals and amateurs. The vice-president of the committee was Major Gordon Fowler, the manager of water transportation for a sugar-beet factory. Godwin described him as 'a massive hearty man'. He had lost a leg in the First World War but, even with what Godwin called his 'ersatz' model, he remained active in 'boxing, hockey and sailing'. Fowler's specialism was roddens, the riverbeds of extinct natural waterways in the fens revealed by the wastage of the land around them, and which show as ghostly serpentine shapes or phantom limbs through crops and ploughed fields. The 'imaginative Ely schoolboy', Anthony Vine, who traced many of these long-abandoned meandering river channels, helped Fowler in his researches. They were joined by the geologist O. T. Jones with his 'quiet but withering Welsh accent'; the archaeologists C. W. Phillips, an 'amiable, generous giant', and Miles Burkitt, who had explored sites in France and Spain with the pope of prehistory, the Abbé Breuil; and the (more recently) celebrated eccentrics, the archaeologist and loony parapsychologist T. C. Lethbridge, and O. G. S. Crawford, the aerial archaeology officer of the Ordnance Survey. Meanwhile, and keeping the gentlemen and scholars on the straight and narrow, Miss Robin Andrew prepared slides of microscopic pollen. It was these, it turned out, that had the most to tell.

Godwin repeatedly took the committee and his students out into the fens, having learned much from his early bike rides. He was famous for his field trips. He walked and talked fast and there are stories of him heading enthusiastically through the densest or wettest of vegetation, resulting in a single file of students, with those at the forefront writing his comments down and passing back the information by word of mouth to the rearguard. What the last undergraduate wrote is not known.' But Godwin and the committee asked, as committees will, what kind of synthesis might be possible if you tie the head of the snake to its tail, if you bring people who know one thing together with people who know another. Out of it came the first multidisciplinary studies of any kind in Britain. Godwin's findings in post-glacial fenland have been called a 'landmark in Quaternary [i.e. the present era] research'. Just a *landmark* would be good enough in the fens.

On the south bank of Burwell Lode I watched a young man, tattooed and pierced, catching an eel. Like all fish it seemed to cool the air as it came wet up into it, but like no other fish it seemed at first to come towards its end, wanting to climb out of the water, twisting on its hook and up the line, refusing to be a fish, and performing some speeded-up account of evolution or of its own past as a sometime land-thing. One silky foot of muscle slalom. A rib of water. An electricity cable shocking itself. I shuddered to remember the country road on the bank of a lough in County Clare where my fishing life began and ended at the age of eleven, with an eel pulled by a worm on a hook from the dark water into the rainy air. And me, terrified by this snake on a string, breathing that same air as I was, and keen, so keen, to live that I couldn't touch it, couldn't still its writhing, couldn't hold it to me to take the hook from its man-mouth, couldn't even cut the line, but instead laid the rod on the road and, as the eel bucked and shimmied like something newly amputated, I picked up a grey breezeblock loosed from a jetty and with both hands launched it on to the fish. Then I first heard that particular sound, the wet fibrous crunch, which is living bone being broken. With the tip of my boot I shifted the breezeblock. The eel was down but not out. I needed it dead. There was another breezeblock and then a third before the thing stopped moving and had lost all of its living shapes and became part of the rain on the road. At the lode I left the eel swimming in the air on its hook and hurried on, asking its fisherman if he would eat it. 'Only', he said, 'if I was Polish.'

*   *   *

John Ray's *Flora* of Cambridgeshire was published in 1660. It was the first-ever county flora in Britain and appeared in the soggy middle of the great fen-adventuring century. Today it seems to have been pulled from a similar fen-trawling net that threw up those more recent books, *The Natural History of Wicken Fen* and Harry Godwin's *Fenland* book. The connection is fundamental: it is to do with kneeling to the wet earth and noting how everything you see there lives together. The effect of the books – on me at least – is also the same. They are works of learning and knowledge, but they are made from such a mixed unfixed place and in such a mixed unfixed way, that they are perfect fen books, and contribute brilliantly to, in Coleridge's phrase, keeping alive the heart in the head.

The *Flora* (more properly the *Catalogus Plantarum circa Cantabrigiam nascentium*) was Ray's first book; he went on to write on fishes, birds, insects and mammals, becoming the country's greatest all-round naturalist. He started out local. He was born in rural Essex; his mother was a herbalist and his father a blacksmith. But he was clever and went to Cambridge University and studied and then lectured in Greek, Mathematics and the Humanities. He knew a lot. The world began to extend away and ripple around him. He became a friend of Thomas Browne among other myth-busters and general-surveyors. Ten years after his Cambridgeshire book he wrote a British flora and, later, three volumes and 2,000 pages of an *Historia plantarum*, describing 6,000 plant species. It was Ray's botanical *Synopsis* (a successor to his British flora) that Jean-Jacques Rousseau carried as his field-guide during his British excursion in 1766.

Ray apologised for any omissions in these books, saying, what else could be expected from one mere man who 'must needs plough the whole field with his own hand'? The Cambridgeshire county *Flora*, a book made from close-looking and local fieldwork or *simpling* (the lovely term for going after – especially medicinal – flowers), was where Ray began. It was mostly written in Latin and my botanising is poor but the *Flora* still reads (translated and explained) as a marvellously fresh-air account of the county (its wetlands especially) coming into focus as flower after flower and grass after grass is picked out in front of us.

Writing later in 1696, Ray was the first to use the word *botany* and the field study of flowers dates from him, and his six years of 'long walks of exploration' into the fens and the wider county. In his preface to the *Flora* he declares that his intention on these journeys was 'to gaze with his own eyes on the nature of things' and to 'gain wisdom by [his] own experience rather than from somebody else's brain'.

Everything swam in those years while Ray knelt to the wet and scrutinised what he saw. Life shifted in front of any observer. The names of things were constantly moving off. Go and stand anywhere on the Equator if you are not from there, and watch its wildlife, and you'll get an idea of what this must have felt like. Plant nomenclature and taxonomy were as unstable as the ground that the unnamed or the misnamed grew from. The boggy elemental fens, half water, half earth, were apt expressions of the dynamism of nature. The world there was turned upside down every winter.

As a concession to the precise specificities of the general wet, Ray moves into English when he describes where he finds the flowers he found. In this way he makes an addition to the great watery plainsong of the fens. But by being faithful to the plants' places and wanting to be clear about their localities, Ray writes a world of local difference and adaptation and, so doing, prepares the ground, as it were, for particular species. One of his plants is found 'in the moory places', another 'on the boggy grounds', a third 'in the osier holts', and so on: 'where toads are found', 'in water courses', 'in moist and marshy localities', 'where waters are stagnant', 'in divers ditches', 'in a Moorish place where they digge turves', 'in damp meadows', 'in sluggish rivers', 'in infinite other ditches'.

There are crops as well as wild plants in the catalogue. There were no potatoes in the fens then, no cabbage, no beet, no celery. But Ray noticed seven varieties of wheat. And with this in mind he poked around in another *crop*, the dissected gut of a fen bustard, and 'found it stuffed with hemlock seeds; [with] only four or five grains of corn mixed with them [s]o even at harvest the bird leaves corn for hemlock'. As he writes this, we can watch how, from the grains that sat in the dead bustard's stomach, Ray can re-walk the bird's last heavy steps through the fields. A single moment, a bird's stride, is raised vividly before us.

At the end of his alphabetical list of plants, as if he knows the A to Z of things is not the best way to make sense of them, Ray gives an outline system for plant classification, and a location-by-location list, a true field-list, of the plants he found in various neighbourhoods – at Gamlingay, and Chesterton, and Ditton, and Stretham, and 'On the bank of the great Ditch called Devils ditch' and several other places. In this list we can see the beginnings of his understanding of habitat and ecosystems; the understanding that gave us, 250 years later, a great encyclopaedia of life from the few acres of Wicken Fen.

Brilliant on the liquefaction of the wetlands, Ray is very good as well on the confusion of grass. Through the words he gives to them we can watch him looking. Among the received common names he notes are the 'Hedge-hog-grass' and 'Grasse of Parnassus' (not a grass in fact, but a bog-star). But we can also *hear* his ordering eye at work as other grass names compound, build up and grow. It is as if speciation itself is happening right in front of his enquiring gaze. Indeed, Ray got closer than anybody had before to defining what we now understand to be a species (Linnaeus later paid his dues to Ray who, he acknowledged, had got there first). Look at the bunch he has picked of 'small foxtail grass' and 'lesser bastard Fox-tail-grass' and 'small rough-eared bastard Fox-tail-grass'. See how sometimes on the fen even the great naturalist was lost for words, or rather flooded with them. Pay attention to 'Water-grasse'; 'Float-grass'; 'Great water Reed-grasse'; '[o]ur great Reed-grasse with chaffie heads'; and '[t]he marsh soft Rush with a round blackish head,' you know the one, yes, the one which is found '[e]verywhere in the watery places of Hinton and Teversham moors, so that he which shall look there cannot doubt what rush we mean . . .'

Ray's little book, which was printed in Cambridge by one John Field, is so beautiful in both its precision and its vagueness, and so stuffed with looking and thinking about looking, that it makes you want to keep it with you, to use it as a true field-guide, to allow it to staunch any wound you might have, to live by it. It couldn't help us when, on my knees at my village roadside, Claire and I grappled with a dead bee orchid next to an orobanche, but it marvellously brimmed full when we got home and read that in the late 1650s there were 'hundreds' of the 'Humble-bee Satyrion' 'in a close behind the Bell Inn at Haverhill', and that the parasitic orobanche then grew 'in barley on the right hand side of the way between Cambridge and Grantchester'.

I can think of nothing more thrilling, nothing that our species has done better, than this benign capture and permanent vivifying of a season, a pathway and a field edge, and its *simpling*, or its lovable mapping of what might be in front of us. He was there and noticed what was there. And now, being all but there, we see it all, 'by the well on the hill not far from the church' or 'along the balks of the plowed fields next the closes, on the left hand of the horse-way to Cherry-Hinton . . .'

OUT FIELD

My son, Lucian, aged five, in December 2000: 'I wish I could be a bird. When I am in heaven I might be an eagle, because you can be whatever you like. Even a drawing pin. Or a piece of fluff. Or a crumb. Or a piece of grass.'

Emily Dickinson, a little older and a while ago, on grass when it dies: 'in Sovereign Barns to dwell – / And dream the Days away, / The Grass so little has to do / I wish I were a Hay – '

Older still. Sir Gawain cuts off the Green Knight's head and it rolls about a bit on the earth. As it bumps past the other knight-spectators they kick at it (as if to send it into the long grass). But the felled Green Knight picks up his own head and carries it off, and you know that when he plants it back on his shoulders it will grow again, that what was cut will not die but will come again, that the Green Knight *is* grass.

You can still catch the smell of the meadow in a city's streets. One May day, in Mount Auburn cemetery on the wooded edge of Harvard near Boston, I watched a female bobolink, a migrant grassland sparrow-like bird, resting on its way north to open fields. It landed on the carved stone wheatsheaf that lies on the tomb of one Caleb Wood. The scene made me think of Bob Dylan saying how he learned 'Baby Let Me Follow You Down' from Ric von Schmidt in the green pastures of Harvard University. Later the same day, outside the Harvard Book Store, an elderly white-haired man in a beret and a chunky Aran sweater, knitted with creamy furrows and ridges, played a tune on a silver-buttoned accordion. It was 'The Bonny Earl of Murray':

> Ye Highlands and ye Lawlands,
>   O where hae ye been?
> They hae slain the Earl of Murray,
>   And hae laid him on the green.

In *Henry V* Falstaff dies talking of green fields at the river's edge as the Thames tide turns. He doesn't appear in the play but Hostess Quickly memorably describes his off-stage last moments and his death:

> Nay, sure, he's not in hell: he's in Arthur's bosom, if ever man went to Arthur's bosom. A made a finer end and went away an it had been any christom child. A parted e'en just between twelve and one, e'en at the turning o' th' tide. For after that I saw him fumble with the sheets and play with flowers and smile upon his fingers' end, I knew there was but one way, for his nose was as sharp as a pen on a table of green fields. 'How now, Sir John?' quoth I. 'What, man? Be o'good cheer.' So a cried out. 'God, God, God!' three or four times. Now I, to comfort him, bid him a should not think of God; I hoped there was no need to trouble himself with any such thoughts yet. So a bade me lay more clothes on his feet. I put my hand into the bed and felt them, and they were as cold as any stone. Then I felt to his knees, and so up-peered and upward, and all was as cold as any stone.

The lines are not totally watertight. Hostess Quickly perhaps mistakes Arthur for Abraham whose bosom was a byword for heaven, though Arthur has a good ring of England or Lyonesse. Other lines are contested. Alexander Pope thought a stage-direction had crept into the text: 'Greenfield was the name of the property-man in that time who furnished implements, etc for the actors, *A table of Greenfield's.*' No other Shakespeare editors follow Pope but many are not happy with 'on a table of green fields'. Variant readings have been proposed and the words emended to 'and a babbled of green fields' or 'and a talked of green fields'.

I like it each way and all ways (and so did Edward Thomas: 'Almost as soon as I could babble', he wrote, 'I "babbled of green fields."').

Whatever the intended words or image, we are watching the green flash at the end of a life. The consolations of a primal experience (to be in a field . . .) are invoked and much else is configured and remembered in a few fleeting moments. An elderly man is in his bed talking of fields – the best good thing that he knows outside and which (at least in his living life) he is on the verge of forsaking forever.

Falstaff at the beginning of his ending and in a kind of easeful delirium dandles a last pastoral plaything at his fingers like a child's toy, the equivalent of a farm-set of animals and implements. He sees flowers and passes his hands over them on the rumpled meadow of his bedclothes, an embroidered pattern mistaken perhaps, but they are also the flowers of the field that will bloom on the turned earth of a grave, making Falstaff alive to his own death like the dying Keats who, having heard his burial place in Rome described, declared back to his friend Joseph Severn from his deathbed that 'he already seemed to feel the flowers growing over him'.

Keats coughed blood on to his sheets during the night of 3 February 1820. He thought its bright red meant it was arterial blood and that his tuberculosis was therefore advanced and probably fatal. In fact tuberculosis invades veins as much as arteries and all coughed blood will look bright because of its contact with oxygen in the airways. But Keats believed he had seen on his sheets what he called his 'death-warrant' and he was right. He died a little over a year later. Ten days after the coughed blood he wrote a letter to his friend James Rice:

How astonishingly does the chance of leaving the world impress a sense of its natural beauties upon us. Like poor Falstaff, though I do not babble, I think of green fields. I muse with the greatest affection on every flower I have known from my infancy – their shapes and coulours [are as] new to me as if I had just created them with a superhuman fancy – It is because they are connected with the most thoughtless and happiest moments of our Lives – I have seen foreign flowers in hothouses, of the most beautiful nature, but I do not care a straw for them. The simple flowers of our spring are what I want to see again.

* * *

Tolstoy is buried at Yasnaya Polyana in a clearing in the wood behind the house. Yasnaya Polyana means 'bright glade' and a sunlit circle has been found or made around his grave. He instructed it thus, though to look at it you might think that nature had decided in any case to comply with the Count. There is no stone and no cross; no lettering of any kind from any time writes its way into the ring of green.

He died on the run like King Lear. In November 1910, aged eighty-two, he fled from his wife and his wider life, his aristocratic class, the state and the religion he had come to hate, those cranky followers who crowded needily around him, his own pride and arrogance that he had never been able to shake off, and the very storm of words which he had lived in for so long. His mad flight also took him from the place that had nurtured him for almost all of his life and that, according to his son Lev, he regarded as 'an organic part of himself'. In the end not even Yasnaya Polyana could save him. The dark green leather sofa Tolstoy was born on, and which he made Sofya Andreyevna use for many of her many labours, is in his study in the white house with its green roof and window frames just down the hill from his grave. The sofa is blackened with age now and dull-polished like the old used skin that it is. Tolstoy died in a stranger's bed in an unfamiliar place. His recent biographers have no truck with his reported last words and W. H. Auden thought they sounded 'too much in character to be credible' but for a time they were said to be: 'But the peasants – how do the *peasants* die?'

Tolstoy's body was returned to Yasnaya Polyana and his funeral was the first public burial in Russia made without religious rites. A hole was scratched in the ground and topped with earth. Tolstoy, Leo or Lev the lion, had requested a pauper's burial and he was granted a simple coffin but hundreds of people followed it up the hill. At the head of the procession two peasants carried a banner made of a white sheet of coarse linen slung between two birch poles. Written on it: 'The memory of your good deeds will not die amongst us.' It was signed: 'The Orphaned Peasants of Yasnaya Polyana.'

His grave must have been repaired over the years but it is still something to look at. The path to it opens to the grassed glade with birch trees towering around, two or three of them leaning over the clearing like comforting parents reaching down to their children. Set to one side of the green is what looks like a table of turf rising little more than a foot from the ground. The entire tomb-barrow, its top, ends and sides, is clothed in grass that, even at the end of September, was still growing and vividly bright. It looked like a delicious place to sit – a table and a bench at once – and I would have if I hadn't known I would be resting on Tolstoy's remains. The raised grave seemed shorter than a body: in my mind's eye, and in the statues of him that are still everywhere in Russia, Tolstoy was taller, but as he aged he shrank. By his last years he was less than five foot four inches high.

Tolstoy is buried in these woods in this way for all sorts of reasons; his whole life took him to his end. But he told one story, a kind of green dream, about why he wanted to end up where he did. When he was about five his eldest brother, Nikolay, who was ten, told him he had discovered the secret of happiness and that it was written on a little green stick which was buried somewhere in the woods just behind their home at Yasnaya Polyana. When the stick was found and its words were read all the world would turn loving and would be at peace. Then everybody would become members of an 'ant brotherhood'. Through their childhoods Tolstoy and his brothers played at being ants, building nests and dens and huddling close, and Tolstoy never forgot the dream and explicitly asked to be buried near to where the stick might lie:

The ideal of Ant-Brothers lovingly clinging to one another, though not under two armchairs curtained by shawls, but of all mankind under the wide dome of heaven, has remained the same with me. As I then believed that there existed a little green stick whereon was written the message that could destroy all evil in men and give them universal welfare, so I now believe that such truth exists and will be revealed to men and give them all it promises.

It isn't clear if the stick was a painted piece of wood or a leafing bough but, whatever it was, when taken back into the ground it offered an endlessly renewable and happy life. So, at the edge of the clearing, it was inevitable that I bent to the earth and peeled from a fallen branch a page of birch bark and, as I pulled it away, several ants hurried like scattering letters and punctuation marks along the rotting wood and into the leaf mould. They didn't like being disturbed and as I stood up I could taste in my mouth and feel at my eyes the smarting metallic vapour that John Ray, sometime fen botanist and discoverer in 1671 of the properties of formic acid, described as *ant juyce*.

In September 1877 at Fort Robinson in the Pine Ridge area (now in northern Nebraska, south of the present-day Sioux reservation), Crazy Horse, the Sioux warrior, was killed as he resisted being taken into prison. He had surrendered at the fort a year after he had helped see Custer into the soil of the Little Bighorn. There are many stories about his death. His life up until then is remarkably unknown. He was never a talker; there is no photograph of him. But as the world closed in the voices grew up. At least twenty people who were at the fort spoke about it subsequently. He was stabbed twice with a bayonet in the stomach during a scuffle. His assailant was probably a soldier called William Gentles from County Tyrone. Still alive, Crazy Horse was wrapped in a sheet or blanket and carried to the adjutant's office where he was encouraged to lie on a cot. He refused. He was perhaps the last man in human history never to sit on a chair. He died on the office floor and Ian Frazier, in his book *Great Plains*, wants to believe that because Crazy Horse spurned the bed he died his own man, claiming his shape on the earth as the only space left to him: 'Lying where he chose, Crazy Horse showed the rest of us where we are standing. With his body, he demonstrated that the floor of an Army office was part of the land, and that the land was still his.' When Touch the Clouds saw that his friend was dead he pulled a blanket over him and said, 'This is the lodge of Crazy Horse.'

He was about thirty-seven. His parents took their dead son by travois forty miles east to the Spotted Tail Agency, which was where he had wanted to move. His body, wrapped in red blankets, was put up on a scaffold on a hill. His parents stayed with it for three days. He had done the same when his baby daughter died of cholera, climbing into her scaffold and lying next to her. A wooden fence was erected around his bier to keep it from carrion-seeking wolves. Later the body was removed to an unknown place. 'Because he possibly said that his bones would turn to rocks and his joints to flint,' Frazier writes, 'Indian boys used to search the hills for his petrified remains. No one knows for sure where Crazy Horse's bones lie.'

The Crazy Horse memorial mountain round the back of Mount Rushmore in the Black Hills is a very sad thing. The mountain top is slowly being carved into the shape of Crazy Horse riding for his life. If you pay your dollars you can go and look at the drilling and blasting. If you don't you are kept from the man and the mountain by a screen of buildings around the car park.

There is a story that before any battle Crazy Horse would paint his pony with earth unearthed by a mole and would rub a smudge of the same earth into his hair. His hope was that the black earth dug by the believed-blind black mole would make both horse and Crazy Horse harder to see.

When T. H. White loses the goshawk that he has been training, 'my lunatic from the Rhine' as he calls it, he tries to get his bird back by hiding out as a field. The story is at the heart of *The Goshawk*. He sets a pigeon as bait and tethers it to the ground. Nearby he slides under a scaffold of ash sticks covered in a sheet. He has sprinkled the sheet with grass and mustard seed and soaked it in water until it has sprouted into a growing green cloth. Sometimes he calls his hide 'the mole-hill' and sometimes 'the grave'. Hidden but primed, he is prepared to wait for days for the pigeon to lure the hawk down from its freedom and for the hawk to come close enough to be grabbed from the grave. The camouflage is good. One day three poachers walked over White without noticing what lay beneath them; one, he says, he could have caught 'by the foot'. But it doesn't work for his bird.

Around the time John Clare started writing poetry he was also saving up for an olive-green coat. He hardly ever had any spare money and was almost always what Robert Graves described as *mouse-poor*. In 1806 Clare had saved enough to buy James Thomson's long poem *The Seasons* from a bookseller in Stamford and was so thrilled he couldn't resist reading it even as he walked home. But he knew he mustn't be seen so he climbed the walls of the estate at Burghley, just outside the town, and hid away in order to read the poem. Soon he started writing himself, and to begin with he buried or cached his words on scraps of paper in holes in the wall of his cottage as if they were not to be known about or were to be held and saved, ready for later.

When his first book appeared in 1820, Clare went to London. He was anxious in the city about many things. Later he rebuked Londoners for claiming they heard nightingales singing everywhere in the capital, but when he first went there he did the same thing, misidentifying street-walking prostitutes in their grabby finery for grand ladies. He was also embarrassed by the poverty of his own wardrobe and his publisher offered him some clothes. His first biographer, Frederick Martin, detailed the camouflage he accepted: 'Clare refused to take anything, except an ancient overcoat somewhat too large for him, but useful as hiding his whole figure from the top of the head down to the heels. In this brigand-like mantle he henceforth made all his visits, unwilling to take it off even at dinner, and in rooms hot to suffocation.'

Clare didn't want to be thought a hayseed but couldn't help playing the part. An old form of his surname was *Clayer* meaning a man who mixes the soil, who marls peaty land with clay. Trying to dress for the occasion on his second visit to London in 1822 he instead gave away the cast of the place he came from, wearing a 'bright grass-coloured coat and yellow waistcoat' and getting himself called, by a magazine editor, 'our Green Man'.

When, in July 1841, Clare absconded from his first asylum in Essex and walked home to Northamptonshire, he was hungry and ate grass from the roadside. The greenery on the verge was known as *flitting grass*; the poor and commoners alike used this marginal herbage to feed their animals. Flitting meant to graze cattle on a tether. Children are attending their family's animals in this way all across Africa today. In revolutionary France, Wordsworth and his friend Michel Beaupuy were horrified by the sight of a hunger-bitten girl being half-dragged by a heifer along such a verge. The grass north of London, Clare said, tasted something like bread.

Later in Northampton Asylum, where he lived for twenty-three years (and was listed on a census first as a limeburner and then, a decade later, as a poet), Clare declared he had been at the Battle of Waterloo where his head had been shot off. He couldn't explain how he came to have it back on his shoulders again. At the same time he told this story to Dr Nesbitt, the medical superintendent, he also reported, clear as day, how his poetry 'came to him whilst walking in the fields' and that he 'kicked it out of the clods'. Writing out of the flat and unedged places of eastern England, he made a horizon with his opening lines, and then dipped below it repeatedly into the fields, noticing what was there. Clare the clayer never stopped being a fieldworker and walked, even in his asylum, like a ploughman it was said, 'one leg seeming to be always in the furrow'.

I always did leave doors open behind me and I still do. It is good to be able to see any available exit and shutting a door has forever seemed rather severe and final, the click of the handle denoting some permanent entrance into a headmaster's study or a doctor's consulting room. Bad news happens behind closed doors. I lock my front and back door but no other door within any of the three places I live is shut. When I was a child, one or other of my parents, who both had known life before central heating and who both now paid the bills for it, would shout after me as I left the room, 'Born in a barn?' But I was happy to be slandered, or to think then of what that would mean. It wasn't a comparison with Jesus that I was seeking – his barn birthplace was, in any case, a stable, with scary horses and other heavy-duty stuff, wise men crowding in and meaningfulness. But to be always on the point of going out – I liked that thought.

I've slept twice in a barn, both times after birds. Once on straw in the crowded birdwatcher's dossing-place at Salthouse, I think it was, on the North Norfolk coast after my first greater yellowlegs, a vagrant from America, in 1975. We were late, it was dark and I tripped over the sleepers already lying in rows, heads to the walls and feet to the centre, scout-tent style. I remember the stirring shrouded figures and the bliss-excitement that took me to sleep, the bird having been seen and all else therefore made good and easy. The other time was in Cornwall a year or so later and near Stithians or Siblyback reservoir, where we'd been chasing another American wader – perhaps a Baird's sandpiper, though I cannot now recall the bird for certain. We hadn't seen it. Antony, one of our carload of bird-boys, had remembered a family friend living nearby and we gatecrashed a dinner party, still slung with our binoculars and heavy in wellingtons. They sat us like tramps or beggars at the distant end of their long farmhouse table, fed us their leftovers, and then pushed us out through the rain into a barn stacked with hay, a loose cap of it just below the roof on top of a solid house of bales. We climbed up, as you might a stepped pyramid, and slept in a fragrant silvery-green pool of dusty cuttings lit from the side by moonlight bruising through clouds. Both nights I recall for the rain galloping on the metal roofs of the barns that woke me every now and then and the complementing prickle of the cut grass on my cheeks as I turned in my sleep, and for the dormitory security of the one barn and my fear in the other of sinking or even drowning into the hay, which seemed so giving and soft in its swimming strew of stems.

I shot and killed a wildebeest one day in Zambia. It was running with its herd through high tawny grass. Then it was a dirty sheet thrown down on the same field. In its abrupt passage from life to death (close in front of me and steered by my trigger-finger) and in the same second that I watched this happen down a telescopic sight (as if from the far side of the world and the other end of time) so all the pages of this book came to call: a field, its contents, its meanings and me.

I killed it because it was sick and a little lame and heading for the chop whether I delivered the final blow or not. I killed it because everyone else where I was staying on the game-farm near Choma had already gone with a gun or a crossbow after one thing or another and I could no longer say not me, not now, not yet. I killed it because my wife is South African and for a time slept with a shotgun under her bed and I thought killing something might let us know one another better. I killed it because, although I had never shot or even held a rifle before, having passed an audition with a cardboard box target wedged in a tree, I felt the dark gun tracking me as we drove out on to the open grass and targeting me until I picked it up once more. I killed it because, although I had watched hours of wildebeest passing me in the grass of the Rift Valley, mooing and mowing there, and being dead there in so many ways, I had never touched one. I killed it because I wanted to mark a field, to cut into it somehow and feel some holding anchor on its grassy floor, to enter a place and to know both it and me more alive even as I made part of it dead. I killed it though I am a student of the Ancient Mariner and his albatross, of D. H. Lawrence and his snake, of George Orwell and his elephant, and Ahab and his whale. I killed it perhaps just because I could.

My knees came close to stopping me. The shooting was to be done from the open back of a Land Cruiser so that we could approach the small herd of twenty-five or so animals and hide from them at the same time. My top half was clouded in a loose camouflage-patterned smock, with my shorts and bare legs, moony and milk-white shanks, hidden behind the cab. I had to steady myself on the bumpy ride across the plain by jamming my knees hard against the chassis. As I looked down they appeared as hopeless as two slices of flabby bread. Something of the very beginnings of my life, of Liverpool and wet days in the playground, came up to me from those knees. But by pushing them harder still into the metal I steadied myself enough, even though my calves and then my thighs juddered as if in shock. Sweat stung my eyes and I had to wipe them with my camouflaged arms to see down the gun-sight. The wildebeest moved on, passing beyond scrub and thorn trees, but the last of them was tiring and lagged a little and I knew my target. It had a limp and, though it could still run, it picked up speed more awkwardly than the others and never got beyond a broken canter. If I was a leopard I would have marked it out in the same way as had Ian. He owns the farm and knows the herd, had tested my gunnery and loaded the rifle, and was driving while quietly mouthing encouragement to both sides of the story, tightening the thread between us as he shortened it. Twice I had the beast side-on as desired and in the sight. But it moved and the moment spooled from me. We drove closer and the herd stopped and Ian switched off. The electric quiet of the outer world came loud into my head and met my nervous pulse. The gun was fantastically solid and sweat had rolled again into my eyes. But looking down the sight calmed me. Years of birdwatching, of tunnel vision and of the magnification of things, helped me arrive in a place without being there and to know that I was looking, without being seen, at a living thing living. The wildebeest turned its old eyes towards me and sniffed the hot air between us. There were lines – cross-hairs – scratched on the lens and my finger was on the sickle-shaped trigger not the focusing wheel of a pair of binoculars, but I was sure that as I squeezed so the wildebeest would sharpen and come closer. That was what I felt I was doing: bringing it to me, getting a gnu with a gun.

It fell before I finished pulling. My muscles dragged behind my optic nerve. I saw a hurry-slump to the grass before I felt my tendons stretch. I heard nothing and registered no kick from the stock. My nerves were looking after that as well. Ian got out of the cab, took the gun from me and started walking into the long grass. The herd had run on over a low rise and we were alone. All the muted noises came back at once and the plain became an itching hot day. I followed Ian in a trance. We walked 163 strides.

There was a dead thing on the ground: big and dirty and already infinitely older than the living morph that had occupied its shape until a few moments ago. Without touching it I could feel the body's warmth but there was no suggestion of any engine running down or ghostly departure. The life had gone out in an instant and everything had changed. Its eyes, like matchboxes now, goatish and new blind, said the same thing. The animal's front sticky legs bent under its chest, and its nose was pushed in the sand between some clumps of grass. It had found its way to the beginning of the earth but couldn't get in.

I did my best for a photograph and tried to cuddle the corpse. Its head was heavier than the gun. I had to take both its horns in my hands and heave and hold on to them like reins. Its mane fell long and black across my pale legs and made me think of pictures of the Ramones outside CBGBs. The animal had been ill. Its hooves were worn with rot to nothing and it had been running on its nails alone. Around its anus a ring of ticks clustered like swollen fruits, already big with blood but buried in bliss in the pink opening and drinking more. At the other end of its body, blood had bubbled scarlet and frothy into the wildebeest's mouth with the final pump of its heart and, strung with slobbery drool, it came dribbling into the sand, pooling darkly as oil will beneath a cracked sump. Its puce tongue had slid out through its slack ruminant mouth. A fly was walking there already. Its teeth showed too, pearly but worn down below the gums, like bulbs uncovered in soil.

Close up its grey-brown body hair might have been the field it fell in. No matter how many apparently uniform runners started at the off, every tight-stretched pelt within the herd makes its own unique tweed. There were scars and swirls of fur, licked places, blemishes and beauty spots, wormholes and bald patches, the signature of a life written into the hills and valleys of a body. And just above its front right leg there was a new bloody nick where the bullet had gone in, finding the lungs and the heart as it ought and blowing and burning them apart before slowing through the rest of the body and coming to a halt inside the top of the front left leg. A punch brought to rest within a punchbag. I could feel the bullet beneath my finger like a loose knuckle just below the skin.

When Ian laid the wildebeest on the concrete of the farmyard his dogs licked its tongue clean of blood and then hurried to stem the bright red gulf that ran from its mouth. Once the dogs had finished on the floor they licked at my bare shins and knees for the specks of blood the wildebeest's death-breath had sprayed on me. Thirty-four portions of meat were butchered from the body. One for each of the thirty women working that day in the fields and four more for each of the compound foremen. The inedible tail was given to the butcher, Samuel, for his 'senior' wife (he has two). Worth one hundred dollars, and more valuable than all the rest of the wildebeest put together, it would be used in dances and, if put under a pillow, could banish bad dreams.

* * *

In the Hungarian novelist László Krasznahorkai's *The Melancholy of Resistance*, a vast stuffed whale travels the small towns of sea-less Hungary on the back of a truck. I once heard the writer say that when he was a child he had seen such a whale when it trundled into the backwater town of Gyula, on the edge of the Hungarian plain close to the Romanian border. Looking at the whale, he said he had thought that if *it* was possible then *everything* was.

Nicholas Redman shares an interest in the *idea* of a whale, though he might not declare it in the same way. He lives in South London not far from the River Thames. Or, rather, his workplace is there: a modern house with blinds drawn on every window, a single army-surplus camp bed in one room, and the rest of the space tight-jammed with the grey hulks of filing cabinets, stuffed bookshelves and splitting cardboard boxes. He uses an ironing board as a desk. Every available inch of the house is made from the details of as many of the whales' bones of Britain as Nick has been able to secure. The bones strewn across the country, that is, that have parted company from their bodies and that have found their way onshore and inland, a skeleton scattered as if dropped from space and made of skulls, vertebrae and ribs, some visible, many lost, a few remembered, most forgotten. In a lockup garage nearby Nick has more boxes and some rescued ribs leaning against the walls like huge half-rotten oars. 'People don't know what to do with them any more and offer them and I feel I must take them,' he told me. A blade of baleen rested on a shelf behind his head like a scythe. From all his findings he has compiled an extraordinary book called *Whales' Bones of the British Isles*, a directory and gazetteer of all of the bones that he knows and of their places. It is a book that nobody else wants as much as he does. He lists whale remains in museums but they can mostly take care of themselves and his real concern is with the farm buildings and barns roofed from bones; the fence posts and field edges made from them driven into the earth; the jawbones donated by a sea captain to the fen town of March and erected in 1850 as Melville was raising *Moby-Dick* on the other side of the sea; the grottoes of marine topiary in forgotten Victorian gardens; the slipway for boats made of a whale ribcage on Harris; the arches of ribs raised into the sky like ruined church entranceways; the half-buried vertebrae near old whaling ports, bone-yard monuments to their own slaughter; the set of jawbones made into a child's swing.

The odd thing is that Nick is not interested in *whales*. A celebrated and publically mourned northern bottle-nosed whale strayed up the Thames in 2006 and came within a few yards of his files and photographs but he didn't go to see it. It was still alive. His fascination is only for what people have thought to do with whalebones. No more than that, but no less than that either. Living whales don't interest him but his is a true work of *nature writing*, an account of how it marks the world, and an answer, like *Moby-Dick*, to its call.

Nick Redman, when I left him, was at work on various European companion volumes to his British whalebone book. Hungary will surface eventually.

I was descending through a crack in the earth, as you must, to the metro station below the Champs-Élysées in Paris and there, at the bottom of the first flight of steps, was a small rabbit, white all over apart from two brown ears, its nose snuffling freely in its slinky lollop between my feet. It stopped me in my tracks. What sort of burrow for what sort of rabbit? But there, sitting against the metro tunnel wall, was its minder, a smiling elderly Maghrebi man, who sat with an opened newspaper in front of him on which was laid one carrot with feathery green tops, his calling card, and their begging bowl – a ticket to another field, another Elysium. I took my train and first came up from the earth at Notre Dame where, at the doors of the cathedral, there was a one-eyed black African beggar, the blue of his clouding cataract as bright as the cloudless sky. He held his arm out, raised in front of him, palm up, St Francis-style, and house sparrows milled there in a halo of blurred and rusty cornlight. I went down again and got out at the Louvre. In the Tuileries, house martins were nesting under the stone flower heads that deck the underside of the Arc de Carrousel and, beyond them, a black and white goat was kneeling into a flowerbed apparently gardening.

*   *   *

One of the sweetest and greenest moments in the *Divine Comedy* comes in Canto 15 of the *Inferno* when Dante meets a friend. Brunetto Latini, the chancellor of the first popular government of Florence, was Dante's guardian after his father died and then became a tutor-figure to him. When they meet Brunetto is dead and condemned, probably for his sodomy, to hell. The damned man appears at Dante's side in the middle of a dark version of the fens, a 'solid mire' with 'fuming mist' and a 'maze of dykes' laid by an 'evil engineer'. Brunetto catches at Dante's sleeve and walks alongside him – the damned must move forever – and they speak of how they both came to be there. It is a tender talk made in the mutuality of love complicated by their shared knowledge (the fallen man and the visitor from the world of life and light), and it continues until Brunetto sees that 'fresh steam is stirring from the sand' and turns from Dante to run back to his place on the night soil of the hot fen and, doing so, Dante says, 'he seemed one of those / who run for the green cloth through the green field / at Verona . . . and seemed more like the one who wins the roll of cloth than those who lose'.

These beautiful last lines drew Robert Lowell, their translator, towards them and as well as making a version of the canto he incorporated them into two of his other poems. In his 1929 essay on Dante, T. S. Eliot wrote of the same passage: 'One does not need to know anything about the race for the roll of green cloth, to be *hit* by these lines; and in making Brunetto, so fallen, run like the winner, a quality is given to the punishment which belongs only to the greatest poetry.' I would only add that I think the *green* helps. The Palio was run outside the walls of Verona on the first Sunday of Lent. In Italian *verde* rhymes with *perde*, but green is for go and the race was towards life and the prize the best badge of it. The loser received a cockerel.

I went out into the fields down a grassed track between olive trees not far from Prato near Florence one late autumn afternoon. Somewhere above me in the sky two woodlarks sang. I couldn't see them. The woodlark's is the song I love the most of all the birds that I have heard. It is tuneful but sad, broken and slight and a little cold. On a beautifully strange LP I bought, when I lived in Budapest in the 1980s, an elderly Hungarian tenor moans a slowed-down version of a singing woodlark. It sounds as if the Earth has cracked open and this sweet, thin and true music is what breaks from its exposed heart. Since I heard the singer and his drifting notes I cannot hear the birds without thinking that theirs is the music of afterwards, a blues, the song of how things have been. Its small sprinkling noise is a modest declaration of limits and is as honest as any song I know. This is where we have arrived, it says to me: a boy standing at the side of a dance floor looking at his feet and expecting nothing.

Of course it is none of this. It is sex and the swollen gonads pushing at the syrinx and warfare over the sky's acres and the olive grove and the horse field below. But I walked under the singing, still not seeing the singers, hearing the threads let down from the sky and feeling the woodlarks only as sad. And their music came then through the chop and burr of human voices that thickened ahead of me in the strange olive wood. And none of it could I understand. On one side of the track there were Chinese men in white shirts and suit trousers crouched in the low crowns of the olives or standing on stepladders leaning against them. One man in each tree. From tree to tree they spoke to each other as they might in a room. They had short-handled rakes and combed as they talked, and the olives rained down through their words and the branches on to the plastic sheets they had laid on the grass to skirt each tree. On the other side of the track West African men in indigo-blue scarves and padded jackets were at the same work. They were taller and moved more than the Chinese and their Wolof remarks jumped loudly from one tree on to another. But the olives fell as before and the woodlarks' song came down through the little grey-green crowns of the trees with their teams of men perching in them like captured birds hung in small cages.

The woodlarks were still singing as, at the edge of a wilder wood of sweet chestnuts and oaks, I crossed the path of an irregular platoon of burly hunters dressed in camouflaged suits and carrying plastic bags of butchered meat dripping blood along the dusty track. There are wild boar in these woods and all day the horizon had popped with gunshots. The woodlarks didn't seem to mind but the woodpigeons were going crazy, first clattering out of any treetop they had stopped down into, then swirling into a bigger nervousness, pulling higher above the woods and leaving the valley as quick as they could. The gunmen, their guns shouldered in cases the same pattern as their clothes, and happy with their bits of boar swinging from their hands, didn't even look up at the larks or the pigeons as they walked to their little runabout cars parked up the lane.

There are no right angles in the seasons, but there are corners and there came a day one late August when I could see round one on the fen and watch the year turning.

The local roads there are cut straight but they slump and humpback following the rise and fall of the ground beneath. Anything driving at more than twenty-five miles an hour fouls with an ugly metal snarl in the tarmac bottoms. The route I take to and from the fen has been laid in sections to give it some stretch-space and so allow for the ebbs and runs of the earth-tide's passage through the moving land. Every twenty yards or so, inch-wide trenches between the sections have opened across the road. Narrow green lines of low grass crouch in them. Crossing these dips in a car the tyres tick; on a bike the repetitive lurch throws your heart into your mouth.

With swallows moving south around me I cycled home from the fens following a tractor pulling a trailer of grain fresh hulled from one of the new harvested fields. It was heading towards the Swan Lake Grain Store where the treasure is tipped into dunes of gold, swimming alive with warmth and weight, and humming with fragrant dust in the dark of the cavernous sheds.

The bumps of the little trenches across the bucking road jiggled a line of grain from the back of the trailer, a thin curtain of English manna. In the fen wind and the machine-blow from the tractor the beads of wheat rolled towards the trenches and gathered in them, joining the grains already captured from earlier journeys. With the lowering sun the evening light made these threads across the road shine warmly. Yellowhammers had already found the golden seams. As I pedalled towards them, three flew up, lifting some of the grain's metal in the shining yellow jewellery of their faces. I stopped and watched as they returned to a glinting trench behind me towards the fen. In my bag I had a pewter flask of sloe gin, the spirit flavoured from the fen edges hereabouts, and warming to the warm moment, I dribbled a little libation, by way of a thank you, on top of the grains at my feet. As I did, I looked back to see the first mist of the autumn growing from the fields and smoking over the road and the rifts of gold, and taking everything – all that was before me – from me, until I could see only the air made thick with water from the earth.

Grass seeds and broken stems and leaves get stuck in the lining of my boots on almost every crossing of a field. When my walking herbarium gets too prickly, I pick the seeds from the weave. All the four fields have met at my feet. I shake them out, my *coup de grâce*, sowing on to my little back lawn at home the seeds from half a mile away and from thousands of miles away, reed flags and sedge-heads, Bushmen's and steppe-feather, prairie and timothy. My days.

'If you want me again look for me under your boot-soles.'
Walt Whitman

Notes and References

Place of publication London unless otherwise stated.

ix   *A man keeps and feeds a lion* – Diogenes, *7 Greeks*, trans. Guy Davenport, New Directions, New York, 1995, p. 173.

Home Field

2   *There was no possibility of taking a walk that day* and other quotations – Charlotte Brontë, *Jane Eyre*, ed. Margaret Smith, Oxford University Press, 1980, pp. 7–8. First published 1847.

3   *a language of my whole life* – Ted Hughes, interviewed in 1995, *The Paris Review – Interviews, III*, Canongate, Edinburgh, 2008, p. 293.

3   *This green plot shall be our stage* – William Shakespeare, *A Midsummer Night's Dream*, III.i.3.

3   *a uniform hieroglyphic* – Walt Whitman, 'A Child Said, What is the Grass?' Song of Myself (1855), poem 6, *Complete Poems*, ed. Stephen Matterson, Wordsworth, 2006, p. 27.

4   *The fields!* – John Ruskin, *Modern Painters*, Vol. III, Part IV, Ch. XIV, +51, *Ruskin Today*, ed. Kenneth Clark, Penguin, Harmondsworth, 1964, pp. 102–3. Based on a journal entry made at Vevey, 3 June 1849.

5   Seamus Heaney's 'Digging' was the first poem in his first collection *The Death of a Naturalist* (1966).

5   *Visionary dreariness* – William Wordsworth, Book Eleventh (1805) 310 and Book Twelfth (1850) 256, *The Prelude*, eds

Jonathan Wordsworth, M. H. Abrams and Stephen Gill, Norton, New York, 1979, pp. 432–3.

9   *all those creatures we behold, are but the hearbs of the field* – Thomas Browne, *Religio Medici* 1.37, *Thomas Browne: The Major Works*, ed. C. A. Patrides, Penguin, Harmondsworth, 1977, p. 107. First published 1642–3.

9   Psalm 103 in the King James version: '*As for* man his days *are* as grass.'

15 *like a very ghost of joie de vivre* – D. H. Lawrence, 'Second-Best', *The Prussian Officer and Other Stories*, ed. John Worthen, Penguin, 1995, p. 115.

17 *The land has been humanised, through and through* – D. H. Lawrence, *Sea and Sardinia*, Heinemann, 1964, p. 123. First published 1921.

Winter Fen

20 *by the height of a man in the life of a man* – Alan Bloom, *The Fens*, Robert Hale, 1953, p. 57.

21 *tench and pike, pearch and eels* – Daniel Defoe, in 1724, quoted in H. C. Darby, *The Draining of the Fens*, Cambridge University Press, Cambridge 1956, 2nd edition, p. 156.

21 *Book-Fish* – see Jennifer Westwood and Jacqueline Simpson, *The Lore of the Land*, Penguin, 2005, p. 60.

22 *great lowland plain* and *harpoon* – Harry Godwin, *Fenland: Its Ancient Past and Uncertain Future*, Cambridge University Press, Cambridge, 1978, p. 25.

28 *aftergrave* – Thomas Browne, 'A Letter to a Friend', *Thomas Browne: The Major Works*, as above, p. 402.

29 Eric Ennion's book: E. A. R. Ennion, *Adventurers Fen*, Herbert Jenkins, 1949. All quotations from Ennion in this chapter are from here. 1st edition 1942, revised 1949.

32 *wrestled for an hour* – see William Yarrell, *A History of British Birds*, John Van Voorst, 1871–4, 4th edition, rev. Alfred Newton

and Howard Saunders, vol. 3, p. 198. The event occurred at about 4 a.m. on a fine June morning.

35   *The only fish that can swim backwards is an eel* – Hilaire Belloc, 'The Sea Wall of the Wash', *Hills and the Sea*, Methuen, 1941, p. 102. First published 1906.

35   *the putrefaction of the earth* – Izaak Walton, *The Compleat Angler*, Dent, 1947, p. 156. 5th edition, 1676.

36   *all those who disobeyed* – Olive Cook, *Cambridgeshire*, Blackie, 1953, pp. 76–7.

38   *out of the ground uprose* – John Milton, *Paradise Lost*, Book VII, 456–74, *Complete Poems*, ed. John Leonard, Penguin, 1998, p. 280. First published 1667, second enlarged edition 1674.

39   *Milton! thou should'st be living at this hour* – William Wordsworth, 'London, 1802', *Selected Poetry*, ed. Nicholas Roe, Penguin, 1992, p. 200.

41   *rigid grid* – Christopher Taylor, *The Cambridgeshire Landscape*, Hodder and Stoughton, 1973, p. 110.

43   *scribbling* and *a tap on the snout* – Arthur Randell, *Fenland Molecatcher*, Routledge and Kegan Paul, 1970, pp. 17 and 34.

43   *hung . . . for traitors* – John Clare, 'Remembrances', *The Oxford Authors: John Clare*, eds Eric Robinson and David Powell, Oxford University Press, Oxford, 1984, pp. 259–60.

45   *the sink of no less than thirteen Counties* – Daniel Defoe, quoted in Dorothy Summers, *The Great Level*, David and Charles, Newton Abbot, 1976, p. 23.

51   *that long-lost, archaic companionship* – Edwin Muir, 'The Horses', *Selected Poems*, ed. Mick Imlah, Faber, 2008, pp. 73–4. Muir's gravestone, the butterfly's rest, is carved with lines from his poem 'Milton': 'his unblended eyes / Saw far and near the fields of Paradise'.

Honeyguide

54 *I had a farm in Africa* – Karen Blixen, *Out of Africa*, Penguin, 2001, p. 13. First published 1937.

85 *Here come the Boer, we must hurry away* – quoted in Julia Martin, *A Millimetre of Dust*, Kwela, Cape Town, 2008, p. 41.

On honeyguides see: H. A. Isack and H. – U. Reyer, 'Honeyguides and honey gatherers: interspecific communication in a symbiotic relationship', *Science*, 1989, 243:1343–5. The standard text remains: H. Friedmann, *The Honeyguides*, United States National Museum Bulletin 208, Smithsonian Institution, Washington, DC, 1955. It includes a survey of references to the birds' behaviour in European literature. The earliest was a Portuguese missionary's account in a book called *Ethiopia Oriental*, written in 1569 and printed in 1609: 'when the birds find a beehive they go to the roads in search of men and lead them to the hives, by flying on before them, flapping their wings actively as they go from branch to branch, and giving their harsh cries'. The next observation was also Portuguese. The *Voyage to Abyssinia* was written in 1659, translated into French, and later into English by Samuel Johnson, who was interested in all things Abyssinian: 'the Moroc, or honey-bird [. . .] is furnished by nature with a peculiar instinct, or faculty of discovering honey. They have here multitudes of bees of various kinds [. . .] some place their honey in hollow trees, others hide it in holes in the ground, which they cover so carefully, that though they are commonly in the highway, they are seldom found, unless by the Moroc's help; which, when he has discovered any honey, repairs immediately to the roadside, and when he sees a traveller, sings and claps his wings; making many motions to invite him to follow him, and when he perceives him coming, flies before him from tree to tree, till he comes to the place where the bees have stored their treasure, and then begins to sing melodiously. The Abyssin takes the honey, without failing to leave part of it for the bird, to reward him for his information.'

86 Thomas Hardy, *Under the Greenwood Tree*, ed. David Wright, Penguin, Harmondsworth, 1986, p. 209.

86 Robert Herrick, 'Corinna's Going a Maying', *Cavalier Poets: Selected Poems*, ed. Thomas Clayton, Oxford University Press, Oxford, 1978, p. 42.

90 *enclosed within the garden's square* – Andrew Marvell, 'The Mower against Gardens', *The Oxford Authors: Andrew Marvell*, eds Frank Kermode and Keith Walker, Oxford University Press, Oxford, 1990, pp. 40–1.

92 *the sleeping green* – Isaac Rosenberg, 'Break of Day in the Trenches', *First World War Poems*, ed. Andrew Motion, Faber, 2003, p. 80.

92 *like autumn corn before the cutter* – anonymous witness quoted in Malcolm Brown, *The Imperial War Museum Book of the Somme*, Pan, London and Basingstoke, 1997, p. 68.

93 *Story about the mole* – Franz Kafka, *Diaries 1910–1923*, ed. Max Brod and trans. Joseph Kresh, Martin Greenberg and Hannah Arendt, Penguin, Harmondsworth, 1972, p. 317.

93 *Does a mole ever get hit* – Edward Thomas, 'War Diary', included in *Collected Poems*, ed. R. George Thomas, Faber, 2004, p. 159.

93 *You see how this world goes* – William Shakespeare, *King Lear*, IV.v.150.

93 *chief organ of sentiment* – John Constable, letter 23 October 1821 quoted in C. R. Leslie, *Memoirs of the Life of John Constable, Composed Chiefly of his Letters*, Phaidon, 1951, p. 85.

95 *an eminent town in the midst of the Level* – Dorothy Summers, as above, p. 71. See also Alan Bloom, 1953, as above, p. 267.

95 On the colony at Manea: Christopher Taylor, as above, p. 204; and www.welney.org.uk and www.utopia-britannica.org.

97 *Wypes* – name for lapwings from 1780, see J. Wentworth Day, *A History of the Fens*, Harrap, 1954, p. 74.

97 *dingy dirty green* – John Clare, 'The Pewit's Nest', cited in Jonathan Bate, *John Clare: A Biography*, Picador, 2004, p. 383.

98   *Moor-lambs* – William Yarrell, as above, vol. 3, p. 344.

98   *Gabhar-athair* – Francesca Greenoak, *All the Birds of the Air*, Penguin, Harmondsworth, 1981, p. 119.

98   *his bump* – John Skelton, 'Philip Sparrow,' line 432, *Selected Poems*, ed. Gerald Hammond, Carcanet, Manchester, 1980, p. 51.

99   *I am in one way better* – William Empson, *Some Versions of Pastoral*, Penguin, Harmondsworth, 1966, p. 19. First published 1935.

99   *pathos of distance* – Friedrich Nietzsche, paragraph 257, *Beyond Good and Evil*, trans. R. J. Hollingdale, Penguin, 2003, p. 192. First published 1886.

100   *[M]y own field* – Hilaire Belloc, 'The Mowing of a Field', *Selected Essays*, ed. J. B. Morton, Penguin, Harmondsworth, 1958, p. 38. All quotations from Belloc in this chapter are from here.

100   *you could have seen me* – D. H. Lawrence, letter to Blanche Jennings, 30 July 1908, *The Letters*, vol. 1, 1901–13, ed. James T. Boulton, Cambridge University Press, Cambridge, 1979, pp. 67–8.

100   *[m]y sheep are thoughts* – Sir Philip Sidney, *The Countess of Pembroke's Arcadia (The Old Arcadia)*, ed. Katherine Duncan-Jones, Oxford University Press, Oxford, 2008, p. 94.

102   *Nature is never journalistic* – W. S. Graham, '[Nature is Never Journalistic]', *Aimed at Nobody*, Faber, 1993, pp. 26–7. The poem continues: 'It does not tell us to tell how / It is faring now.'

104   *Methinks I have a great desire to a bottle of hay* – William Shakespeare, *A Midsummer Night's Dream*, IV.iv.24–5.

105   *Master, our young master!* – Henri Troyat, *Tolstoy*, trans. Nancy Amphoux, Penguin, Harmondsworth, 1970, p. 81.

106   *thinking that he was thinking about what he was thinking about* – John Stewart Collis, *Tolstoy*, Burns and Oates, 1969, p. 15.

106   *The gentleman must be mowed* – J. G. Frazer, *The Golden Bough*, abridged, Macmillan, 1957, vol. 2, p. 566. See also Traffic's 'John Barleycorn (Must Die)' on their 1970 album.

107   *20 April 1858* – Leo Tolstoy, *Tolstoy's Diaries*, trans. and ed. R. F. Christian, Athlone Press, 1985, vol. 1, pp. 150–1. All diary quotations in this chapter are from this two-volume edition.

108   *Bulletin of the Patients of the Yasnaya Polyana Lunatic Asylum* –

quoted in John Stewart Collis, as above, pp. 72 and 86.

108   *lost to literature* – Henri Troyat, as above, p. 265.

114   *Sunk out of knowledge* – Daniel Defoe, *A Tour Through the Whole Island of Great Britain*, ed. and abridged Pat Rogers, Penguin, Harmondsworth, 1971, p. 418.

114   *constant vigilance* – Alan Bloom, 1953, as above, p. 318.

114   *I had almost forgotten Marsh-Earths* – John Evelyn, *Terra: A Philosophical Discourse of Earth*, John Martyn, The Royal Society, 1676, pp. 20–1.

115   *On less competent authority* – John Henry Gurney, *Early Annals of Ornithology*, H. F and G. Witherby, 1921, p. 235.

Buffalo

118   *We use nails to stir the tea* – Wallace Stevens, *British Columbia Journal*, August 1903, in *Letters*, ed. Holly Stevens, University of California Press, Berkeley, 1996, p. 65.

118   *dust scatterers* – quoted in Evan S. Connell, *Son of the Morning Star*, Harper, New York, 1991, p. 86.

119   *Let them eat grass* – Andrew Myrick quoted in Connell, as above, p. 252.

119   *The white people have surrounded me* – Red Cloud, *Our Hearts Fell to the Ground: Plains Indian Views of How the West was Lost*, ed. Colin G. Calloway, Bedford St Martins, Boston and New York, 1996, p. 154.

119   *from the grass roots down* – Custer quoted in Geoffrey C. Ward, *The West: An Illustrated History*, Seven Dials, 1999, p. 292.

119   *I want a sow and a boar* – Red Cloud quoted in Ward, as above, p. 297.

121   *And me they turned inside out* – John Clare, 'The Lament of Swordy Well', *The Oxford Authors: John Clare*, as above, pp. 147–52.

121   *the bosom of a new Atlantic* – James Silk Buckingham, quoted in William Cotter Murray, 'Grass', *American Heritage*, 1968, 19:3.

122   *altered the regimental line of march* – Connell, as above, p. 357.

122   *sang a thunder song* – Connell, as above, p. 320.

123   *a fusillade of pistols* – Richard Manning, *Grasslands*, Viking, New York, 1995, p. 143.

124   *The excitement and heat made our thirst almost maddening* – Lieutenant Edward S. Godfrey, quoted in *Reno-Benteen Entrenchment Trail* guide, Western National Parks Association, 2004, p. 7.

125   *We walked on top of their internals and did not know it in the high grass* – Private John Guthrie, quoted in Connell, as above, p. 130.

125   *sadeh* – translator's note in *The Five Books of Moses*, trans. Robert Alter, Norton, New York, 2004, p. 114.

127   *This was done to improve his hearing* – Connell, as above, p. 422.

127   *double handful* – Connell, as above, p. 344.

127   *When the last stand was made* – Sitting Bull, quoted in David Markson, *Vanishing Point*, Shoemaker and Hoard, Washington, DC, 2004, p. 150.

128   *thousands of dogs* – Ian Frazier, *Great Plains*, Faber, 1990, p. 180.

128   *no longer than a hungry man* – quoted in Ward, as above, p. 302, and Frazier, as above, p. 181.

128   *It was as easy as killing sheep* – Rain quoted in Connell, as above, p. 399.

128   *It was like some Biblical exodus* – Charles Windolph quoted in Connell, as above, pp. 76–7.

129   *disembowelled, with stakes driven through their chests* – survivor Edward Pickard of F troop, quoted in James S. Brust, Brian C. Pohanka and Sandy Barnard, *Where Custer Fell: Photographs of the Little Bighorn Battlefield Then and Now*, University of Oklahoma Press, Norman, 2007, p. 127.

129   *to keep the wolves from digging them up* – Sergeant Ryan quoted in *Where Custer Fell*, as above, p. 129.

130   *A trench was dug* – Lieutenant Charles F. Roe quoted in on interpretation board at Little Bighorn battlefield. See also *Where Custer Fell*, as above.

132   *one of the first permanent structures* and *ghost herder* – *Custer National Cemetery* guide, Western National Parks Association, 2009, p. 6.

134   *saw the whole world* and *they brought back white, greyish earth* – Frazier, as above, p. 42.

135   *We tried to run but they shot us like we were buffalo* – Louise Weasel Bear quoted in Ward, as above, p. 398.

140   Leo Tolstoy, 'How Much Land Does a Man Need', *How Much Land Does A Man Need? and Other Stories*, trans. Ronald Wilks, Penguin, 1993. All quotations are from this edition.

150   Fred E. Miller's photographs are reproduced and his life sketched in *Fred E. Miller: Photographer of the Crows*, ed. Nancy Fields O'Connor, University of Montana and Carnan VidFilm, Missoula and Malibu, 1985.

Summer Fen

153   *Summer* – Coleridge, quoted in *The Charles Lamb Daybook*, Methuen, 1925, p. 135.

154   *a letter 'on the fishes eaten by our Saviour* – Samuel Johnson's 'Life of Browne', in *Thomas Browne: The Major Works*, as above, p. 496.

154   *when, or on what occasion, it was* – Dugdale quoted in Claire Preston, *Thomas Browne and the Writing of Early Modern Science*, Cambridge University Press, Cambridge, 2005, p. 126. I am much in debt to this account of a marvellous man and his mind. Other quotations from the exchange between the two men are from here or from *Sir Thomas Browne: Selected Writings*, ed. Claire Preston, Carcanet, Manchester, 1995.

154   *kild by a greyhound* – Browne quoted in Gurney, as above, p. 203.

155   *that great and true Amphibium* – Thomas Browne, part 1 section 34, *Religio Medici*, *Thomas Browne: The Major Works*, as above, p. 103.

157   *nearly every small grass meadow* – David Lack, *The Birds of Cambridgeshire*, Cambridge Bird Club, Cambridge, 1934, p. 111.

158   *tawny mowers* and other lines – Andrew Marvell, 'Upon Appleton House', *The Oxford Authors: Andrew Marvell*, as above, pp. 53–77.

159 *A sort of living doubt* – John Clare, 'The Landrail', *The Oxford Authors: John Clare*, as above, pp. 233–4.

160 *it is given to them that their sea-longing shall be land-longing* – Ronald Iain, quoted in David Thomson, *The People of the Sea: Celtic Tales of the Seal-Folk*, Edinburgh, Canongate, 2001, p. 175. First published 1954.

162 *level fields / Far from those lovely sights* and *I looked for universal things* – William Wordsworth, Book Third (1850), 94 and 109, *The Prelude*, as above, p. 97.

163 *The wide, wide fens are drear and cold* – James Wentworth Day, *A History of the Fens*, Harrap, 1954, p. 196. All the following quotations from Wentworth Day are from here.

163 *8th March 1852 Fell in with a flock of rare linnets* – quoted in Charles Lucas, *The Fenman's World*, Jarrold, Norwich, 1930, p. 78.

166 Leonard Blomefield, *A Naturalist's Calendar kept at Swaffham Bulbeck, Cambridgeshire*, ed. Francis Darwin, Cambridge University Press, Cambridge, 1922. First published 1903. Written 1846–9. All the following quotations from Blomefield are from here.

167 Georges Perec, *An Attempt at Exhausting a Place in Paris*, trans. Marc Lowenthal, Wakefield Press, Cambridge, Massachusetts, 2010. All the following quotations from Perec are from here.

170 *reading Darwin one admires the beautiful solid case* – Elizabeth Bishop, Letter to Anne Stevenson, 8 January 1964, quoted in Anne Stevenson, *Five Looks at Elizabeth Bishop*, Bloodaxe, Tarset, 2006, p. 82.

171 *live at large, and prey, like pikes* – E. P. Thompson, *Customs in Common*, Penguin, 1993, p. 163.

172 *reeds, fodder, thacks, turves* – *Anti-Projector*, quoted in H. C. Darby, *The Draining of the Fens*, Cambridge University Press, Cambridge, 1956, 2nd edition, p. 52.

172 *Souls of Sedge* and adjacent lines – Samuel Fortrey (attributed), quoted in Darby, *Draining*, as above, p. 90.

172 *mother* – Alan Bloom, 1953, as above, p. 153.

173 *where wee should be now plowing* – quoted in Dorothy Summers, as above, p. 94.

174   *the water, in time of extremity, may go in a large room* – quoted in Dorothy Summers, as above, p. 71.

176   James Ferguson – I owe his story to Richard Holmes.

176   On swifts and their night flights see: http://jeb.biologists.org/cgi/content/full/205/7/905.

Swallow

186   *The old is dying* – Antonio Gramsci, *Selections from the Prison Notebooks*, trans. and eds Quintin Hoare and Geoffrey Nowell Smith, Lawrence and Wishart, 1971, p. 276.

192   *a dying world, like Mars, but glowing still* – J. A. Baker, *The Peregrine*, Collins, 1967, p. 15.

197   *It was a very warm and sunny day* – Nadezhda Nikolaevna Timoshenko's testimony appeared at www.chernobyl.info. Or did. I would be keen to find where it is now.

198   *They say that one swallow doesn't make a summer* – Leo Tolstoy, 5 October 1893, *Tolstoy's Diaries*, as above, vol. 1, pp. 326–7.

Anders and Tim have published their work and findings in Chernobyl extensively over several years in a series of scientific papers. See: Anders Pape Møller and Timothy A. Mousseau, 'Biological Consequences of Chernobyl: 20 years on', *Trends in Ecology and Evolution*, vol. 21 no. 4, April 2006, pp. 202–7.

Autumn Fen

215   *green seraglio* – Andrew Marvell, 'The Mower against Gardens', *The Oxford Authors: Andrew Marvell*, as above, pp. 40–1.

215   *If a man could pass thro' Paradise* – *Coleridge's Notebooks: A Selection*, ed. Seamus Perry, Oxford University Press, Oxford, p. 127.

215   *I have known a riding horse to be bogged* – Sydney Skertchly, quoted in Dorothy Summers, as above, p. 20.

216   *Roman slave chain* – Charles Lucas, as above, p. 9.

216   *what was once a mighty oak forest* – Alan Bloom, 1953, as above, p. 173. Other following quotations from Alan Bloom are from here or from his earlier book, *The Farm in the Fen*, Faber, 1944.

217   *Moore-logs* – Thomas Browne, 'Hydriotaphia or Urne-Buriall', *Thomas Browne: The Major Works*, as above, p. 287.

217   *unguessable* – James Wentworth Day, as above, p. 78.

217   *the Fen cataclysm* – Charles Lucas, as above, pp. 7–8.

218   *Ne'er an axe was heard to sound* – John Clare, 'The Village Minstrel', cited in OED.

219   *Bacchus stands naked* – K. S. Painter, *The Mildenhall Treasure*, British Museum, 1977, p. 26.

220   *they found the dead, dried and pickled body* – James Wentworth Day, 'The Most English Corner of all England', in *Countryside Mood*, ed. Richard Harman, Blandford, 1943, p. 178.

221   *we found leaves that were still almost green* – Alan Bloom, 1953, as above, pp. 173–4.

222   *suction* – Lord Byron, Canto II, stanza 67, *Don Juan*, eds T. G. Steffan, E. Steffan and W. W. Pratt, Penguin, Harmondsworth, 1978, p. 118.

224   *in the watery places* – John Ray, *Ray's Flora of Cambridgeshire – Catalogus Plantarum circa Cantabrigiam nascentium*, trans. and eds A. H. Ewen and C. T. Prime, Wheldon and Wesley, Hitchin, 1975, p. 88. First published 1660.

224   *mowing marsh* – Harry Godwin, as above, p. 180.

227   *acidicolous mosses and liverworts and ferns* – Harry Godwin, as above, p. 181.

228   *I have long tried to find a student* – J. Stanley Gardiner, ed., 'The Natural History of Wicken Fen, Part VI', Bowes and Bowes, Cambridge, 1932, p. 646.

230   *pitchforked* – see www.jitterbrush.com.

231   *a massive hearty man* – Harry Godwin, as above, p. 45. Other following Godwin quotations are from here.

231,232 *enthusiastically through the densest or wettest of vegetation* and *a landmark in Quaternary research* – see www.jitterbrush.com.

233   *must needs plough the whole field* – John Ray, quoted in Anna Pavord, *The Naming of Names*, Bloomsbury, 2005, p. 389.

234   *long walks of exploration* – John Ray, *Flora*, as above, p. 23. Other following Ray quotations are from here.

On John Ray see also: Tim Birkhead, *The Wisdom of Birds*, Bloomsbury, 2008; David Elliston Allen, *The Naturalist in Britain*, Penguin, Harmondsworth, 1978.

Out Field

237   *in Sovereign Barns to dwell* – Emily Dickinson, poem 379, 'The Grass so little has to do', *The Poems of Emily Dickinson*, ed. R. W. Franklin, Belknapp, Cambridge, Massachusetts, 1999, p. 174.

238   *Ye Highlands and ye Lawlands* – 'The Bonny Earl of Murray', *The Oxford Book of Ballads*, ed. Arthur Quiller-Couch, Oxford University Press, Oxford, 1932, pp. 422–3. See also Five Hand Reel's sung version.

238   *Nay, sure, he's not in hell* – William Shakespeare, *Henry V*, 2.iii.7–18.

238   *Greenfield was the name of the property-man* – Alexander Pope, annotation in *The Dramatick Writings of Will. Shakspere, with the notes of all the various commentators; printed complete from the best editions of Sam. Johnson and Geo. Steevens*, John Bell, 1788, Volume 12.

238   *Almost as soon as I could babble* – Edward Thomas, quoted in introduction, *Selected Poems*, ed. Matthew Hollis, Faber, 2011, p. ix.

239   *he already seemed to feel the flowers growing over him* and *death-warrant* – Joseph Severn talking of Keats, quoted in Stanley Plumly, *Posthumous Keats*, Norton, New York, 2008, pp. 65 and 206.

239   *How astonishingly does the chance of leaving the world* – John Keats, *Letters*, ed. Robert Gittings, Oxford University Press, Oxford, 1977, p. 359.

240   *an organic part of himself* – Rosamund Bartlett, *Tolstoy: A Russian Life*, Profile, 2011, p. 12.

240   *too much in character to be credible* – W. H. Auden, *A Certain World*, Faber, 1982, p. 404.

240   *The memory of your good deeds* – John Stuart Collis, as above, p. 124.

241   *The ideal of Ant-Brothers* – John Stewart Collis, as above, p. 12.

242,243 *Lying where he chose* and *Because he possibly said* – Ian Frazier, as above, pp. 119 and 115.

242   *This is the lodge of Crazy Horse* – Larry McMurtry, *Crazy Horse: A Life*, Penguin, New York, 1999, p. 138.

243   T. H. White, *The Goshawk*, New York Review of Books, New York, 2007. First published 1951. All quotations are from this edition.

243   *mouse-poor* – Robert Graves quoted in David Markson, *The Last Novel*, Shoemaker Hoard, 2007, p. 77.

244   *Clare refused to take anything* – Frederick Martin, quoted in Jonathan Bate, *John Clare: A Biography*, as above, p. 167. Other following quotations from Clare are from here.

250   Nicholas Redman, *Whales' Bones of the British Isles*, Redman Publishing, 2004.

252   Dante, Canto 15, *Inferno*, translated in 1967 by Robert Lowell as 'Brunetto Latini' in *Dante in English*, eds Eric Griffiths and Matthew Reynolds, Penguin, 2005, pp. 373–8. All the following quotations from Dante are Lowell's version.

252   *One does not need to know anything about the race* – T. S. Eliot, 'Dante', *Selected Essays*, Faber, 1972, p. 247.

255   *If you want me again* – Walt Whitman, 'Song of Myself', poem 52, 1855, *Complete Poems*, as above, p. 69.

275   *A blade of grass is always a blade of grass* – Samuel Johnson, recorded by Hester Lynch Piozzi, *Anecdotes of the Late Samuel Johnson*, 1786, quoted in Geoffrey Grigson, *Before the Romantics*, George Routledge, 1946, p. 310.

275   *If I want to write about men* – Albert Camus, from 'Notebook I', *Selected Essays and Notebooks*, trans. and ed. Philip Thody, Penguin, 1979, p. 239.

A FEN BOOKSHELF

very fen has its words. My fen chapters draw heavily on the following books, maps and documents. The literature is as deep as the peat and deeper in places. At least one major book is missing from my list. I read Graham Swift's *Waterland* not long after it came out in 1983. I was living in Cambridge and the novel occurred there like weather brought into the city wrapped in the fens to its north. It marked me then, as next to no other modern novel has, going in and staying in. I copied passages from it into my notebooks. In the last few years I deliberately haven't read it again. It was so good I can imagine it easily curtailing other attempts on the fens, raising its own contagious fogs, flooding already drowning minds.

A. K. Astbury, *The Black Fens*, Golden Head Press, Cambridge, 1958.

Dudley Barker, Central Office of Information, *Harvest Home: The Official Story of the Great Floods of 1947 and their Sequel*, HMSO, 1948.

W. H. Barrett, *A Fenman's Story*, Routledge and Kegan Paul, 1966.

W. H. Barrett, *Tales from the Fens*, Routledge and Kegan Paul, 1966.

Trevor Bevis, *Water Water Everywhere*, Trevor Bevis, 1992.

Trevor Bevis, *Flooded Fens*, Trevor Bevis, 2001.

P. M. M. Bircham, *The Birds of Cambridgeshire*, Cambridge University Press, Cambridge, 1989.

Leonard Blomefield, *A Naturalist's Calendar kept at Swaffham Bulbeck, Cambridgeshire*, ed. Francis Darwin, Cambridge University Press, Cambridge, 1922. First published 1903. Written 1846–9. See also Leonard Jenyns.

Alan Bloom, *The Farm in the Fen*, Faber, 1944.

Alan Bloom, *The Fens*, Robert Hale, 1953.

Edward Bond, 'The Fool' in *Plays: 3*, Methuen, 1999. First performed 1975.

British Geological Survey, *Soil and Drift Edition, 1:50 000 series*, Cambridge (sheet 188), 1980, and Ely (sheet 173), 1981.

Mary Chamberlain, *Fenwomen*, Full Circle, Woodbridge, 2011. First published 1975.

Caryl Churchill, 'Fen' in *Plays: 2*, Methuen, 1990. First performed 1983.

Ross Clark, *Cambridgeshire*, Pimlico, 1996.

Olive Cook, *Cambridgeshire*, Blackie, 1953.

H. C. Darby, *Medieval Fenland*, Cambridge University Press, Cambridge, 1940.

H. C. Darby, *The Draining of the Fens*, Cambridge University Press, Cambridge, 1956. 2nd edition.

Anthony Day, *Turf Village*, Cambridgeshire Libraries, 1985.

William Dugdale, *The History of Imbanking and Draining the Fens and Marshes*, W. Wittingham, 1792. First published 1662.

E. A. R. Ennion, *Adventurers Fen*, Herbert Jenkins, 1949. 1st edition 1942, revised 1949.

E. A. R. Ennion, *Cambridgeshire, Huntingdonshire and the Isle of Ely*, Robert Hale, 1951.

John Evelyn, *Terra: A Philosophical Discourse of Earth*, John Martyn, The Royal Society, 1676.

Robin Field, Val Perrin, Louise Bacon and Nick Greatorex-Davies, *The Butterflies of Cambridgeshire*, Butterfly Conservation, 2006.

Laurie Friday, ed., *Wicken Fen: the Making of a Wetland Nature Reserve*, Harley, Colchester, 1997.

J. Stanley Gardiner, ed., 'The Natural History of Wicken Fen, Part VI', Bowes and Bowes, Cambridge, 1932.

Thomas Gibbons, *An Account of a Most Terrible Fire*, James Buckland, 1769.

Harry Godwin, *Fenland: Its Ancient Past and Uncertain Future*, Cambridge University Press, Cambridge, 1978.

John Humphreys, *Hunter's Fen*, David and Charles, Newton Abbot, 1986.

John Humphreys, *Poachers' Tales*, David and Charles, Newton Abbot, 1991.

John Humphreys, *Days and Nights on Hunter's Fen*, David and Charles, Newton Abbot, 1992.

Ernie and Audrey James, *Memoirs of a Fen Tiger*, David and Charles, Newton Abbot, 1986.

M. R. James, *Collected Ghost Stories*, ed. Darryl Jones, Oxford University Press, Oxford, 2011.

Leonard Jenyns, *Fauna Cantabrigiensis*, eds Richard C. Preece and Tim H. Sparks, The Ray Society, 2012.

David Lack, *The Birds of Cambridgeshire*, Cambridge Bird Club, Cambridge, 1934.

G. Lohoar and S. Ballard, 'Turf Digging at Wicken Fen' pamphlet, n.d. (after 1989).

Charles Lucas, *The Fenman's World*, Jarrold, Norwich, 1930.

J. E. Marr and A. E. Shipley, eds, *Handbook to the Natural History of Cambridgeshire*, Cambridge University Press, Cambridge, 1904.

Sybil Marshall, *Fenland Chronicle*, Penguin, 1998. First published 1967.

Arthur Mee, *The King's England: Cambridgeshire*, Hodder and Stoughton, 1965. First published 1937.

K. S. Painter, *The Mildenhall Treasure*, British Museum, 1977.

A. K. Parker and D. Pye, *The Fenland*, David and Charles, Newton Abbot, 1976.

Rowland Parker, *The Common Stream*, Paladin, St Albans, 1976.

Nikolaus Pevsner, *The Buildings of England, Cambridgeshire*, Penguin, Harmondsworth, 1954.

Arthur Randell, *Sixty Years a Fenman*, Routledge and Kegan Paul, 1966.

Arthur Randell, *Fenland Memories*, Routledge and Kegan Paul, 1969.

Arthur Randell, *Fenland Molecatcher*, Routledge and Kegan Paul, 1970.

John Ray, *Ray's Flora of Cambridgeshire – Catalogus Plantarum circa Cantabrigiam nascentium*, trans. and eds A. H. Ewen and C. T. Prime, Wheldon and Wesley, Hitchin, 1975. First published 1660.

P. H. Reaney, *The Place-names of Cambridgeshire and the Isle of Ely*, Cambridge University Press, Cambridge, 1943.

Dorothy L. Sayers, *The Nine Tailors*, New English Library, 2003. First published 1934.

R. S. Seale, *Soils of the Ely District*, Memoirs of the Soil Survey of Great Britain, Harpenden, 1975.

John Seymour, *The Companion Guide to East Anglia*, Collins, 1972.

Rex Sly, *From Punt to Plough*, History Press, Stroud, 2003.

Rex Sly, *Soil in their Souls*, History Press, Stroud, 2010.

Margaret Spufford, 'A Cambridgeshire Community: Chippenham from Settlement to Enclosure', College of Leicester, Dept. of English Local History, Occasional Papers No. 20, 1965, Leicester University Press.

Dorothy Summers, *The Great Level*, David and Charles, Newton Abbot, 1976.

Christopher Taylor, *The Cambridgeshire Landscape*, Hodder and Stoughton, 1973.

Joan Thirsk, 'Fenland Farming in the Sixteenth Century', Dept. of English Local History, Occasional Papers No. 3, 1953, University College of Leicester.

E. P. Thompson, *Customs in Common*, Penguin, 1993.

C. J. R. Thorne and T. J. Bennett, *The Birds of Wicken Fen*, The Wicken Fen Group, Cambridge, 1982.

James Wentworth Day, *Farming Adventure*, Harrap, 1943.

James Wentworth Day, *A History of the Fens*, Harrap, 1954.

B. C. Worssam and J. H. Taylor, *Geology of the Country around Cambridge*, Memoirs of the Geological Survey of Great Britain, HMSO, 1969.

A blade of grass is always a blade of grass, whether in one country or another: let us if we *do* talk, talk about something; men and women are my subjects of enquiry; let us see how these differ from those we have left behind.

Samuel Johnson

If I want to write about men, should I stop talking about the country-side? If the sky or light attract me, shall I forget the eyes or voices of those I love?

Albert Camus

Acknowledgements

My thanks, here, to many who helped me find a way, there. In the fens: Prill Barrett and the late Gabriel Horn, Nick and Jan Davies, Laurie Friday, Martin Jenkins, Ade Long, Helen Macdonald, Ben Phalan (whose science challenges all pastoral complacency and who told me about it as he took me boating above the Earth along the lodes at Reach and Burwell), Rose Thorogood, Geoffrey Woollard, assorted anonymous fishermen and vegetable pickers. Ken Arnold, who cycled with me into the fens in the early 1980s, has been the best of friends ever since. The late Eric Ennion painted his fenny way into my heart long before I even knew where the wet places were. The Cambridgeshire Bird Club is a decent outfit. I also gained much from listening to various participants at a CRASSH conference called Communicating Cultural Knowledge of Environmental Change, in Cambridge in January 2011, and from the annual meetings of New Networks for Nature.

In Zambia: Bruce Danckwerts showed me his fields without knowing I was writing them down; Lazaro Hamusikili and Collins Moya followed honeyguides without knowing quite how much I was following them. Deepest thanks to all three. And also to Ian Bruce-Miller (who trusted me with his gun), Emma Bruce-Miller, the late John Colebrook-Robjent, the late Royce Colebrook-Robjent, Mary Counsell, Ailsa and Dan Green, Chris Wood. Troy and Squacky Nicolle have brought the Colebrook-Robjent farm back to life: it is described here as it was not as it is. In Kenya: Grahame Dangerfield and Lyn Munro, Ben Parker. In South Africa: Mark Johnston, Guy and Jay Louw, Gus and Margie Mills, Christopher and Cécile Spottiswoode.

In the United States: Bill Yellowtail was as friendly and generous as is possible and got up to full speed in a matter of minutes. His insights and honesty turned me round. Thanks also to Steve Alexander and other Custer impersonators, Jeremy Harding (who worked out for me why wolves were interesting and why Melville was too), Fraser Harrison (who first showed me how to look at the Great Plains), and Tim McCleary (who opened the Crow up for me). A Society of Authors award was very helpful in allowing me to travel to Montana.

In Ukraine: Tim Mousseau and Anders Pape Møller took me with them on trust into their field site in one of the world's most troubling places and once there were remarkably patient with my stupidities and generous with their intelligence. Earlier and elsewhere in eastern Europe: Rosamund Bartlett, Michael Hofmann, Gerard McBurney, Simon McBurney, Catherine Merridale, the late Ken Smith, George Szirtes, Miklos Zellei, Zinovy Zinik, and Larisa in Yalta. A British Council studentship in the 1980s to Budapest sent me east and I have been grateful for the kick ever since.

Thanks across the time zones and locales: Simon Armitage, Simon Bainbridge, Jeff Barrett and *Caught by the River*, John Berger, Tim Birkhead, Lesley Chamberlain, Robert Chandler, Susannah Clapp, Mark Cocker, Nigel Collar, Sam Collyns and Antonia Byatt, Christopher Cook, Jonathan Davidson, Jenny Dee and Simon Blackwell, Caitlin DeSilvey, William Earp, Paul Farley, Joe Farrell, Will Fiennes, Roy Fisher, Lavinia Greenlaw, Tessa and Eric Hadley, Alexandra Harris, Louise Henson, Matthew Hollis, Richard Holmes, Jonathan Holloway, Kathleen Jamie, Danny Karlin, Andrew Kelly, Richard Kerridge, James Lasdun, Alastair Laurence, Nigel Leask and Evelyn Arizpe, Kim Lochen, Richard Long, Michael and Edna Longley, Hayden Lorimer, the late Derek Lucas (schoolteacher, word-lover, birdwatcher), Richard Mabey and Polly Munro, Robert Macfarlane, Andrew McNeillie and *Archipelago*, Andy Martin, Andrew Motion, Stuart Murray, Jeremy Mynott, Simon Naylor, Jon Nicholls, Joseph Nichols, Tom Nichols, Adam Nicolson and Sarah Raven, Redmond O'Hanlon and the *TLS*, Alice Oswald, Chris and Helen Parker, Ian Parker, David Perry, Greg Poole, the late Peter Reading, Nicholas Redman, Christopher Ricks and Judith Aronson, Alan Ritch and his *Hay in Art* website, Robin Robertson,

Suzanne Rolt, Colin Sackett, Sukhdev Sandhu, Jo Shapcott, Owen Sheers, Christopher Somerville, Lydia Syson, Matt Thompson, Martina Thomson, Mike Walker, Marina Warner, Christopher Woodward.

At the BBC: Mike Burgess, Kate Chaney, Matthew Dodd, Sarah Goodman, Iain Hunter, Sarah Langan, Clare McGinn, Duncan Minshull, Tony Phillips, Ali Serle, Mark Smalley. In the book world: Sarah Ballard, Zoe Pagnamenta, Joe Pickering, Zoe Ross, Ellie Steel, Clara Womersley. Dan Franklin has made me feel plausible and therefore possible. My thanks also to the estate of Mario Giacomelli for granting permission for the use of the cover image: a picture I have had in my head since 1980 and which I am thrilled to be wrapped in.

In Bristol, my sons Dominic and Lucian have kept me down to earth in all the right departments; I wish I hadn't neglected them as much as I did to get this story dug but I love them for reminding me often enough that there is more to life than grass. Their mother, Stephanie Parker, has (again) been generous and big-hearted. She has done more than her share in many ways and I couldn't have written this book without that. My parents, Kate and John Dee, like my boys, have got used to me looming from behind a laptop and have been, as ever, sweet and encouraging as well as suitably hard to impress. My mother taught me to fold laundered bed-linen with her when I was about six. Something of that comes back in this book with its welcoming sheets of green. She also negotiated the plastic grass that started me off, fixed my subscription to *Farmers Weekly*, and recited poetry at me until a few lines stuck. My father, it turns out, might hail from farming stock. That nothing of this has come through our family line has allowed this book. If only a small, unmuddy, portion of his intelligence, his humour, and his appetite for jokes and ideas has rubbed off on me I would be proud.

Claire Spottiswoode made everything come to life that is here. She gave this book its juice and its heart. I have stolen places and people from her; I have tried to capture some off-cuts of her brilliant way of seeing; and, with her, I have walked and talked almost every sodding inch of these fields. She has been superb throughout and continues so.

Printed in the United States
by Baker & Taylor Publisher Services